Frances Mary Oxenham

Not yet :

a tale of the present day

Frances Mary Oxenham

Not yet :
a tale of the present day

ISBN/EAN: 9783741158179

Manufactured in Europe, USA, Canada, Australia, Japa

Cover: Foto ©Andreas Hilbeck / pixelio.de

Manufactured and distributed by brebook publishing software (www.brebook.com)

Frances Mary Oxenham

Not yet :

NOT YET:

A Tale of the Present Day.

BY

FRANCES MARY OXENHAM.

Dedicated, by permission,

TO

THE LADY GEORGIANA FULLERTON,

WITH

EVERY FEELING OF GRATITUDE

AND RESPECT.

NOT YET.

CHAPTER I.

"Though in Time's record nearly nought,
It was Eternity to Thought."
BYRON.

"A CATHOLIC PRIEST is anxious to obtain the services of an experienced schoolmistress (not certificated), for a country mission, where there are about sixty children. She would be required to play the harmonium, and teach the choir, consisting entirely of men and boys, and would also have the care of the altar, and the charge of the vestments and church-linen. Address, Rev. F. Wilfrid, Stonebridge, Devon."

The foregoing advertisement was read on a certain Saturday morning, in the year of grace 186—, by many anxious candidates for the important and responsible post of mistress in a Catholic school; and the next day's post would have brought Father Wilfrid at least a score of applications, had it not been for that little parenthesis, "not certificated," which caused many of the aforesaid candidates to lay down the paper with an indignant expression of astonishment that any one could be so infatuated as to expect to get a schoolmistress worth any thing with such a condition attached; and a further supposition that Father Wilfrid could probably not afford to pay enough to make it worth any "experienced" person's while to answer his advertisement, especially as nothing was mentioned about salary.

"Depend upon it," said one of the pupil-teachers in a large school, to the mistress, who was longing to exchange her town life for a country one, and had consequently read the advertisement with some anxiety,—"depend upon it, he wants to get some benevolent lady, who wishes to make herself useful, and can afford to do so at her own expense."

"Then he will be nicely sold: benevolent ladies only turn schools into nurseries of spoilt children," was the reply, spoken in a tone of unmistakable contempt for the ladies in question— professors and *amateurs* being natural enemies.

We will not undertake to say whether Father Wilfrid was disappointed or not, to find only one letter on his breakfast-table when he came in after saying Mass on Sunday morning; but he took it up and examined it with some curiosity, first the direction, then the seal, then the postmark, apparently quite oblivious of the fact that he had merely to open it if he wished to know the contents. The address was written in a large, firm, almost masculine hand, and Father Wilfrid shook his head (he seldom indulged in a frown); he had a horror of "strong-minded" women. The seal bore simply the initials, " B. T." "She is not ashamed of her name," thought Father Wilfrid. "I hope it is not Betty." The post-mark was *Warwick*, which was so completely a *terra incognita* to the good priest, that it finally decided him to open the letter without further delay. It was short, occupying only two sides of the sheet: "A sensible woman," he thought, "who does not waste words." The letter certainly *economised* its expressions as much as possible; it said only:

"REV. FATHER,
"I have just read your advertisement, and think your situation would suit me. I have some experience, though I have never been a schoolmistress. I am not certificated. The priest here will answer any questions you may wish to ask about me. I can give no other reference. I am a widow, and nearly forty. I have some means of my own, so that the question of salary is indifferent to me. I have received what is commonly called a good education, and can play and sing. My health is good. If you think I should suit you, I will come to Stonebridge as soon as you like on trial for a month.
"Yours truly,
"MARGARET TRELAWNEY."

"H'm! spasmodic! I don't like that, especially in conjunction with strong-mindedness," soliloquised Father Wilfrid; "but let's see if there are any counteracting qualities;" and hereupon he proceeded to a critical examination of the handwriting as an index of character, occasionally making brief pencil-notes on the opposite side of the sheet of paper. Having completed his task, he deliberately read over his remarks, which ran thus:

"*Quick-tempered, independent, truthful, conscientious, proud, inflexible, trustworthy, refined, artistic.* Rather a dangerous speculation, I am afraid; but I will, at all events, write to the priest, and see what he can say for her. I will wait to answer her letter till I hear from him." Having arrived at this conclusion, he betook himself to his breakfast, a very frugal one, though it was late in the morning, his Sunday Mass being at ten o'clock.

In due time he received the following answer to his inquiries:

"My dear Father Wilfrid,

"I can conscientiously recommend Mrs. Trelawney, who is really a most invaluable person. Though she has never been a schoolmistress, she has constantly supplied the place of mine, when the latter was absent or ill, and I have always been thoroughly satisfied both with her teaching and management of the children. She is quite a lady, both by birth and education, and only desires such a situation as your advertisement offers, from motives which I must leave her to explain for herself, as far as she is inclined to do so. She is a good musician, and sings well, and is clever in church-embroidery; she has patched up some of my old vestments so as to look better than when they were new. She is a convert of about five years' standing; her husband, who was a Protestant, was one of the leading barristers in Warwick, and universally liked and respected. I

certainly should strongly advocate your proposing
a month's trial to Mrs. Trelawney.
"Yours truly,
"EDMUND GORDON."

"A mystery! I hate mysteries! I won't have
any thing to do with it," was Father Wilfrid's
first impulse after reading the letter; but as no
other answers to his advertisement were forthcoming, and he was really in distress for a schoolmistress, a few hours' calm consideration of all
the *pro's* and *con.'s* finally decided him to offer
Mrs. Trelawney the month's trial she had proposed, being at the same time fully determined
that, unless she could satisfactorily clear up all
that seemed mysterious or doubtful, he would on
no account engage her. Accordingly, he secured
two quiet rooms for a month, over a stationer's
shop in the village, and, mindful of the hint that
Mrs. Trelawney was "quite a lady," as well as of
the evidence of her handwriting, he caused two
very staring coloured prints to be removed, and
replaced them by two small, but well-executed,
engravings of religious subjects from his own
study, and also placed a vase filled with fresh
flowers from his garden on the table a few hours
before the time fixed for her arrival. He had re-
quested her to drive from the nearest station
direct to the presbytery, and now sat waiting to
receive her, with, it must be confessed, some little
curiosity.

As the fly drove up, he went himself to the
door, wishing to give her as kind a welcome as
possible; but the kindness seemed quite lost upon

Mrs. Trelawney, who replied to his greeting with a formal bow, and a cold, "Thank you, but I should prefer going at once to my lodging, if you will allow me." This was in answer to Father Wilfrid's hospitable offer of tea, which in fact stood ready on the table.

Of course, nothing remained for him but to give the necessary directions to the driver; and saying, "Well, perhaps it will be more comfortable for you; I will call upon you in the morning, when I hope you will feel rested after your journey," he returned to his study, and his solitary tea, not, it must be owned, with the most favourable impression of his new schoolmistress, except with regard to her personal appearance, which was decidedly prepossessing.

"Certainly quite a lady," he remarked to himself, "and looks intellectual, but inconveniently independent, I fear, for the position she has chosen; however, time will show."

Meanwhile Mrs. Trelawney, with her luggage, was duly deposited at the private door of the stationer's shop, and received by the stationer's wife with every mark of civility: would the lady prefer dinner or tea?—there were eggs and mutton-chops in the house.

Mrs. Trelawney preferred tea, but would like a mutton-chop with it if convenient; while it was preparing, perhaps Mrs. North would kindly let her see her apartments.

It must indeed have been a fastidious person who could have found fault with the view from Mrs. Trelawney's bedroom-window; scarcely any thing of the village was visible, but, on the other side of the lane, a hoed meadow sloped down to the richly wooded dell, through which, to judge from the sound that met her ears, a river was dancing and leaping in its rocky bed; while in the far distance one of the Dartmoor Tors rose in silent majesty against the sky, now flooded with the light of a brilliant October sunset. Did Mrs. Trelawney think that her lines had fallen in pleasant places, as she gazed on the scene before her? Did she think of her native Cornish moors, as she threw open the window and inhaled a breath of pure mountain-air? What deep emotion suddenly brought the tears to her eyes as she fixed them with a painful eagerness on that rocky summit, now burning in the glow of the setting sun like the sacrifice upon an altar? It was but for a moment; then, turning abruptly away, and passionately grasping a crucifix in both hands, almost as though she would have crushed it into powder, she flung herself on the ground, and buried her face in her hands.

A few minutes passed, and there was a knock at her door. Quite calmly she rose, began to search for something in one of her boxes, and said, "Come in."

"If you please, ma'am, your tea is quite ready," said a pleasant voice belonging to a young girl, Mrs. North's niece and helpmate.

"Thank you; I will come down directly," replied Mrs. Trelawney, without turning towards the speaker, who instantly vanished. In the sitting-room a pleasant fire was burning, the kettle hissed cheerfully on the hob, the candles were lighted, the tea was set out on a table-cloth as

white as snow; while on a little work-table near
the fire stood Father Wilfrid's vase of flowers,
and a low easy-chair was drawn towards it. Altogether the room looked as *cosy* as a room in a
lodging-house could well be made to look.

Mrs. Trelawney stood for a moment looking
at all this in a dreamy kind of way, and might
perhaps have so stood for much longer, had it
not been for the presence of the girl, who was
waiting to fill the tea-pot and take the cover off
the dish of mutton-chops.

"Where do those flowers come from?" she
asked suddenly.

"Father Wilfrid brought them, ma'am, this
morning, from his own garden."

"Thank you; you can go now," replied the
lady, not ungraciously, though Katie thought it
rather hard to be so summarily dismissed when
she had looked forward to "a bit of chat."

Mrs. Trelawney, instead of beginning her tea, as
might have been expected after her long journey,
sat down in the easy-chair, drew the vase of flowers
towards her, and, quickly passing her hand across
her brow, said to herself with a strange sort of
terror, which seemed wholly uncalled for by the
occasion: "Oh, what shall I do if he is going to
be kind to me! Thank God, he is not coming
here to-night!"

She would not, perhaps, have felt so secure,
had she known what was passing at that moment
in the presbytery. Good Father Wilfrid, whose
charity sometimes a little outran his discretion,
bethought him in the course of the evening that
his new schoolmistress was, perhaps, feeling very

lonely in her strange lodging, and, saying to himself, "I will try to make her feel at home with me," was in the act of going out, when he met his housekeeper in the passage.

"I shall not be long," he said, pausing for a moment; "I am only going to see if Mrs. Trelawney has every thing she wants."

Mrs. Morris, who sometimes used the privilege of an old and confidential servant, ventured to do so on the present occasion. "Shall I step up and inquire for you, father?" she said. "The lady seemed very tired; perhaps she would rather not be disturbed, when she has got to unpack her things, and settle herself, like."

"Very well; you can go, then; I suppose women understand each other best, after all," he continued to himself in an undertone, and with a somewhat mortifying conviction that he had as yet quite failed in understanding them himself in many cases.

So Mrs. Trelawney was spared for that evening, Mrs. Morris bringing back word to her master that the lady was "much obliged, and found her rooms very comfortable, and the people very attentive."

CHAPTER II.

*" How sharper than a serpent's tooth it is,
To have a thankless child!"*
SHAKESPEARE.

MRS. TRELAWNEY was not an early riser, and Father Wilfrid looked in vain for her after Mass the next morning. Not that he really much expected to see her after her long journey; but still he would have been better pleased if she had come, especially as it happened to be a day of devotion. He was strong, active, and energetic himself, and, though ready enough to make allowance for others, he had not in his heart much toleration for any thing in the shape of indolence. Perhaps, if he had been a Protestant, he might have been drawn into the ranks of "muscular Christianity;" but, being a Catholic, he was "under the unfortunate delusion that he had to save his soul," and, further, believed that the training thereof was more important than the development of his physical powers.

As soon after breakfast as he conveniently could, he went to call upon Mrs. Trelawney. She was, no doubt, expecting him; for a chair was drawn near the fire opposite to her own, and she was employed only on a piece of knitting, which evidently occupied none of her attention. As he entered the room, she rose and came forward to meet him, with the graceful ease of a lady accustomed to the ways of the world, and thoroughly at home in them. All the *brusquerie* of the evening before had wholly disappeared; but it was perhaps from a consciousness that it could not be wholly forgotten, that Mrs. Trelawney said:

"I am afraid I must have seemed rude and ungrateful to you yesterday; I am so little used to travelling, that the long journey had quite knocked me up."

"Oh, pray don't mention it. I saw you were very tired. I hope you feel rested now?" said Father Wilfrid kindly, but with a lurking fear in his heart, that a lady who was so terribly knocked up with a few hours' railway journey as to be unable to go to Mass the next morning, could hardly be strong enough for an energetic schoolmistress.

"Yes, thank you, quite rested, and ready to begin my work as soon as you can introduce me to it," was the reply. "Is your school under the charge of a pupil-teacher, or have the children holidays just now?"

Mrs. Trelawney might be an *amateur*, but she evidently *meant business*, and meant it a little more decidedly than Father Wilfrid was quite prepared for.

"A lady here has kindly taken charge of the school for this week," he said. "I thought you would be glad of a few days to settle down, and get acquainted with the place and people, and that Monday would be time enough for you to begin with the school" (it was then Thursday); "but if you would like to see it now, I shall be happy to take you there this morning, and introduce you to the children."

"Thank you," she replied; "I should like it,

if it will not be giving you too much trouble; but there are a few little matters I should like to settle with you first."

She spoke with a little constraint of manner; and Father Wilfrid, putting his own interpretation upon this, said:

"Yes, '*business first*' is a wise maxim, I believe. You were kind enough to say in your letter that the question of salary was not a very important one to you, which I am thankful for, as I fear I cannot offer you more than—"

"Pardon me," interrupted Mrs. Trelawney, looking down, and colouring so deeply that he feared he had offended her. "I did not say that the question was not important, but that it was *indifferent* to me; in fact, it is not any question at all. I want no salary."

Father Wilfrid looked at her with a puzzled expression of countenance, and began, "But, indeed, I could not allow you—"

"Excuse me for interrupting you again," she said; "but will you allow me to explain myself?"

"Certainly, my dear madam," he replied; "pray feel no scruple in telling me any thing you wish to explain."

"It is only this," she said, with a little return of the bluntness he had noticed on the evening before; "I have an income of 800*l.* a year, and therefore I do not require any salary. I should be simply robbing you if I were to take it. The case is simply this: I wish to make myself of use to some poor mission, and I have a fancy for teaching a poor-school. It will be some benefit to you, I suppose, to be saved the salary of a schoolmistress and an organist; and I shall also be able, I hope, to help you in other ways—that is," she added, in a stiff, formal tone, " if you are satisfied with my services at the end of a month's trial."

She had spoken so rapidly, that it had been quite impossible for him to interrupt her; and now, when she suddenly ceased speaking, like some piece of machinery that has performed its allotted task, he felt almost too much bewildered to realise what she had said.

"I hardly understand you," he said, after a moment's pause; " do you mean that you wish to try the experiment of having a poor-school entirely under your own independent control and management?"

An indignant flash shot from Mrs. Trelawney's eyes, as she replied, with outward calmness, " No, Father Wilfrid, that is not what I mean. If you allow me to teach your school, it must be entirely and absolutely under your own control and management: I will not undertake it at all, except on that condition; and I must further beg that you will treat me in all respects as if I were your paid schoolmistress; and feel no more scruple in reproving, correcting, or, if you desire it, dismissing me, than if you paid me a quarterly salary. There must be no misunderstanding between us on this point—to others I shall be simply the schoolmistress; forget, as far as possible, that I am any thing else to yourself. If you engage me after a month's trial, let there be a written agreement between us that three months' notice is to be given on either side in case of removal."

Father Wilfrid sat in silent amazement during this speech. Such a cool, business-like way of performing what seemed to him an act of heroic generosity perplexed him, and, without desiring to insinuate any thing uncharitable, it must be honestly confessed, he began to have doubts as to the real motive of such apparently self-sacrificing conduct. By way of gaining time, more than any thing else, he said:

"You will not, I hope, object to my taking the chief part of the religious instruction myself?—I always like to do so, as I feel responsible for it, especially"—he hesitated a moment, and Mrs. Trelawney, suddenly looking him full in the face, rather to his discomfiture, and there reading the want of confidence he found a difficulty in repressing, interrupted him by saying:

"Especially with so recent a convert as myself. Do not be afraid to speak plainly to me, father; I never could see the advantage of calling a spade an agricultural implement; and, to say the truth, I think you are quite right to distrust converts: if I were an old Catholic myself, I should hate them."

There was a fierceness in the tone of the last words, and Father Wilfrid thought he had not been far wrong when he had characterised Mrs. Trelawney, from her handwriting, as "strong-minded, independent, truthful, and proud." He smiled as he answered:

"But you would hardly think it *quite right* to hate them?"

"I don't know; it is quite natural," she replied.

"Is it?" he said, with great simplicity. "But then, you see, Catholics—*old* Catholics, at least—are apt sometimes to be *not* quite natural in their feelings."

Was it meant for reproof, or satire, or what? Mrs. Trelawney said no more about converts; but perhaps she was still thinking of the expression of distrust she had witnessed, for she said rather abruptly:

"I dare say you are thinking that my wish to be a schoolmistress is a mere whim or caprice; but I am not a capricious or speculative person: I have other reasons besides those I have already given you, which perhaps I may tell you some day, but not now, and," she added significantly, "*not here.*"

The priest was silenced at once—so completely silenced, indeed, that, after a short and somewhat awkward pause, Mrs. Trelawney found herself obliged to continue the conversation herself. With an entire change of tone and manner, she said:

"I have not yet thanked you for providing me with such comfortable lodgings; they suit me exactly, and the people seem very civil and attentive; but if I remain here, I shall want two more rooms: do you think Mrs. North can supply them, or shall I be obliged to move?"

"H'm, yes, decidedly spasmodic," was Father Wilfrid's rather irrelevant mental comment, before he answered:

"I really do not know, but we can ascertain easily. You wish, I suppose, for a dining-room, and a bedroom for your maid?"

A rigid, stony look settled on Mrs. Trelawney's features. In cold, hard, metallic tones, she said :

"I shall want a room for my daughter."

Though not easily taken by surprise, Father Wilfrid positively started; good, simple-minded man that he was, it had never occurred to him that Mrs. Trelawney, being a widow, might possibly have children, and the revelation rather dismayed him. He had no objection to one lady schoolmistress, but he didn't want two; and being of the Honourable George Lawless's opinion, that "women are kittle cattle to deal with," the prospect was by no means agreeable to him.

Perhaps he had "a tell-tale face," an inconvenient possession for any one, especially for a priest ; for Mrs. Trelawney, after a moment's pause, added :

"She will only come here occasionally."

"She does not live with you, then ?" he replied, considerably relieved, it must be confessed, though at the same time thinking it was all very strange, and beginning to wish he had adhered to his first impulse, and refused to have any thing to do with such mysterious people.

"No," replied Mrs. Trelawney, "she is living with friends, as companion to a young lady. My daughter," she continued stiffly, "is not a Catholic."

Father Wilfrid did not quite see how that excused her mother for having apparently refused her the shelter of a home ; but he felt that any further questioning would be impertinent just then, and merely said :

"Let us hope and pray that she may soon become one."

"Never!" exclaimed Mrs. Trelawney, with startling emphasis; "it is utterly hopeless;" and there was a ring of despair in her tone, which haunted the gentle-hearted priest for many a long day.

"God forbid!" he said; "nothing is hopeless; faith does not recognise impossibility."

Mrs. Trelawney stooped to pick up the ball of cotton which had for some time been lying unheeded at her feet, and as she did so she said quietly:

"Will it be too late now, father, to go to the school this morning?"

Father Wilfrid had quite sufficient tact to follow lead; he took out his watch, and replied:

"If we go at once, we shall just have a quarter of an hour to see the children before they go home to dinner; but perhaps you would rather wait till the afternoon?"

"Oh, no, not at all; I will be ready in a moment," she said, rising, and tossing her piece of knitting all in a heap into a work-basket on the floor. In less than two minutes she reappeared with her bonnet on, and a crape veil so thick that it entirely concealed her face. During the five minutes' walk to the school, she did not speak a word; but just as they reached the door, she said in a business-like tone:

"You do not keep the children in all day, then; how many hours are they in school?"

"From nine to twelve, and again from two to four," he replied. "I find a break in the middle of the day quite necessary both for scholars and teachers, the latter especially: I think keeping schoolmistresses hard at work for five or six hours on a stretch ought to be punishable under the Act for 'Prevention of Cruelty to Animals.'"

"On the principle that 'a good man is merciful to his beast,'" she answered, with a smile; "but I have heard Catholics say that animals have no rights, and are entitled to no protection."

It is rather embarrassing to be taken *au pied de la lettre* when you only intended a harmless joke, and Father Wilfrid laboured under the further disadvantage of not in the least recognising the text Mrs. Trelawney had quoted. Instead, therefore, of attempting any reply, he opened the school-door, revealing to view a neatly furnished and tidily kept room, in which about fifty children, ranged in rows, were standing with slates in their hands, evidently just prepared to show the result of their calculations to a lady, who was pacing up and down the room, for the apparently very needless purpose of keeping order. She had her back to the door, and had not heard it open; but the children both heard and saw, and, with a good deal of unnecessary noise and confusion, knelt down for the priest's blessing.

"Good morning, Miss Crofton," he said; "allow me to introduce Mrs. Trelawney to you; she was anxious to see the school this morning."

A young, fair girl turned towards them, and, putting out her hand instead of only making a formal bow, said frankly, "O Mrs. Trelawney, I am delighted to see you; my hands are not strong enough to hold the reins of government, and I am in daily dread of *une jolie petite révolution.*"

Mrs. Trelawney glanced for a moment at the children, hoping none of them understood a word of French; they were all sitting as quiet as mice, and staring hard at her: they had not understood a word of Miss Crofton's speech, as she probably very well knew before she ventured on making it; even the elder ones only dimly supposed her to mean that she was not physically capable of thrashing them.

"I have interrupted your arithmetic-lesson," was all she said; and Father Wilfrid wondered whether it was *her way* always to put on a blunt and repelling manner to strangers. But Miss Crofton was neither proud enough nor sensitive enough to be easily repelled; she laughed merrily, and answered:

"No; it was just over; I was only going to look at the sums before dismissing the children: but I can leave them now till the afternoon, unless," she added, suddenly roused to a sense of *the fitness of things,* "you would like to see what they can do. Janie, bring me your slate," she said, turning to the children, and speaking in a more authoritative tone than seemed quite consistent with her former profession of incompetence.

A tall, awkward, red-haired girl came forward, holding out a slate; Miss Crofton took it, and, without even glancing at the sum, handed it to Mrs. Trelawney, who at once apparently devoted her whole attention to it. After a few moments she returned it to the child, who had stood meanwhile looking very shy, and blushing literally to the roots of her hair.

"I think, my dear," she said, in a gentle, winning tone, which made Father Wilfrid turn round suddenly to see who was speaking,—for he did not recognise the voice,—"you will find a mistake in the shillings, which you can easily correct for yourself; 7 and 5 make—what?"

"Twelve, ma'am, if you please," replied Janie quite readily: half her shyness seemed gone already.

"And if I don't please, too, I suppose," replied the lady, smiling; "but you see you have put down 11, and cheated yourself of a shilling."

Father Wilfrid now came forward, and told the children they might go home, adding, that perhaps Mrs. Trelawney would pay the school a longer visit the next day. They went out quietly and orderly, only three or four being left, who lived at a distance, and brought their dinners with them.

"And now," said Father Wilfrid, speaking to Miss Crofton, "I will leave you two ladies together, for I have some business in the town; perhaps you can show Mrs. Trelawney where the books and things are kept, and tell her," he added, laughing, "how many black sheep she may expect to find among her scholars;" and without waiting for a reply, he turned to go; but Miss Crofton stopped him by saying:

"O father, have you forgotten that it is Benediction night?"

"Forgotten!—no, certainly not," he replied; "but what of it?"

"Only that I hope you don't expect *me* to play the harmonium again, because—"

Father Wilfrid checked her by saying quite gravely, "I should be glad if you would play to-night, if you please; I will not trouble Mrs. Trelawney before Sunday."

But here Mrs. Trelawney herself interposed; looking up kindly, she said, "If Miss Crofton would prefer it, I shall be very happy to play to-night, if she will kindly tell me what music is used."

But Father Wilfrid's grave look had subdued Annie Crofton for the moment, and she made no reply.

"Well," he said, "I will leave you to settle it together;" and in another moment he was gone.

CHAPTER III.

"Child of earth, with the golden hair!"
OLD SONG.

"Do you really mean it? Would you really not mind playing to-night?" said Miss Crofton.

"Not in the least. I shall be very glad to be of use, if you think the choir will not be put out by it before we have practised together," was Mrs. Trelawney's reply.

Miss Crofton laughed merrily. "Put out by it!" she exclaimed; "they will only be too thankful not to have *me* to put them out. I play abominably, and always get myself and every one else into a scrape. Last Sunday I scandalised the whole congregation, and nearly sent the choir into fits, by beginning 'Daily, daily,' instead of the *Asperges*." Mrs. Trelawney laughed too, now; Annie Crofton was like sunshine, brightening every thing that came near her.

"Let me see," she said, "what did Father Wilfrid say I was to show you? Oh, the books *and things*. How like a man! they always speak so contemptuously of what they don't understand! They would say, ' Have you got *your things* on?' to a peeress arraying herself in her coronet and ermine! But I beg your pardon," she continued, unlocking the school-desk; "here are books, pencils, slates, samplers, babies' shirts, and—well, here are *things*, with a vengeance!—dirty bits of crotchet-work, two marbles, three peppermint-lozenges, and a peg-top! I remember, now, I took them from some of the children yesterday, and forgot to give them back after school. I can't cure them of bringing things to eat or to play with; I hope you may be able to succeed better."

"Perhaps you are not very fond of children?" suggested Mrs. Trelawney, at the same time taking up and examining some of the lesson-books.

"Well, I don't know; I like them well enough sometimes; but I don't like to be plagued with them, and I get out of temper when they tease me, which I fancy people who are fond of children don't do. Are you fond of them?" she asked suddenly.

"I love them; I could do any thing for them," replied Mrs. Trelawney eagerly.

Miss Crofton looked up so quickly that she surprised a tear in Mrs. Trelawney's eye. "How stupid of me!" she thought to herself; "perhaps she has lost her own children;" and taking up one of the books, she opened it at a list of names, and said, "Here is the school-register; we have about seventy names down; but I think only about fifty children come regularly. Oh, dear, I forgot to mark the attendances yesterday; it is lucky Father Wilfrid did not ask to see the book— he is terribly strict. ,I fancy he prides himself on having his school under better discipline than the government ones. Woe betide you if your books are not always ready for inspection at a moment's notice."

Miss Crofton had talked on, with the kind intention of giving Mrs. Trelawney time to recover herself, in which she fully succeeded. It may, perhaps, seem a little strange that she should have been so free and unreserved with a person she had never seen before, and who, moreover, must have been more than double her own age; but Annie Crofton was almost a child, quite a child in many things, and a spoilt child, too—the darling of a widowed father and an only brother. She had been the plague of nurses and governesses, from the day when she first stamped her tiny foot, and said, "I won't!" on being desired to kiss an old lady, whose personal appearance did not please her. Not that she was a naughty child; her fits of temper were quickly over, and left no trace behind; and she was always so genuinely sorry for them, that no one could be angry with her. No need to teach her acts of contrition; they came spontaneously. As she grew older, her impulsiveness of character was always getting her into scrapes, by blinding her to even the most obvious consequences of her actions; while an almost inexhaustible fund of high spirits and good temper rendered her all but inaccessible to warnings or reproofs. She only laughed at the former, while to the latter she would reply, with upturned face, shaking back her sunny curls, "O Miss Bailey, I am so sorry—I am, indeed; please don't be angry this time; I won't do it any more;" and Miss Bailey's wrath was always instantly appeased, though she knew from many past experiences that "any more" might safely be interpreted "till next time." On one of these occasions Father Wilfrid had happened to be present, and to remark that, as she broke her promises so often, it was difficult to believe that she really meant what she said. With flushed cheeks and dilated eyes she had exclaimed:

"I *do* mean what I say, Father Wilfrid, you *know* I do; you *know*, if I break my promises, it is only when—There!" she continued, rushing past him out of the room; "you dare not say another word now!" Of course he dared not; she had her revenge; but the taste thereof was by no means sweet to her. This was the first, the last, the only time she had ever been really in a passion.

She was now nineteen, emancipated from the restraints of the schoolroom, and mistress of her father's house,—for her mother had been dead some years; and during the last few months she had been perpetually admonished—*persecuted*, she called it herself—to be less childish, less impulsive, more restrained, more conventional: whether or not she had profited by these admonitions, we shall, perhaps, discover before long. A few days before that on which we have made her acquaintance, she had said to Father Wilfrid:

"They scold me for being *childish;* I know I wish I could feel more *childlike;* I think sometimes I try to cheat myself into it by talking nonsense."

But we have made a long digression.

"Perhaps you would like to mark the attendances before you forget them; I will not interrupt you," was Mrs. Trelawney's very matter-of-fact reply to Miss Crofton's speech.

"Bless the woman!" thought Annie; "has the fairy *Order* stepped out of the story-books, and come here to torment me *in propriâ personâ?*"

But the fairy (a somewhat substantial one, certainly; and, moreover, who ever read or dreamt of a fairy in widow's weeds?) had moved away, and was diligently coaxing a poor little child, sitting forlorn in a corner, to eat its dinner. Annie watched her curiously for a few moments. The child, who had begun to cry at first, gradually relaxed into a smile, then stuffed a large mouthful of bread-and-butter half-way down its throat, and—marvellous to behold!—swallowed it without choking; then, holding out another piece in a very dirty little hand, said: "Oo have some, too!" To Annie Crofton's infinite astonishment, Mrs. Trelawney stooped down, opened her mouth, and suffered the dirty little fingers to deposit themselves therein. Yes, there could be no sort of doubt that she had spoken the truth when she said that she loved children, and would do any thing for them.

The child now burst out into a merry laugh; and Annie, taking up the register, with just a little shadow of a sigh, as she thought, "*I* couldn't do that—I wonder why not?" began slowly and carefully to mark the attendances.

In a few minutes Mrs. Trelawney came back to her. "I should never have supposed," she said, "that Father Wilfrid was strict."

"No?" replied Miss Crofton. "Just wait till you know him a little better; he is as kind as ever he can be; but I believe he thinks order and punctuality hold at least equal rank with the three theological virtues. You know the daily Mass here is at eight; well, every morning he opens the sacristy-door with the first stroke of the clock, and exactly as the eighth stroke sounds he is at the altar."

"I think that *is* a great virtue," said Mrs. Trelawney; "want of punctuality wastes so much time, not only one's own, but other people's."

"It is horribly like a machine," replied Miss Crofton, a little impatiently.

"Like a machine," repeated Mrs. Trelawney; "yes, and yet, you know—" She stopped, and would have turned off her sentence in some way, if Miss Crofton had not caught it up rather eagerly, saying, "No, I don't know; what is it?"

Mrs. Trelawney turned a little away, and looked dreamily out of one of the windows towards the far-off Dartmoor hills; "You know," she said, "to be a saint, one's very heart itself must beat by rule."

"Then I shall never be a saint—that's very

certain," said Annie; "if I were to try ever so much, I couldn't turn my heart into a machine, like the mainspring of a watch."

Mrs. Trelawney made no answer; she still gazed dreamily out over the low rounded Tors, which seemed to heave and swell like the bosom of an unquiet sea; it must surely have been some weakness of sight that caused so strange an optical delusion. The mighty heart of ocean breathes and palpitates with a passionate life, though even in its wildest storms it beats by rule; but what can move the unutterable calm of the everlasting hills?

Miss Crofton was not troubled with delusions either of mental or of bodily vision; and after wondering for a few moments at her companion's evident abstraction, she said:

"After all, I believe you would enjoy a ramble over those hills, even if it were out of bounds and against rule."

Mrs. Trelawney woke up from her dream, whatever it was, with the most perfect self-possession; she even laughed lightly, or what seemed lightly, as she replied:

"*Out of bounds!*—are we prisoners on parole here, then?"

Annie laughed a ringing, joyous laugh, as she answered, "To be sure we are, with Father Wilfrid for our gaoler. I don't know what amount of liberty he may allow *you;* but he gave *me* a pretty scolding last week for cantering over Hillsborough Tor by myself, though I have the quietest pony in the world, and I didn't meet a soul except Robert Hatton."

For the first time during the conversation, Mrs. Trelawney put up her veil, and looked into the bright young face that was turned towards her. "Beautiful exceedingly" it was, with its childlike, fearless innocence and contempt of danger. She had taken off her hat, and her hair, of a rich sunny brown, was swept back from her brow and gathered into a large knot (she had always stoutly refused to wear that fashionable deformity, a *chignon*), which somehow kept itself marvellously close and compact without the restraint of a net. Her features were perhaps hardly regular enough to be called handsome, but they were all the more charming in their changeful playfulness of expression; her eyes sparkled with fun and mischief, and her mouth was pursed up into the prettiest little pout imaginable as she complained of the interference with her roaming propensities. Mrs. Trelawney thought Father Wilfrid might have good reason to object to her running wild over Hillsborough Tor, even on "the quietest pony in the world," and with no chance of meeting "a soul except Robert Hatton," whoever he might be—though her free and unreserved mention of him proved clearly that as yet, at all events, he was nothing to her. She did not, however, put her thoughts into words, but merely said:

"Are you fond of riding?"

"I like it better than any thing else in the whole world," was the reply, spoken in rather an excited tone; "I wouldn't give up my pony for all the Queen of Spain's diamonds; but I don't half enjoy it, except when I go by myself, and explore all the wild bits of moor that other people are afraid of."

"You are never afraid yourself, then?"

"Not I! What should I be afraid of? *They* are only afraid of breaking their horse's legs, or getting stuck in a bog; but my pony is mountain-born and mountain-bred, and knows better than to slip backwards down a granite-quarry, or rush headlong into a bog; he can take very good care of himself, even if I were foolish enough to ride him carelessly—which, however, I don't do," she added quickly; "so they need not be so afraid to trust me. I don't ride with the reins on my horse's neck, like a forlorn lover making sonnets to the moon, or a travelling friar overtaken by an ecstasy."

Mrs. Trelawney looked at her in speechless amazement; and Annie, rather shocked, to say the truth, at the result of her own impulsiveness, said penitently:

"Oh, I beg your pardon; I am afraid I have quite scandalised you; the truth is, papa threatened yesterday to send a groom out with me, whenever Charley—my brother, I mean—is not able to go; and I do so hate to have a man dangling after me, watching every thing I do, and reporting afterwards to all the servants how many ditches I jumped over, and how often I dropped my whip, and got off to pick it up."

"A groom would at least save you that trouble," suggested Mrs. Trelawney; "or, at all events, help you to remount your pony—you must find it rather awkward to do that alone."

"If I couldn't do it, I certainly should not be

fit to ride alone," replied Miss Crofton, with just a shade of annoyance in her tone, which warned Mrs. Trelawney that it would be better to change the subject of conversation.

"Do you stay here all day," she said, "without any luncheon ?"

It was turning the corner at right angles, certainly; but Miss Crofton was evidently relieved.

"No," she replied; "I generally go home to luncheon at one, and turn these little ones into the playground ; it is hardly five minutes' walk to our house, so I can easily get back by two o'clock ; but," she continued, looking at her watch, "it is after one now, and I shall only just have time. Will you come with me ?—we shall be quite alone. Papa never comes home to luncheon, and Charley is gone to a crôquet-party at Abbotsleigh."

"Thank you very much; but I ordered dinner at half-past one, and Mrs. North will be expecting me."

Miss Crofton had quite enough tact to understand when it would be bad taste to press an invitation, and she did not attempt it in the present instance, but said at once :

"Well, then, good bye, for the present ;" and was proceeding to open the door, when she suddenly turned back, saying, "Oh, but I had forgotten about Benediction ; when would you like to look over the music ?"

A quiet smile played round Mrs. Trelawney's mouth, without affecting any other part of her face.

"Thank you," she said; "if you would be kind

enough to come to the church a few minutes before Benediction, and give me the music that is to be played, I shall be much obliged to you."

"But suppose I give you a Litany you don't know?" suggested Miss Crofton. "Had you not better allow a little time to try the music over? You see," she added apologetically, "our choir can only sing what they have learnt and practised."

Again that smile of the lips only, as Mrs. Trelawney said quietly: "I think I know most of the Litanies in use, and at all events I can play at sight sufficiently for that. I have been accustomed to accompany a choir, and am not afraid of breaking down."

Miss Crofton coloured with the painful consciousness that she had committed "worse than a fault, a blunder," and endeavoured to retrieve it by saying hastily:

"Of course not. I beg your pardon; I am so nervous myself about playing in church, that I fancy every one else must be the same."

If Mrs. Trelawney had intended to amuse herself by making her companion feel awkward, she would certainly have attained her object; but she was quite incapable of such vulgarity (not to say rudeness), and was really sorry for the impression she saw her words had made. She smiled this time with her whole face, as she said:

"And you charitably follow the golden rule of doing to others as you would have them do to you; it is very kind of you, and indeed I feel most grateful: it is only that as, somehow, I never am nervous myself about playing, it is difficult for me to realise the feeling."

"Never nervous about playing! how I envy you!" exclaimed Annie. "Well, then, we will meet in the organ-gallery—I wish it were really an *organ*-gallery; harmoniums are an abomination fit only for savages!—a little before eight."

CHAPTER IV.

"Press the loud organs! roll the living psalm,
In jubilant thunders, o'er the prostrate crowd!"
F. W. FABER.

MRS. TRELAWNEY did not do much justice to her dinner that day, or show herself duly grateful for the trouble Mrs. North had taken to prepare it "to her liking," as she said; and the good woman was consequently just the least bit disposed to be cross and disobliging, when Mrs. Trelawney sent a message in the afternoon to say that she would be glad to speak to her for a few minutes.

"I'll be bound," she said to Hannah, her maid-of-all-work, "she is one o' them fine ladies as can't abide plain, wholesome food, and wants it made into all sorts of messes, and what they calls *kickshoes*; but I knows nothink about all that there, and I'm too old to learn; so if she can't eat a good mutton-chop or beefsteak, she must find some one else to cook for her, that's all."

"Lawk, ma'am!" replied Hannah, a somewhat rough country-girl, as untrained as an Exmoor pony, but kind-hearted withal, "her be only a bit *whisht;* folks can't cut their dinners when they're a-crying after their husbands; her ha'n't a-been a widdy many months, her caps is all so new."

Half amused at Hannah's logic, and half angry with her for the impertinent curiosity—so naively confessed—of peeping into Mrs. Trelawney's cap-box, Mrs. North jumbled up both feelings together, exclaiming:

"How dare you go meddling with Mrs. Trelawney's caps, or her husband either, you little fool!" (whereat Hannah stared, feeling quite guiltless of any desire to disturb the ghost of the late Benjamin Trelawney, Esq.); "crying after him, indeed! much *you* know about widdies! You may thank the Lord you never had no husband to cry after."

Which pious counsel Hannah did not follow, not feeling in her heart any special gratitude on that particular account. She made her escape more quickly than elegantly, muttering to herself, "Her *were* a-crying, though, when I bust into the room so orkard-like to fetch away her dinner," much in the same spirit that Galileo is reported to have muttered, *E neppur si muove.*

It was not, however, to complain about her dinner that Mrs. Trelawney had summoned her landlady, but to ask if she had any more spare rooms in the house. Mrs. North's ruffled feathers were smoothed down instantly; and though, in honest truth, she had not any more spare rooms, it immediately suggested itself to her fertile brain that she might create them by giving up her own best parlour, and sitting in a sort of store-room at the back of the shop, and by condemning the unfortunate Hannah to sleep in a garret used at

D

present only for lumber. She had only one scruple on the subject. Father Wilfrid had engaged two rooms for his schoolmistress, on the understanding that he should pay the rent himself; would he be willing, or indeed able, to indulge her fancy for a larger suite of apartments? Mrs. North was a good-natured woman, but her good nature was not of so exalted a kind as to dispose her to give up her own sitting-room without ample security for the *quid pro quo*. Consequently she hesitated a little, cleared her throat, and was troubled with a slight fit of coughing, before she replied :

"Well, you see, ma'am, it depends—"

"On what?" asked Mrs. Trelawney, breaking into the solemn pause.

Mrs. North had another fit of coughing. She had been concocting a little speech, and this ill-timed question interfered with it. It was "not in the bond."

Guessing somewhat of the state of affairs, Mrs. Trelawney proceeded, "If I remain here, I should wish to have the use of two more rooms, though I shall not always occupy them; Father Wilfrid has not told me what rent you ask for them, but I presume it is not unreasonable. I shall, of course, be willing to double it if I take four rooms instead of two."

After this very satisfactory piece of plain speaking, Mrs. North no longer hesitated, and her troublesome cough appeared greatly relieved. With some regard, however, for consistency, she said :

"I was a-going to say, ma'am, as it depended on how many more rooms you was pleased to want." It was not in the least what she had been going to say, but some people have a convenient theory that "all is fair" in trade as well as "in love or war," and seem to expect that the scales of God's Eternal Justice will measure by false weights like their own. "But," she continued, "if it's only two, I think, ma'am, as I could let you have them."

"Very well," replied Mrs. Trelawney; "in that case, I shall probably remain here. For how long did Father Wilfrid engage these rooms?"

"For a month certain, ma'am, and with the refusal of them afterwards."

"Ah! yes, very right; and the rent?"

Mrs. North felt a strong temptation to add a little to the price she had agreed upon with Father Wilfrid; but, in the first place, she was a tolerably good Catholic, and had been taught the obligations of the seventh commandment, and, in the next place, it would have been very short-sighted policy, for, of course, her duplicity would have been speedily discovered. On the whole, therefore, she preferred being honest, and said:

"I told Father Wilfrid, ma'am, he should have them for a guinea a week, but I gets five-and-twenty shillings for them from ladies in the summer; you see, ma'am," looking complacently round the room, "the furniture is very good; that sofy, now—my poor 'usband bought it at a sale, and—"

Whether the reference to "my poor 'usband" was too much for Mrs. Trelawney's feelings, or from some other cause, she cut short her landlady's inventory of the furniture very unceremoniously—the more so, perhaps, from the conviction that her interruption would not be an unwelcome one.

"If I remain," she said, "I will give you two guineas and a half for the four rooms; I shall use the second sitting-room always for breakfast and dinner, but the bedroom will probably not often be occupied."

Mrs. North executed her very best courtesy, and professed herself abundantly satisfied with this arrangement, offering, at the same time, to have the two other rooms "put to rights" immediately.

"That is not necessary," said Mrs. Trelawney; "I have not yet decided on remaining; in a month's time, I will let you know. I should like tea at half-past six, if you please."

Feeling that this was intended as a dismissal, Mrs. North retired in a state of good temper and general benevolence, which overflowed upon Hannah, to the extent of her giving that damsel leave to go out to tea with a friend in the village, saying she would wait upon Mrs. Trelawney herself. In her own mind she argued, and not altogether illogically, that a lady who was so anxious to secure additional rooms, was not likely to change her mind and go away at the end of a month; and, in truth, Mrs. Trelawney had not the smallest intention of going away. With a woman's quickness of perception, she felt convinced that she should suit Father Wilfrid; and if he did not exactly suit her, she was accustomed to fitting herself into adverse circumstances, and would not so much mind it; "and besides," she said to herself, "if I am to be a slave, I don't care who is my master, and I would rather wear real iron fetters than sham golden ones."

Was she thinking only of the self-imposed drudgery of a schoolmistress's life, or of any thing further? She was a Cornish woman, and traced her descent from the ancient Britons; there might be Saxon blood in her veins; that mattered little: Briton and Saxon are one pure race, the " old original" children of the soil, untainted by Danish ferocity or Norman pride. But what roused the old heathen spirit in her just then? and was it a dream or a trick of the imagination that filled the air with clashing cymbals and a chorus of wild voices, shouting,

" Rule Britannia! Britannia rules the waves!
Britons never, never, *never* shall be slaves"?

St. Francis of Sales says, that there are two kinds of ecstasies, one coming from God, and one from the devil: the ecstasy of Divine Love, and the ecstasy of frenzied passion; it may be that there is also a third kind, neither divine nor diabolical (unless, indeed, it spring from that pride of intellect which is the devil's own sin), neither spiritual nor animal, but human and intellectual. Mrs. Trelawney's dream (if such it were) had, at all events, one attribute of an ecstasy—it rendered her stiff and motionless as a statue, as she sat with closed eyes and clasped hands. But it was only for a few minutes; the clattering of a horse's hoofs brought her to her senses (if she had ever been out of them), and, looking up, she saw Miss Crofton cantering past the window on a pretty gray pony, alone and unattended, except by a tawny Newfoundland dog.

"Out of bounds for to-day!" thought Mrs. Trelawney. "I wonder if she is going over Hillsborough Tor to meet Robert Hatton."

Apparently not; for she passed the narrow sunk fence leading up towards the moor, and turned down the road into the village.

"And she thought I should want to *practise* a Litany and *Tantum Ergo!* She is afraid of a *fiasco* to-night. Ah! well, I wonder what sort of harmonium they have."

Half an hour afterwards, when she was unpacking her "things," she took out a large crucifix of somewhat rough workmanship, and, suddenly kissing it fervently, exclaimed, "Thank God, I am a Catholic!" It was the answer of grace to nature, the victory of the divine over the human spirit; but it was only a victory, not a conquest—not yet.

Punctually at a quarter before eight she was at the church-door; Miss Crofton was already there looking out for her. *She* was nervous about the music, if Mrs. Trelawney was not. The harmonium stood in a sort of gallery over the sacristy, at one side of the sanctuary, which was reached by a staircase leading from the former. As they passed through, Father Wilfrid, who was there, said:

"It is very kind of you, Mrs. Trelawney, to play to-night without any preparation. I think we have a tolerably docile choir, but you must keep them in good order—make them *feel* that you are choir-mistress, and must be obeyed."

"There! didn't I tell you he was strict?" said Annie, as they went up the stairs. "Charley says he is a martinet, but that is not quite a nice word for a priest. All the same, I should not like to go into a monastery where he was novice-master. However, he will uphold *your* authority in the school and in the choir, which is a good thing."

"Had we not better look out the music?" suggested Mrs. Trelawney.

Annie felt rebuked, and, like a spoilt child as she was, answered pettishly:

"Very well, here it is," at the same time opening a book containing the *O Salutaris* and *Tantum Ergo* most commonly used, on two opposite pages. A glance was enough for Mrs. Trelawney, who said, "Thank you; and the Litany for to-night?"

Annie took out a small manuscript-book. "Any one of these that you like," she said; "they know them all."

Mrs. Trelawney turned over three or four leaves, and then, having apparently found one to suit her, laid it open on the desk.

"Do you sing the *Adoremus in Æternum* afterwards?" she asked.

"Yes, instead of a voluntary, after the priest has gone out; 'Blessed be God,' is said directly after Benediction."

By this time the church was about half-full of people; four men and six boys had assembled round the harmonium, and an acolyte had begun lighting the candles on the altar. Annie Crofton disappeared, and Mrs. Trelawney was left "alone in her glory." She seated herself very quietly at the harmonium, pulled out four stops, and began to play softly, "Lift up your heads, O ye gates," from Handel's *Messiah*. As the procession from the sacristy entered the church, the strain gradually swelled louder and fuller, till, as the priest mounted the altar-steps, a sudden burst of triumph seemed to announce, " The King of Glory shall come in." Then all was hushed and still while the tabernacle was opened, and till the moment when the King of kings took possession of His throne, when softly, like the breath of sweet incense, rose clear and distinct, from tones and voices in unison, the hymn of praise, *O Salutaris Hostia !"*

Never before had the choir sung as they sang that night, never before had they made the discovery that they *could* so sing. Guided and sustained by what seemed to them some mysterious power, their voices, rough and untutored though they were, rose as if wafted on angels' wings; and yet Mrs. Trelawney did nothing but play the simple notes of the accompaniment exactly as they were written. She was even too considerate to risk embarrassing the singers by any change of time in the Litany after the *Kyrie Eleison*, but only accelerated it so gradually as to be almost imperceptible, till, with the triplet beginning, *Causa nostræ lætitiæ*, it swung from side to side (the alternate verses were sung in the sanctuary), like the unfettered song of some joyous bird; but after the last *Ora pro nobis*, there came a momentary pause, and then the *Agnus Dei* followed in slow, measured tones. Slowly and solemnly, too, rolled the glorious *Tantum Ergo* over the heads bent low in silent adoration; and after the prayer, during the few moments whilst the

Blessed Sacrament was taken down from the throne, there came a gentle strain, like the breath of a "moist whistling wind," dying away into an echo as the priest took his Lord into his arms, that with a holy boldness he might bid Him bless His people.

Having been told that the *Adoremus in Æternum* was sung "instead of a voluntary," it had not been Mrs. Trelawney's intention to play any thing after it; but the choir had stopped in the sacristy instead of merely passing through, and she overheard Father Wilfrid talking to them. She felt shy of passing through their midst, and she was still sitting before the harmonium; the notes were under her very fingers; the temptation was irresistible, and a sound like the plaintive warbling of nightingales in a grove filled the church. Those of the congregation who had not gone out, remained entranced; and after listening for a few moments, Father Wilfrid mounted the stairs of the organ-gallery, accompanied by Miss Crofton. Before they reached it, however, Mrs. Trelawney had closed the instrument, and was quietly putting on her cloak and gloves.

"I really don't know how to thank you," began Father Wilfrid; when she rather bluntly interrupted him with, "Indeed you have nothing to thank me for; I am used to playing in church, and it is no trouble to me."

"Oh, but do tell me," exclaimed Miss Crofton, "where you found that beautiful *vox humana*; I thought only organs could have it."

Mrs. Trelawney laughed. "Only organs *can* have it," she said; "I found none here; I used only the ordinary stops."

"Well, I never heard any thing so like the *vox humana* in my life," declared Annie.

"But I hope my voice *is* a human one," was the quiet reply.

"*Your* voice! you don't mean to say it was your own? But there were no words!"

"Perhaps," said Mrs. Trelawney, "you have never heard the Cologne Singers, or a Manchester *Lieder tofel;* it is nothing very wonderful to produce sounds without words. But may I say good night to you now?—I feel a little tired, and I think Mrs. North is waiting in the church for me."

"And papa is waiting for me," replied Annie, with ready tact; "so good night, Mrs. Trelawney;" and she ran down the stairs.

Mrs. Trelawney turned to Father Wilfrid: "May I come to the school to-morrow morning?" she said.

"Certainly," he replied; "if you will allow me, I will meet you there at eleven."

CHAPTER V.

"But if the judgments are untrue, what then?"
F. W. FABER.

ANOTHER week found Mrs. Trelawney duly installed as schoolmistress at Stonebridge, greatly to the satisfaction of all parties concerned. The children were delighted; for though she held "the reins of government" with a firm hand, and even occasionally inflicted summary punishment for offences which Miss Crofton had allowed to go scot-free—as, for instance, for unpunctuality, or wilful breach of school-discipline—they all felt and understood that she cared for them, and took an interest in them, and sympathised with them, in a way to which they had not hitherto been accustomed; and they appreciated her accordingly, and were fast learning to love her,—for children quickly find out who are their real friends.

Father Wilfrid, too, was satisfied—abundantly satisfied—so far as the school was concerned; for Mrs. Trelawney could not have been a better or more efficient teacher, if she had been certificated a hundred times over. And as regarded the choir, he was more than satisfied, he was delighted ; on that first night, at Benediction, he had been a little afraid that she might turn out *too* accomplished a musician, and wish to substitute Mozart's Masses and elaborate *cantiques* for the grand old Gregorian music which alone he thought fitted to express reverence or adoration, and which he had himself taken infinite pains to teach his choir; and he consequently came with some little trepidation to "assist at" the Saturday practising; but Mrs. Trelawney speedily relieved his mind by saying, as she turned over the portfolio of music:

"Then we really *may* 'sing to the praise and glory of God,' as they say in the Protestant churches, and not for the entertainment of the congregation ?"

"I hope so," replied Father Wilfrid. "I would rather have no music in my church all the year round, than turn the Holy Mass into a concert or an oratorio."

"And yet," said Mrs. Trelawney, throwing out a *feeler*, "the elaborate music in Catholic churches often attracts Protestants into them."

"And as often drives them out again disgusted, and complaining only too justly that we turn our churches into theatres."

"You are severe," said Mrs. Trelawney.

"Is there not a cause?" he replied. "I have heard Mozart's Masses sung on solemn festivals by men and women whose lives were a public scandal—actors and actresses fresh from *Lucrezia Borgia* and *La Traviata!* And the Mass," he continued, turning towards the tabernacle with a rapt gaze, and in a voice trembling with emotion, "is the offering of the Son of God for the sin of the world!"

There was a pause. The tone of Father Wilfrid's last words had fairly taken Mrs. Trelawney by surprise, and given her a new insight into his character; he had an almost morbid horror of "*seeming* to be religious," and would have been an excellent disciple of St. Philip Neri,—for nothing pleased him better than to be caught reading the last number of *Punch*, or mixing a salad for his dinner, when any one came to him for advice; and once, in the latter case, he had shown so much interest in his occupation, that his visitor went away fully impressed with the idea that the worthy priest of Stonebridge was not much given to mortifying his taste, and very decidedly *eat mustard with his beef.* Had the good gentleman returned an hour later, however, he might have met Father Wilfrid's housekeeper carrying the salad to a poor invalid, who had no relish for any thing else ; and if he had proceeded to look in through the parlour-window, he would have seen the priest himself dining on oatmeal-porridge and bread-and-butter—coarse bread and salt butter, moreover. But he did *not* see these things.

When at last Mrs. Trelawney's reply came, it was in the blunt but energetic form :

" I hate Mozart's Masses."

" Do you?" said Father Wilfrid, looking rather surprised. " I thought I had heard you tell Miss Crofton you admired his operas ; and it seems to me they are very much alike."

" Yes, that is just it," replied Mrs. Trelawney in a decisive tone.

The conclusion was not quite so self-evident to Father Wilfrid ; but the choir now began to assemble, and practising had to take the place of conversation.

After going steadily through the Mass, and occasionally repeating a passage, with a view to ascertaining the exact power of voice she would have under her command, Mrs. Trelawney remarked that, as the next day was the Feast of the Maternity of the Blessed Virgin, they ought to sing something in honour of our Lady at the Offertory, " if Father Wilfrid has no objection," she added deferentially, turning towards him.

" No," he replied, smiling, " I am not so severe as all that. Sing what you like at the Offertory, so that it is solemn and devotional ; I think I can trust you for that."

Mrs. Trelawney slightly bent her head, and, addressing the first tenor in the choir, asked if he could sing Schubert's *Ave Maria*, at the same time playing a few bars of the exquisitely touching accompaniment.

Of course he could not; he had never heard of it, and knew about as much of Schubert as of King Theodore.

"You sing it yourself, perhaps?" suggested Father Wilfrid.

She stopped playing suddenly, and a strange light shone in her eyes as she turned them full upon him.

"Not here," she replied; "I mean, not during the Mass."

"No, that is right; I am glad you think so, too," he answered, looking pleased, and feeling pleased; for he had made the suggestion very unwillingly, and only from a kind-hearted wish not to insist on forbidding her to sing if she wished to do so. The *Ave Maris Stella* was substituted for Schubert's prayer, and, being sung in unison, there was no reason why Mrs. Trelawney should not join in it as well as any one else in the congregation.

But if Father Wilfrid was satisfied as regarded his school and his choir, he was not altogether without misgivings as to the wisdom of his experiment. Mrs. Trelawney went through all her duties with scrupulous fidelity and unerring punctuality; but, except now and then with the children out of school-hours, there was something unpleasantly mechanical about her, something giving an impression that she either could not or would not trust herself to act naturally, and suggesting the further impression, that a nature requiring such severe self-control might be dangerous if suffered to break loose. A little incident, moreover, occurred, which strengthened this impression. On coming into the sacristy one day to look for something, Father Wilfrid heard the sound of the harmonium; he had begged Mrs. Trelawney to practise there whenever she liked, and had given her a key of the church for that purpose,—so it was all right so far. But what was the use of practising the accompaniment of Schubert's *Ave Maria*, when no one in the choir could sing it? and yet Father Wilfrid, who had a good ear for music, recognised the notes at once. He had a good memory, too, however, and recollected that she had qualified her refusal to sing it by adding, "I mean, not during the Mass." There could be no harm, certainly, in singing for her own pleasure, or her own devotion it might be, in an empty church. Empty? Nay; God forgive us for so speaking of His earthly dwelling-place: but there was no human ear to listen, and to drink in the poison of mere sensual gratification. Moved, it must be confessed, by a spirit of curiosity, Father Wilfrid quietly sat down and listened. The notes seemed to rise and swell, and heave and toss, like rolling waves; the hands that passed over them, and bade them speak, were no mere piece of mechanism, but thrilling and palpitating with life in every touch. Then presently words came, resting at first on the sustaining chords, and then soaring freely out above and beyond them. A few moments, and suddenly words and accompaniment blended together in one loud, passionate cry for mercy,—entreating, imploring, pleading, with the desperate energy of a soul in agony, *Ora pro nobis peccatoribus, nunc, nunc,* as though ten thousand devils were dragging it down to hell; the tones were no longer those of mere agony, but of terror. Father Wilfrid started up, but a moment's reflection reminded him that the intrusion he meditated would be cruel and unfeeling. All at once the music stopped; there seemed no courage for the last words of the prayer. There was no sound, no movement, for a few moments, and then, in rich, full tones, but still a voice of passionate entreaty, came that masterpiece of touching eloquence from the *Messiah*, "But Thou didst not leave His soul in hell," which is like the patient, sorrowful pleading of the holy souls in purgatory. Father Wilfrid was literally entranced; he had never heard it, or any thing the least like it, before, and could hardly understand what it was that drew tears from his eyes as he listened to it. He did, however, fully understand, and gratefully appreciate, Mrs. Trelawney's refusal to sing solos during Mass or Benediction.

The sound of the closing of the harmonium warned him to make his escape before he was discovered, and Mrs. Trelawney never knew that there had been any witness to that outpouring of her heart's bitterness. To him it was as though he had heard it in the confessional; but he could not help feeling a little troubled at the glimpse he had thus unintentionally obtained into the inner life of one who was outwardly so cold and calm and mechanical; who treated him always with the studied deference and respect of a paid schoolmistress, and drew back with a sort of haughty independence whenever he attempted to show her any thing like kindness or sympathy.

Her month's trial was nearly over, and he knew almost as little of her as on the first day; indeed, she had never again spoken so freely to him as she had done on that first day, or given the slightest intimation of any desire to follow up the hint she had then thrown out, that perhaps she might give him more of her confidence "some day." It was natural enough, certainly, that she should prefer waiting to do this till she was more secure of remaining under his direction; people, especially reserved, undemonstrative people, do not like sowing their confidences broadcast wherever they may happen to go; still, in the present instance, he could not help wishing that he could see his way more clearly towards making the important decision, " to be, or not to be." And now the little glimpse he had accidentally obtained was more of an embarrassment than a help to him; he could neither use it, nor altogether ignore it.

Annie Crofton, who might, perhaps, indirectly have helped him,—for she would have *drawn out* Mrs. Trelawney,—was away on a visit which had been postponed till the school was off her hands, and would not return till long after the decision must be made.

After all, however, Mrs. Trelawney had stipulated for a written agreement that three months' notice should be given on both sides in case of dissatisfaction; and she was so evidently a person who *wished* to be taken at her word, that he could feel no scruple in doing so: if, therefore, *the worst came to the worst,* he could at any time

E

give her three months' notice, "or three months' salary,"—no, there she had outwitted him; there was to be no question of salary, and he would never be able to get rid of her in less than three months. But no great harm could be done in so short a time; as a schoolmistress she was invaluable, and in other ways she was of course a clear gain and a standing benefit to the mission.

On the whole, therefore, he had made up his mind to accept her, when, on the very day before the decision was to be made, he received, to his great surprise, a letter from Miss Crofton—to his surprise, because she had never written to him before in her life, though she was often away from home; when he had once asked her to do so, she had replied:

"Well, if any thing extraordinary happens, I will; but I hate writing letters, and have no taste for supplying my friends' waste-paper baskets, or for seeing scraps of my handwriting in their match-holders."

And as nothing extraordinary ever had happened, Miss Crofton had never written.

But here was a letter four pages long, and closely written, too—as closely, at least, as Annie could contrive to write; for her contempt of order and regularity manifested itself in as straggling and untidy a hand as a lady could well write.

Something extraordinary had evidently happened; what was it? We will take the liberty of looking over Father Wilfrid's shoulder as he reads his letter, having first ascertained that it is not marked *private and confidential*, though certainly it was intended for no eye but his own: but authors and readers have special privileges.

"DEAR FATHER WILFRID,

"The mere fact of my writing to you at all is a proof that I have something to say, and I hope you will not think me impertinent or meddling for saying it; but I think, before you engage Mrs. Trelawney, you ought to know some things that I have heard about her here. She has a daughter living here as companion to the eldest Miss Vivian, who, as you know, is a great invalid, and requires constant watching; in fact, she suffers from epileptic fits, and can never be safely left by herself. Well, so far as I can make out,—for they are all very mysterious on the subject, in consequence, I believe, of my being a Catholic,—it seems that Mrs. Trelawney treated her husband very unkindly in his last illness, and also interfered, in some not very honourable way, to make him alter his will and deprive this daughter of her fortune, on account of her being a Protestant (but of course they are shy of saying much about this to *me*)—at all events, the whole property was left to the widow, and only a very small annuity to Miss Trelawney. Why she and her mother separated, they do not seem to know, or, at all events, they won't tell me; but they evidently lay all the blame on poor Mrs. Trelawney. The daughter was obliged to look out for a situation, as she had not enough to live upon without it; but the Vivians were greatly astonished when I told them that Mrs. Trelawney was at Stonebridge on trial as a schoolmistress, as they say she has an ample fortune at her own free disposal. They have hit upon the marvellous supposition that she is employed as a cat's-paw by the Jesuits to get money for them!—a pretty little Protestant invention, of course; and, in fact, the whole story may be that, for any thing I know; but the Miss Trelawney who is here as companion to Maggie Vivian certainly *is* the daughter of our Mrs. Trelawney, and I thought you might as well know what is said about her here. Please don't accuse *me* of rash judging, or, if you do, let it be rash judging of *Miss* Trelawney, for I can't endure her (and she seems to hate all Catholics, so I suppose we are natural enemies); and I don't and won't believe any thing bad of our new schoolmistress, with her lovely *vox humana*—a woman's logic, you will say; but never mind that. I have fulfilled my duty and discharged my conscience as informer, and I must discharge my wrath by adding, that I don't believe a word of it.

"Your affectionate child,

"ANNIE CROFTON."

"Poor Annie!" thought Father Wilfrid; "she is a warm-hearted little special pleader, but I would not like to trust my case in her hands if she were a Q.C."

Seriously, however, he acknowledged that she had been quite right in telling him what she had heard, and it troubled him considerably; there is always *something* at the bottom of every idle tale, even though the something may be to the credit instead of the blame of the person whom it concerns; but this, *on the face of it*, was certainly *not* very satisfactory. As to the notion about the Jesuits, it was of course mere nonsense; Mrs. Trelawney was not *getting* money at all, but *spend-*

ing it, and that too with a liberal hand, even already, at Stonebridge. But there was the broad fact, as yet unaccounted for, that with so ample an income, she had allowed her only child to live as a dependant in the house of strangers; and even if there were family reasons sufficiently strong to justify a separation between mother and daughter, surely no reason could justify a parent who had such liberal means in leaving her child unprovided for. Was it possible that Mrs. Trelawney could have cheated her husband out of his money, and was now devoting it to the service of the Church as a sort of act of restitution? But that would imply a marvellously distorted conscience, and she was a particularly clear-headed and straightforward person; moreover, there was something about her which made it difficult to suspect her of any thing the very least dishonourable. He could fancy there might be a vein of cruelty in her nature; perhaps she had tormented her husband with controversy on his death-bed, which would be quite enough to make Protestants think her "unkind" to him; but that she should have deceived or cheated him—no, he could not fancy that; and yet, and yet—there have been swindlers and adventurers whom all the world trusted implicitly up to the last moment, when the bank broke, or the speculation turned out a mere invention of its promoters.

In short, poor Father Wilfrid felt in what our American cousins would call "a neat fix," and more heartily than ever did he wish that Mrs. Trelawney had never crossed his path. But something must be done, and that at once, too; what should it be? Though she had so emphatically declared her preference for " plain speaking," it would be a little awkward, to say the least of it, to ask a lady point-blank if she had embezzled her husband's money, and hardly less awkward to ask why she did not provide a home, or at all events a maintenance, for her daughter. Something, however, must be said, and perhaps she would relieve him by taking the plain speaking upon herself, as she had done on a former occasion.

Hoping most earnestly that this would be the case, Father Wilfrid set off the next afternoon to pay a visit to his mysterious schoolmistress, feeling something like the unfortunate man in one of Paget's tales, who got up to make a speech " with the impression strong on his mind that he had nothing to say."

CHAPTER VI.

> " True, true, constant thought
> Will overflow in words unconsciously;
> But when another speaks of Greece, it wounds me."
>
> BYRON.

MRS. TRELAWNEY received Father Wilfrid with her usual calm dignity of manner, and without any apparent nervousness or embarrassment.

" You have come, father," she said, " to tell me the result of my month's probation; do you consider me capable of undertaking your school, and conducting your choir in such a way as to satisfy you ?"

This was going straight to the point, certainly. Mrs. Trelawney had evidently not been educated in the Circumlocution Office, and the very directness of her question supplied him with a ready answer; there could not be a moment's doubt that she was eminently capable of filling both offices to perfection.

"I am very glad you are satisfied with my services," she replied; "I hope, as that is the case, you will allow me to continue them."

Halte là! Here was the real point at issue, the "tug of war," and it behoved Father Wilfrid to stand his ground firmly. Firmly, yes; but he was resolved it should also be kindly.

"Nothing," he said, "would give me greater pleasure than to have you permanently settled here, if you can feel satisfied that it is right for you to give up other ties and duties so entirely."

Her face flushed, but she said coldly, "What ties or duties do you refer to? I have none any more in this world."

But for the habitual self-control of a priest, Father Wilfrid would have started; but he betrayed no surprise as he said quietly, "You have a daughter."

"A daughter! Who says so? who has spoken of her?" demanded Mrs. Trelawney fiercely.

"Yourself," he replied calmly; "do you not remember telling me you should want a room for her, and also that she was not a Catholic?"

Like a wounded creature, Mrs. Trelawney's head drooped. "Yes, yes," she said, in a low, sad voice, "I remember now."

There was a few moments' pause, which he

did not interrupt; and then, raising her eyes for a moment, as if asking to be believed, she dropped them again, and said:

"You think the circumstances require explanation; though you are willing to dispense with a certificate of scholarship, you would like a certificate of morals with your schoolmistress?"

Her words, blunt as they were, so exactly expressed his own feeling, that he had nothing to say, and, like a wise man, having nothing to say, he said it,—though perfectly aware that, under the circumstances, silence was almost an insult; but she had set him the example of plain speaking, and he was only following it by an equally expressive silence.

She hesitated a moment, and then continued: "Unfortunately, there is no one to whom I can refer you, except the priest at Warwick, who has already, I believe, written to you, and whose testimony, as he was my confessor, is not worth much; my own word is worth, perhaps, still less, —but it is all I have to give you: such as it is, will you take it?"

Once more she raised her eyes, with a pleading, beseeching look in them, that would have melted a harder heart than Father Wilfrid's; if it was a mere piece of acting, she was more perfect in her part than the arch-deceiver himself.

"Of course I will," he replied. "But I am sorry to distress you in this way; do not say more to me than you think right and necessary. Perhaps I ought to tell you," he continued, taking a leaf out of her own book, "that Miss Crofton is staying now with the Vivians, of Carew Castle—" He stopped, out of sheer pity for the look of keen suffering produced by these words; but Mrs. Trelawney's lips only trembled slightly, as she said:

"I understand you now; will you have the charity to tell me what has been laid to my charge?"

She was helping him out certainly as much as he could wish, and yet he hesitated; somehow, as he looked at her, he could not bring himself to deal so cruel a blow.

"Will you not tell me?" she said. "How can I satisfy you without knowing?"

Ay, how indeed? This woman was either singularly straightforward or diabolically subtle.

Seeing that there was no help for it, Father Wilfrid said, as gently as he could:

"The Vivians are old-fashioned Protestants, and strongly prejudiced against Catholics, so that I do not attach much importance to any thing I hear through them; but they seem to have an impression that—" How on earth was he to say it? Would she not help him? No, not this time; she sat still and silent as a statue, and almost as white. When we find we *must* do a thing, we generally do it; and Father Wilfrid did not pause more than a moment before he continued, "that it could not have been Mr. Trelawney's intention to leave his only daughter unprovided for, and that he may have been influenced during his last illness to alter his will."

Not a single muscle of her face relaxed, as she said slowly:

"*Influenced* to *alter* his will! Are you sparing me, father? do they think I forged his will?"

It was an ugly word to speak, but she spoke it clearly and distinctly; and as Father Wilfrid looked up at her, she neither coloured nor flinched.

"No, indeed," he said; "there is not even the least hint of such a thought, of any thing so dreadful."

"I don't see much difference," she said, "between forging a will, and getting it altered; the guilt may be greater in degree, but it is the same in kind."

"Hardly, I think," said Father Wilfrid; "forgery must always be in itself a sin; but influence, if not used dishonourably, may in some such cases be justifiable."

"You think so? Well, then, you will not be scandalised when I tell you that I *did* try to persuade my husband to alter his will; but not as they think, not as they think," she repeated, as if speaking to herself. "I was unsuccessful in my attempt—he refused to alter it; they might have remembered," she continued, while an indignant light flashed for a moment in her eyes, "that the will was dated five years before his death, six months before I became a Catholic, and that there was neither alteration nor addition made afterwards. So far I can prove my words by a reference to the will itself; for the rest I must be dependent on how far you can trust me."

"I think I understand you," said Father Wilfrid, anxious to spare her as far as possible; "and, indeed, I could not for a moment doubt your word.

You wished, I suppose, after you became a Catholic, to persuade Mr. Trelawney to provide a separate maintenance for his daughter?"

He meant it kindly; but he had laid his finger on a wound that would not bear the lightest touch. A low, half-stifled cry broke from Mrs. Trelawney: "My child! my own child!" and before he had time to speak another word, she had risen, and her hand was already on the door.

But she was stronger than she had given herself credit for; and before she had opened it, she turned back, turned back slowly and calmly, and turned towards him eyes not full of tears, as he had expected, but eyes which seemed to have utterly exhausted all their power of weeping, from which all expression seemed to have died out—eyes which told, to such as could read their language, of an anguish too deep for outward show, too bitter for tears; a grief, moreover, which was "too proud to bear a pitying eye;" for, seeing that he was about to speak, she silenced him by a quick movement of her hand, and then, resuming her seat, said, in a low but perfectly distinct voice:

"You have a right to a clear explanation, and I will give it to you, as far as it is possible for me to do so. No; do not stop me. I can say it now; another time I might not be able. There is a very painful misunderstanding between my daughter and myself. Her father idolised her, and she—God forgive me! for I taught her to do it—I believe she almost worshiped him. He educated her himself, except the few things she learnt from me,—taught her, as he would have taught a boy, Latin and Greek and Euclid; even in his last illness, their greatest delight was to read together passages from Horace or Euripides. And other things, too, he taught her: she learnt to write like a lawyer's clerk, and copied all his legal documents for him; so that, you see—"

Father Wilfrid's countenance so evidently expressed that he did see, that Mrs. Trelawney was spared further explanation on this point. She continued:

"My husband was a Protestant—such as one rarely meets with now—sincere, earnest-minded, deeply religious in his tone of mind; but so strongly prejudiced against Catholics, that he would scarcely even admit them to be Christians. This, too, he taught his child—my child. I thought they would hate me for being a Catholic, and I concealed it; out of human respect—no, human *love*—I was false to God. I deceived my husband and my child for four years, then an accidental circumstance betrayed me; the shock was my husband's death-stroke: he never recovered it, and my child looks upon me as his murderess."

She stopped. Those tearless eyes were still fixed upon him like piercing swords.

"But during his illness," said Father Wilfrid,— "it was a long one, I think,—were you not able to soften any of his prejudices?"

Her face contracted with a sudden spasm of pain. "No," she said; "oh, no; I dared not even try—I could not; I was in despair. I thought I had killed him, and I dared not speak to him, dared not stay more than a few minutes at a time with him, dared not *see* him suffer, dared not listen to his voice, lest—lest—"

"Lest what, my child?" he said kindly, seeing that she needed a word of help.

"Lest I should apostatise," she said bluntly, but in a thick, hoarse voice, "lest I should give way to the longing, the intense, consuming desire, to save his life at the cost of my own soul. They thought I was cold, indifferent, that I didn't care, that I didn't love him—and *she* thought it; she thinks it now, my own child thinks it, and spurns me from her: and a thousand times I was on the point of going straight to hell for love of him. I would do it now, now this moment!" she exclaimed wildly, "if it would bring him back to me."

For all that he was so simple and unassuming, Father Wilfrid was an experienced master in the spiritual life, and he knew full well that these words were wrung in a moment of agony from the inferior will, and that she was scarcely even responsible for them. A fierce storm had made wild havoc with the surface of the stream, but down deep below it followed its appointed course, calmly and evenly. He neither reproved nor contradicted her, but reverently made the sign of the cross over her as he said:

"God has been very good to you, my child."

"*Good!*" she repeated, in a bitter tone; "He is very cruel to me."

"Listen," he said authoritatively. "God has kept you, by a miracle of grace, from committing a great mortal sin, and more than that: He has given you a cross to bear, which is like a perpetual martyrdom, and may merit for you a martyr's crown."

She seemed scarcely to have heard, much less understood, his words; part of her task was still unfinished, and she was gathering up all her remaining strength to accomplish it.

"I have been congratulated," she said, in a stiff, constrained voice, "on having *lost nothing* by becoming a Catholic, on not being reduced to work, or to be dependent on charity for my living, like many converts. *Lost nothing!* I lost—" She stopped, and clenched her hands tightly together, then went on more calmly, "You are a priest. You cannot understand—pardon me, I was only going to say that this money is hateful to me. I cannot use it: I dare not waste it. For God's sake, take it, either with me or without me, and let it do some good if it can!"

He was about to speak; but she quietly stopped him, and went on:

"I told you some time ago that I had motives for taking the situation of a schoolmistress that I might, perhaps, speak of to you at another time, and in another place. Is this a confession-night?"

It was not so much the suddenness and abruptness of the question that struck him, as the extraordinary absence of mind which it seemed to evince, especially in so very methodical a person as Mrs. Trelawney, who ought to have known perfectly well that Tuesday was not a "confession-night," under ordinary circumstances. Perhaps she did know. Perhaps she asked literally "for the asking," to gain a little breathing-time;

but such an idea never occurred to the unsuspicious mind of the good priest.

"Tuesday? No; not generally," he said. "But you know I am always ready to hear you at any time. I shall be at home all the evening after six o'clock."

"Thank you!" she replied. "I have only one word more now to say. I shall, of course, follow your direction as to whether it is right for me to undertake such a life at all. But, supposing that it is, could you *now*"—she looked up for a moment, as if to remind him of all she had before told him—"could you *now*," she repeated, "feel satisfied to retain my services for your school and choir here?"

It was a return—and he felt that it was *intended* to be a return—to the business-like tone of the first part of their interview. That look told him plainly enough that she had no more strength left for any thing else, and that the kindest thing he could do would be to say simply, "Yes," or "No," and leave her. But should it be "Yes," or "No"? Father Wilfrid was by no means an impulsive person, or easily carried away by any transitory feeling; but as he met that look, he hesitated only for a moment before he said:

"Yes, Mrs. Trelawney, quite satisfied."

She tried to thank him, but her eyes filled with tears, and she could not speak. He rose to go, merely saying, with a kind smile, as he gave her his blessing:

"Don't trouble yourself any more now. I will see you again to-morrow."

She saw him that evening at the church, and came away with the knowledge that—for the present, at all events—she was schoolmistress of Stonebridge.

CHAPTER VII.

"To be wroth with one we love
Doth work like madness in the brain."
COLERIDGE.

It is time to return to Annie Crofton, who is just now waiting impatiently for Father Wilfrid's reply to her letter, several days having elapsed since her own had been despatched. It is to be feared she had not profited much by the lecture given her by her governess on a certain occasion when she had scandalised that good lady by characterising patience as "one of the tiresome virtues, like prudence and perseverance; very good for old maids, but quite useless to any one else." It was really too bad, she thought, of Father Wilfrid to keep her in such suspense. He must know she was dying to hear from him; and, besides, it was really and positively a sin against charity in him not to clear Mrs. Trelawney's character at once from such cruel suspicions,—what could he mean by it? Was it possible—? No, Annie was determined *not* to think it possible; how could a woman who so loved children defraud her own child? How could a Catholic, constantly frequenting the Sacraments, continue in unlawful possession of her husband's property?

"No, I don't, and I won't, and I sha'n't believe it," Annie declared over and over again to herself. "What *can* Father Wilfrid be dreaming of, not to write and stop this plague of tongues?"

For the Vivians, whose curiosity seemed wonderfully excited about Mrs. Trelawney, were constantly cross-questioning Annie on the subject, though they dared not, after the first few days, insinuate any thing against her; for Annie had met their somewhat incautiously expressed suspicions with a downright refusal to listen to any repetition of them. With Miss Trelawney she held no communication whatever, except what the barest civility required at the breakfast- or dinner-table; for that young lady devoted herself entirely to her invalid charge, and never joined the rest of the family except at meals. If they chanced to meet each other in the house or grounds, they exchanged the coldest and stiffest of all possible salutations; Miss Trelawney, indeed, would sometimes gather up the skirts of her dress, as though to guard against its possible contamination by contact with that of a "Papist."

Annie would simply have laughed at this in any one else, but between her and Miss Trelawney there seemed a sort of instinctive antagonism; and she had occasionally, with *malice prepense*, it must be confessed, contrived to meet her in a very narrow path, having previously put on an extra-large crinoline, which extended her dress across its entire width. It was an irresistible source of

F

amusement to her, when drawing aside to let Miss
Trelawney pass, to hear the grating sound produced by the friction of her silk skirt across the
crape flounces of her enemy, who would walk
majestically past, with a slight inclination of her
head, as cold and stately as if she had been
Empress of all the Russias, and Annie the most
insignificant of her attendants. For Maude Trelawney was in every possible respect a contrast to
Annie Crofton. She was tall, slight, and dark ;
Annie was little and fair, not fat, certainly ; but
still far too well proportioned to be called lean.
Maude was silent, reserved, and grave—more than
grave, she was sad—sad with that gloomy sadness
which sorrows without hope ; not even the faintest shadow of a smile ever lighted up her eye, or
played upon her lip. Annie seemed to live in a
perpetual flow of animal spirits and merry talk,
with a capacity for mischievous fun, which would
have got her into endless scrapes, if she had indulged it freely, and which did often get her into
trouble, or what would have been trouble to any
one else,—but nothing ever seemed a trouble to
Annie. If people were cross to her, she laughed
at them ; if they were offended with her, she
begged their pardon with such perfect good temper that it was impossible for them to bear malice.
And when Father Wilfrid lectured her gravely for
her imprudence, she would listen very demurely
till he came to a pause, and then say: "Is the
sermon over, father? because, if so, it is time for
the benediction," and kneel down for his blessing
without saying another word, so that he found it
really impossible to be angry with her.

The two girls were the same age, eighteen; but Maude Trelawney seemed to have already lived out her life, while Annie Crofton had not even begun it. There was a worn, spent, almost haggard look in Maude's face, which might have belonged to that of a woman of fifty; while there was a certain absence of expression in Annie's countenance, which betokened a child's ignorance both of deep joy and deep sorrow. It was Maude's nature to brood silently over her own thoughts, till they took exaggerated and distorted forms, haunting her imagination, and exciting her brain to a degree that would have driven a weak-minded person to the verge, if not over the verge, of madness; but Maude was emphatically strong-minded, —her wildest imaginations were under the control of a sharp curb; and, with the exception of certain prejudices, too strong to be concealed, nothing appeared on the surface to denote any mental agitation. Annie Crofton, on the contrary, seldom troubled herself to go through any process of thinking at all; and, as to brooding over a thought, she had not even the faintest idea of what was meant by such a proceeding: to her impulsive nature, thinking and acting were synonymous terms. Often, indeed, the action came first, and the thought afterwards—a propensity that had earned her the nickname of *Scatterbrains* from her father, and the less polite, but more expressive, one of *Little Blunderbuss* from her brother. It would have been possible to Maude to commit a great crime, but she had a supreme contempt for *mistakes*. Annie would have shrunk back terrified from the faintest suggestion of a sin, but never realised a blunder till after she had committed it.

One of Maude's strongest prejudices, as we have already seen, was against Catholics; and with her a prejudice amounted almost to a mania. She had encouraged and fostered it till she had come seriously to believe, or to *think* she believed, that every Catholic was an incarnation of diabolical wickedness, a slave bound over hand and foot to work out the designs of the Prince of Darkness; and her inflexible nature made no allowance for exceptions in what she had laid down as a general rule.

Brought up in the belief that the whole Catholic priesthood, *en masse*, was a sort of secret society, having for its object the corruption of faith and morals all over the world, her own imagination had further invested it with a kind of witchcraft, or sorcery, acting like a charm on all who came within its influence, withering up whatever natural virtues they might possess, and gradually *educating* them in every refinement of vice and hypocrisy.

Too passionate to reason with her feelings, she became their slave. What she loved, she worshiped; what she hated, she spurned and trampled on; and she hated Catholics with that bitter and special hatred which in all ages has been the chief touchstone of obstinate heresy.

And this thing that she hated, this thing that she despised and scorned, this thing that to her was utterly vile and shameful, had suddenly and unexpectedly revealed itself to her in the person of her own mother!

On the morning of the day when this shock fell upon her, Maude Trelawney was a high-spirited, enthusiastic girl, loving and warm-hearted, radiant with the freshness and beauty of "sweet seventeen." In the evening she was cold, stiff, passionless; the fire of her eyes was quenched, and their light extinguished. She moved and spoke as though her body were a mere machine, suddenly deprived of the living soul which had inhabited it. It was a state of mental paralysis, but it was soon succeeded by a still sadder one. The first use she made of the full power to realise what had happened, was to tear herself violently from the arms that held her in a mother's strong embrace, and, exclaiming, "Don't touch me! Don't come near me!" to fly from her as from a deadly serpent, and lock herself up in her own oom.

We have said, that what Maude loved, she worshiped; and she had loved both her father and mother with all her heart, and all her mind, and all her soul, and all her strength,—for God was more an object of fear than of love to her; and she knew nothing as yet of any other human affection. But though she loved both equally, she had always been more peculiarly her father's child. Having no son, he had educated her as gentle-natured, warm-hearted men will often, in such cases, educate a daughter. He had taught her all that he knew himself, made her his companion and friend; and latterly she had prevailed upon him to let her share not only his favourite pursuits and studies, but, as far as it was possible or right for her to do so, his business also, and he would sometimes laughingly call her his private secretary and confidential clerk.

She had thus grown to feel herself first useful, and then necessary to him; and the natural result was to increase and intensify her affection, till her whole being seemed wrapped up in him. She loved her mother as only mothers can be loved, with fond, yearning, tender affection; but she literally idolised her father. If *he* had become a Catholic, the shock would have killed her; as it was, she lived on, sharing her father's grief, and, alas, increasing it tenfold; for his more yielding nature would have led him to take a calm and dispassionate view of the step his wife had taken, and perhaps in the end to understand and follow it. But Maude would not hear reason. Just *because* the iron had entered into her soul, she let it sink in as deeply as it would. Just *because* it was her own mother who had done this thing, she avoided and shunned her, lest, by the influence of human affection, she should be led to look compassionately on what she had obstinately determined to hate. Just *because* she *loved* her—loved her, perhaps, now more than ever—she could not bear to see her, to be near her; and lest her forced sternness should give way, she spoke to her roughly and harshly.

No wonder that poor Mr. Trelawney's health broke down under this accumulation of misery. A few short weeks after he knew of his wife's reception into the Church, he was laid upon a bed of sickness from which he never arose again, though he lingered for nearly a year; and, in a moment of uncontrollable bitterness, Maude had accused

her mother of being his murderer. Did *he* think
so too?—did *he* accuse her of it? Mrs. Trelawney
never knew; she knew only that he was, if possible,
more kind, more affectionate, more gentle with
her than he had ever been before. Did this mean
pity for an error, or forgiveness for an injury?
She dared not ask, dared not even try to discover; she never even had the courage to tell
him of the agony she endured in witnessing his
grief: and knowing that she herself was its cause,
she dared not expose herself to the temptation of
apostasy. Perhaps it was want of faith, want of
confidence in the power of divine grace. Perhaps
the counsel of a wise director would have spared
her some part of the suffering she thus inflicted
upon herself, and spared others many painful
misunderstandings; but she could never bear to
speak of this part of her trial. She told her confessor "half her sorrows, all her sins;" and because he knew only half her sorrow, his advice
was often just the contrary of what he would have
given had he known all. It was a fatal mistake,
as she knew now when it was too late to remedy
it; but it was the mistake of a generous heart
and a self-sacrificing spirit.

And thus it came to pass that the care of her
father devolved chiefly upon Maude, and that the
hand which most often smoothed the invalid's
couch, bathed his burning temples, and administered to his every want, was not that of his wife,
but of his daughter; it was Maude who read to
him, prayed with him, watched by him while he
slept,—and this was the bitterest drop in Mrs.
Trelawney's cup of sorrow. What would she not

have given to take Maude's place by his side for only one half-hour, and soothe, by the outpouring of her heart's love, the suffering she was compelled, for the sake of God's truth, to inflict!

It would have been better both for him and for herself had she done so, but she dared not; she was never, indeed, long absent from the room,—for she could as little bear to be away from him as to be with him; but she stayed only a few moments, and often merely asked some trivial question with regard to his food or medicine, both of which she scrupulously refrained from touching; for had not Maude accused her of desiring her father's death, and did they not think a "Papist" capable of any crime?

Sometimes, when he was asleep, she would stand over him, gazing down with fixed, glassy eyes upon his face, during minutes that to her were like hours or years; then she would bend down as if to kiss his forehead—very, very rarely she did actually kiss it; but for the most part she drew back, shuddering through her whole frame, and passed quickly out of the room. Was it altogether unnatural that Maude, who saw only the blanched cheeks and the tearless eyes, and knew nothing of the after-agony of passionate weeping, witnessed by God alone and her guardian angel,—was it altogether unnatural that even her own child should have had strange thoughts of her, and suspicions that she shrank from clothing in any tangible form? Would it be strange or impossible if even her husband, who knew the strength of her love for him, should think that her new religion had hardened her heart, frozen her affections, stifled her love? She knew, she felt, that they thought this, and perhaps even more than this, of her; and she knew that one moment's intermission of the torturing self-restraint she had imposed upon herself, one moment's flinching from the sacrifice she had felt it necessary for the salvation of her soul to offer to God, would undeceive them: and she longed, with that death-like heart-sickness which only they who have felt it can understand, to let human nature and human love burst the flood-gates which held them captive; longed, that is to say, with her inferior will, —for when did Jesus, the King of Martyrs, ever require a martyrdom, either of the flesh or of the spirit, for which He did not give sufficient grace? When did He ever refuse the prayer: "Give what Thou commandest, and command what Thou wilt"? By His grace, Margaret Trelawney endured her martyrdom even to the end; and though, as we have said before, it might be that a fuller confidence in her director would have lightened her burden, who shall say that it might not also have stolen the brightest jewel from her crown?

Once, and once only, except on the very day of his death, she had asked to be left alone with her husband; it was when she had pleaded with him not to leave their child dependent entirely on her, and, as we know, unsuccessfully; for Mr. Trelawney, who loved his wife not only fondly, but, what is far more rare, generously, would not listen to a proposal which seemed to imply a doubt of his perfect confidence in her, an unwillingness to trust her with her own child. Whatever misgivings he may have felt, he had at least no fear that Maude's interests would not be safe in her mother's hands, and he said decisively:

"No, dearest, *you* must take care of Maude: I leave her to you;" and the trusting look which accompanied these words was the one only little ray of comfort in her dark sorrow.

What had passed in this interview, Maude, of course, never knew; but she could not doubt that it had some reference to her father's will, as he immediately afterwards sent for his lawyer, and desired to be left alone with him. The only service, however, that he required from that gentleman was to add a codicil to his will, to the effect that he desired then and there to ratify all its contents, bequests, and provisions.

Again we ask, was it altogether unnatural that, when Maude heard this will read, she should have attributed the codicil to her mother's influence?

But whatever may have been her thoughts, she never spoke them to any living being, nor would she ever suffer the least word to be spoken in her presence that reflected even the lightest blame on her mother. The Vivians knew nothing of Mrs. Trelawney from her own child; what they had told Annie was only the common gossip of Warwick.

From the day on which these two interviews took place, Mr. Trelawney sank too rapidly, and suffered too acutely, to bear any further allusions to matters of business. Once only he had said to Maude:

"Try to be a comfort to your mother, my child, when I am gone; be gentle and loving to her, never reproach her."

Unhappily, Maude had misinterpreted these last words, and supposed them to refer to some injury done, or sought to be done, to her by her mother; and when she heard the will read, she thought she had found the explanation she could never have asked for.

When all was over, and mother and daughter were left alone together, Maude made a violent effort to fulfil her father's dying words; and it was not for *lack* of love that she did not succeed, but from the very strength of her love, which made it a bitterness unspeakable to her to find that it was not in her power to give consolation. With almost savage fierceness, Maude hated the sight of the good priest, whose least word, whose mere blessing even, seemed to give more comfort than her utmost efforts could accomplish. Mutual misunderstandings arising, as such misery almost always does arise, from unwillingness on both sides to speak freely, and that proud reserve which shrinks from pleading its own cause, widened the breach, and at last Maude could no longer endure so painful a state of things.

"Mother," she said one day, "let me go away somewhere, any where. There is a gulf growing between us, and I cannot live upon its brink; I cannot bear it—I must go away."

Had it come to this, then, that her own child forsook her? Had the edge of that fiery sword, which Jesus came to send upon earth, not yet done its work in her heart? Did He require a more perfect sacrifice from her? Had she not given Him enough? No, not yet, not yet. "To whom much is given, of him shall much be required." He had given her the priceless gift of faith; He had illuminated her soul with the light of His truth, and given her efficacious grace to correspond with that light; He had not only "called," but "chosen" her; He wanted her for Himself, and He is a jealous God—He will bear no rival. And for all that He had done for her, what return could He ask that would be too much to give? What height or depth, what "other creature," what thing present, or thing to come, is worthy for one moment to be compared with the love of Jesus for His elect? He had greater and higher graces in store for her, but He could not give them without her coöperation, without more perfect detachment than she had yet attained.

But she knew nothing of all this, knew nothing as yet of the law which made her very salvation depend on her reaching the degree of perfection to which she was called; neither did she know that, if it were possible to attain it by any other path than that of suffering, she would have been spared even the lightest touch of pain; for it is only when "the keen edge must come, or we must perish," that the loving Heart of Jesus inflicts a wound.

As yet she saw only that a further sacrifice was demanded of her, and felt only that she dared not refuse it. Her daughter was to be taken from her,—well, be it so; her whole soul rebelled and revolted, her whole heart was turned into bitterness against God; but coldly, sternly, without a word of regret or remonstrance, she let Maude take her own course. Was it altogether unnatural and unaccountable that this poor girl should suppose her mother no longer cared for her? Was it to be wondered at that she refused, obstinately and indignantly, to be dependent on her for a maintenance?—that she preferred earning a livelihood to accepting what she supposed would be grudgingly given? Would this have been strange, even had she not believed what she did about the disposal of her father's property?

Mrs. Trelawney urged, entreated, besought her to accept a fixed annuity, but all in vain; Maude only replied:

"I will never touch what my father left to you;" and the reply cut the poor widowed mother to the heart, for she felt keenly all that it implied; but she let it pass, as at that time she let any thing and every thing pass, with that forced calmness which is one of the saddest signs of despair.

And so it came to pass that, a few months after her father's death, Maude Trelawney engaged herself as companion to Maggie Vivian, and her mother answered Father Wilfrid's advertisement for a schoolmistress.

CHAPTER VIII.

"That sarcastic levity of tongue,
The stinging of a heart the world hath stung."
                                            BYRON.

THE long-expected letter came at last; Annie caught it up eagerly from the breakfast-table, and, as she was generally the first to come down in the morning, had time to read it in peace, before any one else appeared.

It was a very short letter, only a few lines; for Father Wilfrid could not reckon "the pen of a ready writer" among his accomplishments,— and moreover, in the present instance, there was so little that he *could* say without betraying Mrs. Trelawney's confidence.

With characteristic impatience, Annie looked at the end of her letter first—it was at the bottom of the second page; she tore off the blank half-sheet, crushed it up in her hand, and threw it into the fire, exclaiming:

"There, that's all *you're* good for !" and, with a little shade of disappointment on her face, began to read her letter in a rational manner.

It began by acknowledging her own, and telling her that she had acted wisely in writing it.

"*Wisely !*" repeated Annie to herself. "I declare, I don't think he ever paid me a compliment before in my life !"

As she went on reading, however, a grave, troubled look came over her face; succeeded presently by a somewhat abortive attempt to laugh off the trouble, whatever it might be, as she exclaimed aloud:

"I declare, it is too bad! I can never amuse myself with the least little bit of mischief, without getting into some awful scrape!"

"And pray what awful scrape has your ladyship got into now? Is that a scolding from Arthur Hatton?"

The speaker was Charles Crofton, who was spending a week at the Vivians', before escorting his sister home, and who had just entered the room, unperceived by Annie. She coloured furiously, and turned upon the unlucky youth a pair of flashing eyes, which might have been fatal to the peace of mind of any one but a brother.

"Good gracious, Annie! what's the row? You look like a little tigress!" he exclaimed.

But the tiger fierceness was already dying out; Annie could never keep up indignation for more than a few moments.

"Do let me alone; there's a good boy," she said. "It is nothing to do with—I mean—this letter is from Father Wilfrid."

"The deuce it is!" he exclaimed, forgetting himself for a moment, in sheer astonishment at the excitement produced by such a cause.

"Charley, be quiet, can't you! the servants will hear you."

"Well, they might hear worse," replied the incorrigible boy,—"themselves, for instance; that puritanical old butler can swear like a trooper when he is angry, for I heard him yesterday. And so Father Wilfrid has honoured you with some ghostly counsel and advice? You don't seem to find it very comfortable doctrine ; so I can only hope it was necessary for these times."

"What nonsense on earth are you talking, Charley ?" exclaimed Annie, now unmistakably out of temper, to her brother's great amusement.

"*Nonsense !*—you had better not say that to Miss Trelawney ; she believes in the Gospel according to the Thirty-nine Articles."

Now, Annie had never so much as heard of the Thirty-nine Articles, those " forty stripes save one" wherewith the " Church of England" so unmercifully scourges her children; and this exposure of her ignorance did not tend to improve her temper; neither was Miss Trelawney's name calculated just at that moment to do so. Crushing up her letter in her hand, she was turning quickly to leave the room, when the door opened almost in her face, and Maude Trelawney confronted her.

" Excuse me, Miss Trelawney," said Annie, as, with unwonted consideration, she drew back a little to let her pass unscathed. " Beg them not to wait breakfast for me ; I shall be down again in five minutes ;" and she flew up-stairs, before Maude had half understood what she was saying ; but noticing Charley's look of astonishment, she said rather stiffly :

" I hope nothing is the matter, Mr. Crofton ? —is your sister ill ?"

" Not that I know of, thank you," he replied ; " but girls have such queer whims, I can't pretend to understand them."

Somehow, no one, not even a mere boy like

Charley Crofton, ever looked upon Miss Trelawney as a *girl;* but a slight flush, which his words had called into her cheeks, reminded him that he had made a decidedly rude speech,—and not being good at apologies, he stammered out rather awkwardly :

"I beg your pardon, Miss Trelawney; I quite forgot"—that you were a girl yourself, he was on the point of saying; but suddenly remembering that this was not exactly the most polite form of apology, and nothing else immediately occurring to him as a substitute, he stopped short, and covered his confusion by going to the farthest end of the room to fetch a chair.

Maude took not the slightest notice either of him or of his apology, but busied herself in her usual office of cutting the bread.

What use was Annie making, meanwhile, of the five minutes she had secured to herself for the purpose of cooling down her temper? She was sitting on the floor in the middle of the room, with Father Wilfrid's letter, also on the floor, in front of her, and her eyes were intently fixed on one sentence thereof, namely this : "You have it perhaps now in your power to do a great act of charity, and heal many wounds, by softening Miss Trelawney's prejudices against Catholics, and I hope you will be very careful to avoid any thing that might even innocently give scandal; you little know, my child, the mischief that may be done by an imprudent word or act. In your present position, you may do either great good or great harm; for the love of God, take care that it is not the latter."

"But it *is* the latter, and I can't help it now. Oh, dear, how dreadfully wicked Father Wilfrid always makes me feel!" burst out Annie presently, with a keen recollection that her chief amusement for the last fortnight had consisted in scandalising Miss Trelawney, and that only the day before, being Friday, she had met Mrs. Vivian's regret that she could not take meat, by gravely asserting that Catholics always eat more good things on Friday than on any other day in the week; whereupon Miss Trelawney, slightly raising her eyebrows, had remarked that no doubt it would be very easy and pleasant to read the commandments backwards, and Protestants must be very stupid not to have yet learnt the accomplishment.

Annie's five minutes lengthened into ten before she could summon up courage to descend to the battle-ground of the breakfast-table; for, to her dismay, she remembered that it was the eve of All Saints. "A plague upon all fast-days!" she mentally ejaculated; but it was a fast-day, and no mistake, and Father Wilfrid's letter had come just in time to make it a very black fast indeed, she thought,—for she would have to eat humble-pie for breakfast; and if even the best of us are apt to find it somewhat unpalatable food, to a spoilt child, like Annie, it was positively revolting.

"It will choke me," she thought; "but no matter: I will take as large a mouthful as I can swallow;" and with this magnanimous resolution, she at last entered the breakfast-room, briefly apologising for her lateness, — for the Vivians were old-fashioned people, who liked punctuality.

"Finished your sermon, Annie? I hope you feel the better for it," remarked Charley, with a view to improving the occasion by a little teasing, after the manner of brothers.

"Reading sermons before breakfast! I declare that's too much of a good thing," exclaimed Mr. Vivian, a prosy old gentleman, who always took every thing *au pied de la lettre*, and made himself very troublesome to his friends by his incapacity to understand a joke.

"Exactly so, sir," replied Charley, enjoying the fun; "I quite agree with you—never do it myself, lest it should give me an indigestion."

"It seems to have taken away Annie's appetite, at all events," said Mrs. Vivian. "My dear, you are eating nothing: Miss Trelawney, will you be good enough to pass the toast?"

"No, thank you," said Annie, with the humble-pie sticking too unpleasantly in her throat to say more, and quietly helping herself to a small piece of bread.

"Some butter, Annie?" said her brother, at the same time putting a large piece on her plate.

She made no reply, but left it untouched, while she eat the dry bread.

"My dear," said Mr. Vivian, "I know you are fond of fresh eggs, and these were only laid this morning; Miss Trelawney, will you be good enough to pass them?"

"Bother the people!" thought Annie; "are they all bent upon plaguing me?" but she only said, "No, thank you; I am not hungry; at least, I mean," she continued, suddenly resolving to swallow a large mouthful of her pie, "it is a fast-day."

Charley looked up in amazement.

"But *you* haven't got to fast," he exclaimed, "for another three years yet, unless you want"—but suddenly recollecting the *un*fitness of things involved in discussing this subject at a Protestant breakfast-table, he turned off into "unless you want to make a fool of yourself."

"I thought," said Maude, "that Miss Crofton considered it orthodox to eat nice things on fast-days; she said so yesterday: but perhaps it is only Fridays that have that privilege."

Every one looked annoyed, for Maude had certainly made a rude speech,—every one, at least, except Annie, who coloured furiously, and was evidently on the point of bursting into tears; but choking them down with a violent effort, she looked straight at Maude, and said:

"I am sorry I made such a foolish remark, Miss Trelawney, for it was untrue as well as foolish; and pray do not judge of Catholics from me."

"Heigho!" thought Charley; "now I've found it out; we've had a whipping this morning, and come down with our tail between our legs!"

Miss Trelawney *thought* she had found it out too, and took the apology only at what she believed to be its worth, saying:

"Oh, of course I understand that it is not an *acknowledged* article of faith, and may require to be supplemented with, '*Tell it not in Gath;*' it needs no explanation, thank you, Miss Crofton."

Poor Annie! she had only made matters worse, and suggested an additional scandal, instead of removing the former one; and she would have eaten her breakfast now, to escape further observation and ridicule, if she could have done so; but she could only with great difficulty manage to drink her tea,—even the piece of dry bread was left unfinished.

"Poor child!" said Mrs. Vivian, "you really have teased her appetite away amongst you;" and, to Annie's great relief, the party broke up.

Though so late in the year, it was a warm, sunny morning; for "St. Luke's little summer" was keeping its brightness for All Saints, and the soft south wind played lovingly among the leaves that were soon to be ruthlessly scattered by the stern November blasts.

Annie opened one of the French windows, and passed out into the garden, where her brother presently joined her.

"I say, Annie," he began, "does Father Wilfrid send penances by post? I don't believe it's canonical: I shall appeal to the Bishop."

"Penances! nonsense, Charley; and please go away now, I want to think about something."

"All right—I'm going; but where did you leave your brains last? you'll want them, if you are going to think; I'll fetch them for you, if you will tell me where to find them!"

"Oh, do be quiet!" exclaimed Annie, with such unmistakable earnestness, that Charley began to think there was really something the matter; and dropping his teasing tone, he put his arm affectionately round her, and said, "What is it, dear? any thing wrong?"

"Wrong?" she repeated; "yes—wrong enough; but *you* can't put it right: I've made a fool of myself, that's all," she concluded, trying to laugh the matter off.

"Been flirting with somebody, and made Hatton jealous?" he asked, putting a boy's interpretation upon her confession. "By Jove! Annie, you'd better not; he'll make you pay dear for it; you won't find the game worth the candle."

"Charley, I am ashamed of you!" said Annie, drawing herself up with as much dignity as her fairy-like little figure was capable of.

"What is it, then?—in what particular form have you made a fool of yourself?" persisted Charley, meaning to be kind, but irritating poor Annie almost beyond endurance.

"Well, we've both done it," she burst out, to his great astonishment.

"Both done *what?* *I* haven't been and gone and done *nothing*, that I know of—at least, not just now," he added, with a convenient mental reservation.

"Yes, you have," replied Annie, with a gravity that rather puzzled him; "we have both teased and scandalised Miss Trelawney shamefully."

"Whew!—that's the crime, is it? and some one has caught us *in flagrante delicto*, and told tales to Father Wilfrid, eh? Well, never mind; teasing isn't a sin; and as for scandalising, Protestants are fair game: no need to keep faith, hope, or charity with heretics, you know."

"Oh, don't, Charley; you are worse than a Protestant, I declare,—for they believe it, and *you* know it's a lie; how *dare* you say it?"

"Come, come; you're making a fool of yourself *now*, Annie, and no mistake. Are your wits so blunted this morning, that you can't take a joke?"

"There! read the letter, if you like, and don't plague me any more about it," said poor Annie, at last fairly *run to earth;* and taking the letter out of her pocket as she spoke, she offered it to him, and, sitting down on a grassy slope, covered her eyes with her hands, by way of a preparation for the process of *thinking out* the whole matter.

"Judgment pronounced before hearing the cause; that's not fair," said Charley, dropping the letter into her lap. "If he knew how tough Miss Trelawney's prejudices are, he wouldn't expect you to soften them."

"But at least we need not have hardened them," said Annie in a penitent tone.

"'*Why don't you speak for yourself, John?*'" replied Charley, laughing; "*I* don't plead guilty to the hardening performance; I have only tried to laugh a little of the nonsense out of her, which I think ought to come under the head of softening. I don't know what *you* may have done, for I believe women are born persecutors from Jezebel downwards; as for me, I have only tried to provoke a smile out of those great, glorious eyes of Maude Trelawney's, that can flash such bitter scorn; and, upon my word, I think it would be an act of charity to do it."

"Great, glorious eyes, indeed!" repeated Annie contemptuously; "great, fierce, cruel eyes, I call them."

"Of course you do; never praise one woman to another, as Solomon says, or somebody,—perhaps it was Shakespeare,—some one who knew what he was talking about, at all events. I tell you, Annie, Miss Trelawney is a magnificent creature, and, after all, it's a thousand pities she should be a Protestant; take Father Wilfrid's advice, and convert her by all means, if you can."

"A magnificent creature!—what a disgusting expression!" exclaimed Annie. "By the by," she continued, suddenly changing her tone into that of mischievous banter, which was more natural to her, "though I never read the Thirty-nine Articles, I did read something the other day in Miss Trelawney's Prayer-Book, and a very sensible thing it was, too : '*A man may not marry his grandmother.*'"

"Oh, indeed! well, as I have no grandmother, the personal application does not strike me," replied Charley, as he walked off, leaving Annie to her meditations, which was precisely the result she intended.

"Grandmother, indeed!" Charley half said, half whistled to himself; "why, she's only two years older than I am."

It was true—Maude Trelawney was eighteen, and Charles Crofton was sixteen; but it was also true that had she been twenty-eight, or thirty-eight, as indeed many persons might have supposed her, it would have made no difference, it being a well-attested psychological fact, that many a boy's first fancy has been for a woman more than double his own age.

Left in peace at last, Annie began to consider first what she had done, and secondly the best means of undoing it. The first part of the matter was unfortunately clear enough; she had not only increased and intensified Maude's hatred of Catholics, but had done all in her power to give her a thoroughly false and scandalous impression of the Catholic faith itself. Looking at this in the new light thrown upon it by Father Wilfrid's letter, poor Annie perhaps somewhat exaggerated the real measure of her fault, which after all had been one of thoughtlessness, not of malice; but she had always been subject to intermittent fits of remorse, seemingly disproportionate to their immediate cause: whether really disproportionate, let that pure-hearted young saint make answer, who thought a life of severe penance the fitting reparation for having once when a child stolen a little fruit hanging over the wall of a neighbour's garden.

But now, secondly, what could she do to repair the evil, to counteract the scandal? One thing at least she did at once, spontaneously: she took the whole blame, every bit of it, to herself. It never even crossed her mind to lay any part of it on Maude, though, to say the truth, she might justly have done so,—for Maude's cool contempt and perpetual sneers had irritated her like a sort of chronic blister; and it is unquestionably a greater sin to take scandal than to give it, under ordinary circumstances. But Annie was generous in the fullest and widest sense of the word, and never rested any part of her burdens on other people's shoulders, either literally or metaphorically.

Beyond this interior act, however, it was a little difficult to see her way. The experience of the breakfast-table that morning had proved to her that merely contradicting herself would not answer the purpose, and had rather unpleasantly demonstrated the truth, that the opposite of wrong is not always right; moreover, she felt instinctively that any sudden change of manner on her part would be attributed by Maude to some secret influence, and set down to "priestcraft." And yet she must change,—she could no longer, with a clear conscience, go on as she had done,—and she had only a few more days to spend with the Vivians; so she had no time to lose, if any thing was to be done towards breaking down the barrier between Maude Trelawney and her mother.

At this point in her meditations, she was disturbed by the rustle of a dress, and the next moment Maude herself appeared, supporting her invalid charge, who had been tempted by the fineness of the morning to come out. Annie sprang forward:

"O Maggie, dear," she said, "I am so glad you are well enough to come out; do sit down here and rest a little; and you, too, Miss Trelawney,—you look tired."

Maggie looked irresolutely at her companion; the poor girl was incapable of deciding for herself, even in such a trifling matter.

"It is too cold for Miss Vivian to sit out of doors, thank you," replied Maude stiffly; "and I am not tired,—I have not exhausted my strength by fasting, as you have;" and, drawing Maggie's arm closer within her own, they both passed on. It was Maude's fault that time, certainly; but Annie would not allow herself to think so, and reproached herself for her want of tact.

At luncheon-time, Mrs. Vivian said, "Come, my dear Annie, you really must eat something; you had no breakfast; I think you would like this omelette."

Now, it so happened that Annie detested omelettes, and, feeling besides utterly disinclined to eat, she refused it, and took some bread-and-cheese.

"Do have some, Annie; it's delicious," said Charley, who was enjoying the omelette.

"I prefer this, thank you," replied Annie.

"Do you really," asked Maude, "or is it only to entice back the cat you let out of the bag this morning?"

Annie flushed scarlet, and was on the point of launching a barbed arrow at her adversary, but controlled herself in time, and said, with a demureness which provoked a smile from every one:

"I am particularly fond of bread-and-cheese."

"You see, Miss Trelawney," said Charley, charitably coming to the rescue, " Catholics are so accustomed to fasting, that they don't think it worth making a fuss about, and we don't want to imitate the Pharisees."

He spoke with such perfect good temper that it was impossible for Maude to be offended, and, greatly to Annie's relief, the subject passed off.

During the few days that remained of her visit, she saw scarcely any thing of Maude, who seemed more than ever to avoid all society; but the day before her return to Stonebridge, she resolved to take the bull by the horns, and knocked softly at the door of Miss Vivian's sitting-room.

"Come in," said Maude; and Annie entered.

She started. Could this be the same Maude whom she had known in the dining-room and the garden, stiff, erect, haughty, cold, sarcastic? The Maude she now looked upon was a dreary, listless figure, crouching over the fire, with that utter disregard for appearances of which women are popularly supposed to be incapable under any circumstances; the perfect picture of one sorrowing without hope.

"O Miss Trelawney, I am so sorry to disturb you," began Annie; but in a moment Maude had risen, and stood, cold, proud, defiant, before her.

"I did not know it was you," she said; "I thought it was one of the servants."

"But you are not going to turn me out, I hope?" said Annie, with her brightest smile; "I will not stay more than a few minutes; but I am going home to-morrow—to Stonebridge, you know; and I came to ask if I could take any thing for you to Mrs. Trelawney."

A quick observer, and Annie *was* a quick observer, might have noticed a slight trembling of the lower lip at the mention of her mother's name.

"Nothing, thank you, Miss Crofton," she replied; then suddenly added: "Do you see much of my mother?"

"As much as I can," replied Annie, grateful for the opening; "I am very fond of her."

Maude turned away with a weary look, as she said: "Perhaps, then, you would give my love to her, and tell her I am well, and comfortably situated here."

"And happy, Miss Trelawney?" Annie suggested timidly.

Maude turned fiercely upon her.

"Happy!" she repeated; "oh, yes, if you like; happy as a queen, as the Queen of England."

Annie looked pityingly at her; she remembered that the subject of conversation that morning at breakfast-time had been the inconsolable grief of the widowed Queen for her husband.

"Come to Stonebridge," she exclaimed; "it is so beautiful, you couldn't help being happy there; come and spend a month with me, if Mrs. Trelawney has no spare room for you; I won't tease you or be cross to you, indeed I won't. I am so sorry for all that now; will you forgive me?" She stopped short; for, in her excitement, she had talked herself quite out of breath.

Maude looked at her with the sort of half fear, half curiosity, with which one watches the movements of some strange animal; she had been impulsive herself once,—but it was so long ago, and she felt so deadened now, so weary; why did this bright young girl come to startle her?

Then all at once she roused herself: it was no sudden impulse, but a deep-laid plot, a conspiracy to get her among Papists; she bowed stiffly, and said: "Thank you for your kind invitation, Miss Crofton, but I cannot accept it; and now will you excuse me?—Miss Vivian is waiting for me."

Poor Annie was not accustomed to having such very cold water thrown upon her, and the tears started to her eyes; but, without attempting to say another word, she took her departure: nor had she any opportunity of speaking again to Maude before leaving the Vivians.

CHAPTER IX.

"Talk not of books—thou hast not been with me,
Free and bareheaded, where the wind was wildest,
Or riding fast o'er Loughbrigg's tufted knolls."
F. W. FABER.

ON the morning of Annie's return to Stonebridge, Father Wilfrid received the following letter from her:

"DEAR FATHER,
"I have done every thing you told me not to do, and made nothing but mischief."

Perhaps she would have been a little mortified if she had known that he laughed as he tore up the note and threw it into the fire, saying to himself: "Poor child! Well, at all events, if her arrows are sharp, they are not poisoned; and perhaps she has done less harm than she thinks,"—which was true; for, though Maude had received her apology so ungraciously, she had been a good deal impressed by Annie's evident indifference to all her cutting sarcasms. She had at least learnt that Catholics could not be made ashamed of their religion.

"Miss Crofton is coming home to-day," Father Wilfrid said, after he had dismissed the children from afternoon school; "so you will see her to-morrow."

"To-morrow!" dreamily repeated Mrs. Trelawney; "do you think so?"

"I am sure of it; she would never have patience to wait longer. Will you not be glad to see her?"

Mrs. Trelawney shivered in that peculiar manner which a popular superstition has set down as the effect of a cock walking over one's grave, as she replied:

"I don't know; perhaps she will be much changed."

"I think not,—it would be very unlike her; but if she should be"—he paused a moment, and then added, "are you already so much attached to her as to mind it?"

She turned away, answering not a word.

"I will tell you," he said, "what a holy Bishop said to me before I was ordained priest: '*You will never be fit for any thing till you have learned perfect indifference;*' rather 'a hard saying,' was it not?"

Still no reply for a few moments; then she said, in a low, *shy* voice:

"Did *you* think it hard?"

"Well, to own the truth," he replied, smiling, "I believe I was conceited enough to think indifference a very easy virtue. I mistook it for the *Don't care,* whose untimely end used to be held *in terrorem* over me as a boy, and who is so fond of dressing up to imitate it."

"Like *cui bono,*" she said bluntly.

"Nay, that comes a little nearer the truth,"

he replied; "it might almost be translated into 'What does it profit a man—'"

"And *quite* into *no matter*," she broke in, catching up his words with a touchiness that was unusual with her.

He gave one moment's quiet, searching look at her, as he said quietly, "Well, yes, it might;

'For self-disturbance hath the skill
To turn the words which way it will.'

But I am keeping you from your dinner; and you earn it well after your hard day's work here," he added kindly, taking up his hat to go.

"*That* is not hard," she said quickly, as she knelt for his blessing.

"Is it to be *this* ?" she said to herself, as she walked home; "is *every* cord to snap ?"

Perhaps, but not yet; He who spared His disciples "many things," because they "could not bear them" yet, deals more gently, more lovingly, more tenderly with us, than often we dare to ask or hope. In His own time, He will bring us to the mountain-top; but if we grow faint and weary, He will let us "drink of the brook by the way."

The next morning, after Mass, Annie ran after Mrs. Trelawney, and stopped her, saying:

"May I come and see you this afternoon after school ? Shall you be disengaged ?"

She was not changed, then; *that* cord had not snapped yet.

Having received the desired permission, she darted back, and knocked at the outer sacristy-door.

"Come in," said Father Wilfrid; but he had

not finished making his thanksgiving; and she was obliged to wait, with what patience she might, till he was ready to speak to her.

"Well, my child," he said, "so you have come back from your sojourn *in partibus?* are you glad to come home?"

Annie gave him a little odd, puzzled look, and, instead of replying to his question, asked him if he had received her letter the day before.

Father Wilfrid laughed. "Oh, yes," he said, "I had it; are you in a great hurry for an answer?"

A few tears of sheer vexation gathered in Annie's eyes; she was prepared for a scolding, but not for being laughed at, which to many persons is a far greater mortification, as Father Wilfrid knew well enough. Perhaps it was rather hard upon her by way of a first greeting; but, in the first place, she had herself provoked it, and in the next, Father Wilfrid had set his heart upon making a saint of Annie, and consequently never let slip an opportunity of mortifying her—a practice which, as she was quite ignorant of its motive, she may perhaps be pardoned for not always appreciating.

"O father, don't be so unkind," she burst out; "why don't you scold me at once, and have done with it?"

"But what am I to scold you for?" he replied, in a tone very much the reverse of unkind; "you have not told me."

"Yes, I have; I told you in that letter," she answered bluntly.

"Which was much too mysterious for my poor

II

understanding; I was going to ask you for an explanation of it," he said, "but not now, when you ought to be going home to breakfast."

"Bother breakfast!" exclaimed Annie impatiently.

"Perhaps you would be glad of it, if you had been six miles for a sick call since three o'clock this morning," said Father Wilfrid quietly. He might have added, that finding his pony was lame, he had walked the whole twelve miles; but he probably thought that little fact of no consequence, for he did not mention it.

He judged rightly that he had said enough, for Annie's whole manner instantly changed.

"O father, I beg your pardon; how selfish I am!" she said; "but indeed I have been very naughty at Stretton, and I want to know how to put it right."

"Well, I will do my best to help you," he replied; "you can come and tell me all about it this evening, if you like."

"Now, that is tiresome," thought Annie, as she went home. "I wanted to know what I had better say to Mrs. Trelawney. However, it can't be helped now; I must say what comes uppermost, and take the consequences."

Certainly Annie had a spice of recklessness in her nature. A phrenologist had once told her that she had "the organ of destructiveness so strongly developed as almost to amount to murder." "Good gracious! you don't mean to say I could kill any one!" she had exclaimed in horror. "No, no, my dear young lady," was the reply; "not intentionally, of course; but don't be too fond of playing with edged tools :" a counsel which Annie utterly set at nought in practice, but which nevertheless she sometimes remembered with a little uneasiness. She did so on the present occasion, for she felt that Maude Trelawney was an edged tool of the sharpest description ; but whether she played with it or not, she was at least resolved to handle it. Perhaps, if she had done mischief at one end of the breach, she might do something to repair it at the other; at all events, she would try.

Mrs. Trelawney received her a little stiffly, and with a quiet dignity of manner, which, for a moment, checked Annie's impetuosity, but only for a moment. She was in the habit of taking all things and all people by storm; and instead of appropriating the chair she was evidently intended to occupy, she seated herself on a low stool at Mrs. Trelawney's feet, saying :

"This is so much more comfortable; you will not mind? Please don't make a stranger of me, or a visitor, which is a thousand times worse."

Mrs. Trelawney felt half inclined to say, "And yet you really are both," but she had not the heart to repulse this bright young creature.

"I have all sorts of things to say to you," began Annie, "but first I must give you Miss Trelawney's message: she desired me to give her love to you, and to tell you she was well, and comfortably situated."

Annie instinctively felt that it was safest to repeat Maude's exact words.

At first Mrs. Trelawney merely said, "Thank you," but after a moment's pause she added,

"Did you see much of Maude?"

It was the very same question Maude herself had asked about her mother, as Annie could hardly help noticing; but she answered it very differently.

"No," she said, "not much; Miss Trelawney was almost entirely taken up with poor Maggie Vivian; you know she has fits, and is obliged to have some one always with her. Is it not sad?"

"Poor child! yes, very sad," replied Mrs. Trelawney, thinking, in truth, of her own child, and not of Miss Vivian,—but she asked no more questions; it was not to a young, light-hearted girl, however compassionate, that she could speak on such a subject. But Annie was not going to let it drop so easily; with more zeal than discretion, she said:

"O Mrs. Trelawney, do ask your daughter to come here for a little while; she would not accept my invitation, but of course she will come to you; and I do so want her to see Father Wilfrid—I am sure he will soon make her a Catholic."

So, then, Annie had actually invited Maude to stay with her! Mrs. Trelawney was surprised, but she did not express any such feeling; she only said:

"You are very good, Miss Crofton, and I know you mean kindly; perhaps Maude may come here some day, but not just at present; and she would never consent to see Father Wilfrid, so he could not do much for her."

"Come here, and not see Father Wilfrid!" exclaimed Annie; "but that would be impossible;

she *shall* see him, dear Mrs. Trelawney; and even if she does not," continued she, with a little disregard for consistency, " he can convert her all the same with his prayers. Oh, do let her come!"

"Maude will never be a Catholic; let us talk of something else," said Mrs. Trelawney, with a decision of tone which effectually silenced Annie; she felt hurt, too, for she had intended to give sympathy, and had hoped to win confidence, and could hardly understand why it was not given to her.

However, she was determined not to be altogether baffled, though she clearly perceived that she must not venture to talk of Maude again.

"Well, then," she said, "let us talk about Hillsborough Tor: I want you to come there with me on Saturday; is not that your half-holiday? You can't think how beautiful it is,—and there is such a glorious view; you see right over the Tamar into Cornwall, and the whole range of Dartmoor, and the white ships out beyond Plymouth Breakwater; and the wind is so delicious —you feel as if you could fly like a bird, and it blows every thing dismal away; you don't know, you can't think, how glorious it is up there, quite away from every thing, and a little bit nearer to heaven. Do come; you shall ride my pony, and I will take Charley's—they are both very quiet, and even Father Wilfrid won't mind if you are with me."

Did she not know? could she not think? Had she not, years ago, ridden wildly over the shaggy heath of the Cornish moors, and learnt

"How mountain-winds, and cold, pure breaths of sea,
Unclasp the pain that girds the aching brow"?

Had she not sat and gazed from her window on those gray Dartmoor Tors, with that intense yearning known only to those who are mountain-born and mountain-bred? She had even sometimes had wild thoughts of hiring a pony, and wandering off alone, and certainly would have done it, had not all energy been crushed out of her in the last few months.

And, now, what she had dreamily longed for, as something that had long since passed away out of her reach, was suddenly brought face to face with her, and laid down, as it were, at her very feet. But it was so like a dream, that she hardly realised it—hardly recognised it as a definite proposal requiring a definite answer; and instead of making any reply, she turned and looked out over the hills which could be seen from her window.

"Oh, do say you will come!" pleaded Annie. "You are not afraid to ride, are you?"

The spell was broken. Mrs. Trelawney turned rather quickly back from the window, and said:

"*Afraid?* oh, no; I have been accustomed to it all my life. I used to enjoy it so much!" she added, with flushed cheeks and kindling eyes.

Annie looked at her in astonishment; it was the first time she had ever heard Mrs. Trelawney express the very least pleasure in any thing, or seen her eyes flash with excitement; and their resemblance, at that moment, to Maude's, quite startled her. She enjoyed riding herself, and felt exhilarated by it; but that this grave, sad-faced, broken-hearted woman should be so strangely moved at the thoughts of mounting a gray pony was a thing quite beyond the limits of Annie's philosophy.

After a moment's hesitation, she wisely gave up the problem, and merely said :

"Then, of course, you will come, and we will have a famous scamper over Hillsborough, and down towards Tavistock Heath; then we can ford the Lewin (you won't mind tucking up your feet? the water will be above our stirrups), and come home through Ringtor Wood, and by the sunk fence."

Yes, twenty, or even ten years ago, and with her husband by her side, Margaret Trelawney would have welcomed such a prospect as the summit of earthly felicity; even now, if she might only go alone—only go free, untrammelled, unwatched; but with a companion—with Annie Crofton, who would talk, and expect her to talk again—expect her, perhaps, to *admire* the rocky moor, the breezy heath, the leaping, gurgling river, the shadows on the hill-side, the sunlight in the foam-bells—no, she could not thus lay bare the innermost shrine of her human heart, weary as that heart had grown of all its holy places,—for they still *were* holy places, and would be till the end of time, and all rude touching of them was a sacrilege.

To Annie's utter discomfiture, she said very quietly :

"I am afraid I cannot come; but thank you very much, all the same, for your kind thought."

"But why not? what should hinder you?" persisted Annie, for once failing in tact, owing to her extreme eagerness. "If you have any tiresome scruples, take them to Father Wilfrid; I am sure he will think you a sufficient *chaperone* for me; and if not, well, rather than give it up," she continued, making a wry face, like a child on the point of taking a dose of medicine, "I will take our old coachman with us, on condition, you know, that he never comes within a quarter of a mile of us."

Scruples! perhaps Mrs. Trelawney had scruples of some kind; but they did not, apparently, need Father Wilfrid's help to remove them; for she suddenly revoked her refusal, and said:

"I was wrong, Miss Crofton; I beg your pardon for being so ungrateful: I will come with you on Saturday."

"But," said Annie, looking puzzled, as well she might, "I don't want you to come, if you would rather not; I hate teasing people to do what they don't like,—it's just persecution; I want you to *enjoy* it, not only to *do* it."

"And I shall enjoy it, indeed I shall, very much," said Mrs. Trelawney, with one of those rare smiles that seem to have more of heaven than of earth in them, and which had begun occasionally to light up her face within the last few weeks. She was not one to do any thing by halves; to make a sacrifice with an *arrière pensée*, or embrace a mortification with a frown. If a martyr could salute his cross with affectionate rapture, cannot an interior suffering be welcomed with a smile, and counted as a joy? But our first beginnings in the supernatural life are as awkward and unsteady as an infant's first attempts to walk, —often unsuccessful, sometimes even ridiculous to the bystanders. Mrs. Trelawney could not sustain the effort she had made, and had barely presence of mind enough to say that she had a bad headache (which was quite true), as an apology for being unable to talk any more.

Annie took the hint, and departed.

CHAPTER X.

> " Heaven fades away before our eyes,
> Heaven fades within our heart,
> Because in thought our heaven and earth
> Are set too far apart."
>
> F. W. FABER.

ANNIE had no cause to complain that she had not been sufficiently scolded after her interview with Father Wilfrid. It was not commonly his "way" to be stern or severe, but there were certain faults for which he had no toleration; and giving gratuitous scandal was one of them. That any one should find amusement in such a practice, was simply incomprehensible to him; and when Annie told him that she had startled and shocked Miss Trelawney *for fun*, he asked, with unfeigned astonishment:

"For *what?*"

"Well," replied Annie, "it was rather dull there with nothing to do all day, and I wanted a little amusement."

Father Wilfrid looked up with such severe eyes, that Annie quailed under them, as he said quietly but sternly:

"And you thought it worth having at the risk of your neighbour's soul, as well as your own? Did you forget that our Lord Himself said it would be better for a man to be thrown into the sea, with a millstone hung round his neck, than that he should scandalise a child?"

"What!" exclaimed Annie; "our Lord said that? I didn't know; I don't understand. Don't frighten me out of my senses, father. What have I done? Maude Trelawney is not a child."

The last words sprang from her natural quickness in seizing upon the weak point of any argument, but she spoke them from mere impulse, and not with the slightest idea of contradicting Father Wilfrid. She was a great deal too much frightened for that.

"I *want* to frighten you," he replied; "though I hope you have not done very much harm *now*—perhaps not so much as you think; but unless you break yourself of this habit of amusing yourself at all costs, and even at our Lord's expense, you will some day dishonour Him grievously. Don't distress yourself now, my child," he added, for Annie had thrown herself at his feet in an agony of mixed grief and terror; "you have only been thoughtless, and acted from the impulse of the moment; but it is a dangerous habit, and I want you to try and control yourself a little sometimes."

"But I can't!" cried Annie. "I can't help saying whatever comes into my head, though I should often like to bite my tongue out for it afterwards."

Father Wilfrid smiled. "Then I suppose you must keep things out of your head," he said.

"Keep things out of my head!" she exclaimed; "why, thousands of them are rushing in and out all day long. I could no more stop them than I could stop the Falls of Niagara. You don't understand me a bit!" she added, a little impatiently.

"Don't I?" he said quietly. "Well, then, you had better find some one who does; if I don't understand you, I certainly cannot help you."

She sprang suddenly to her feet, stood for a moment as if transfixed, and then said slowly, "Do you mean that? Do you give me up? Do you want to get rid of me?"

"Not just this moment," he said, smiling; "I don't think we need act a sensation scene together. Sit down quietly; I want to talk to you."

"You want to drive me wild," she exclaimed; but she dared not disobey him, and sat down.

"Well," he said, "now we have both been saying exactly what came into our heads, and you see what comes of it, or what *will* come of it if we take each other at our word. Think before you speak this time, and tell me if you really mean that you don't think I understand you a bit."

Annie looked straight at him for a minute, without speaking; then she said:

"I can't *think*, but I suppose you do understand me, all but the impatience; you can't understand that; you have no impulses yourself."

Father Wilfrid laughed, as he replied:

"Then you did not really think I was out of

patience with you, and wanted to give you up? I suppose you gave me credit for one of your own impulses, by mistake?"

Annie gave him a puzzled look; she was beginning to feel quite confused, and, to own the truth, began to think that perhaps he did understand her impatience a little. She did not care to argue the point further, and was content to let judgment go by default.

"I have been very foolish, father," she said; "will you forgive me, and tell me what to do about Maude Trelawney?"

"Do *nothing* about her," he replied, "except pray for her; let her alone, and don't talk to her mother about her."

"But I have done it already, of course I have; and, besides, I couldn't help it. She gave me a message to her," exclaimed Annie, with a supreme disregard of logic and grammar.

"Well, never mind," he answered; "of course, you were bound to give a message; what else did you say?"

"I'm sure I don't know; I never remember what I say," replied Annie bluntly. She hated being "brought to book" in this way.

"Well, then, it can't have been any great harm," he replied; "but you had better say no more, if you can help it; the subject can only be a painful one to Mrs. Trelawney."

"I remember now," exclaimed Annie, who had not paid the slightest attention to the last words; "I said I wanted Maude to come here, that you might convert her, and she—Mrs. Trelawney, I mean—seemed vexed, and said Maude would never be a Catholic. Wasn't it very wrong of her to say that, father?"

"We must hope she is mistaken," he replied gravely; "and now, if you really want my advice, here it is: Be as kind as you can to Mrs. Trelawney, and don't distress her by talking of what is only painful."

"I thought a little sympathy would be a comfort to her," said Annie, looking hurt; "I'm sure it would be to me."

Father Wilfrid looked at her compassionately. What did he pity her for? was she not young, and innocent, and bright, and joyous?

"My child," he said, "don't meddle with sorrow till you know what it is. It is a holy thing, and should be touched reverently."

Something in his tone silenced Annie. She sat looking at the floor, and made no reply.

"I will tell you what you can do," he said presently. "Ask Mrs. Trelawney to walk with you sometimes; take her to the waterfall in Lussleigh Wood, and show her the ferns at Stinchcombe. I think it will give her pleasure."

"I can show her something better than that. I am going to take her to the top of Hillsborough Tor, on Saturday; that *can't help* doing her good," replied Annie, delighted to find herself met half-way in her plan.

"To the top of Hillsborough Tor!" he exclaimed; "up four good miles of steep, rough road! What are you thinking of? Poor Mrs. Trelawney could not walk half the distance."

"I don't want her to walk; we are going to ride," Annie replied demurely.

"To ride!" repeated Father Wilfrid, greatly astonished; he could not conceive the possibility of Mrs. Trelawney riding, and would as soon have thought of offering her a velocipede as a horse.

"Yes, why not?" asked Annie.

"Can Mrs. Trelawney ride? I hope you don't propose mounting her on one of your father's hunters?"

"Papa would not thank me for taking a hunter over those stones," she replied; "Mrs. Trelawney will ride my pony, and I shall take Charley's. She is used to riding, and likes it very much, so we shall be all right; I settled it with her to-day. Are you not glad? don't you think it will do her no end of good?"

"I don't know; indeed, I hope it may. But I wonder you ventured to ask her; I should never have thought of proposing it."

"Ah! that's just where it is, you see," said Annie. "*I* should never have *thought* of proposing it; I should always be afraid to do things, if I thought about them first; but I don't: I do them without thinking, and so sometimes they're wrong, and sometimes they're right, and I never know which till afterwards; but it is not wrong this time, is it?"

"Not if Mrs. Trelawney likes it; she must judge for herself," he replied, a little doubtful how far the plan really had her consent, and yet feeling that perhaps, after all, Annie's impulsive nature had done good service for once in a way; he had made a friend of Hillsborough Tor himself before now, and knew something of its value in that capacity.

Annie went home more thoughtful than she had ever been in her life before, and, as a practical result of her meditation, asked Mrs. Trelawney the next day whether she still felt quite inclined for their proposed expedition,—finding herself, however, greatly relieved by a very decided reply in the affirmative.

Perhaps a dull, gray November afternoon was not what most persons would have chosen as the most favourable time for exploring Dartmoor; and as they cantered along the sunk fence, Annie said:

"There will not be much view to-day ; I wish we had gone before I went to Stretton. All we can hope for now is to be spared a November fog; mist is an inevitable necessity, but we shall not have worse than that to-day."

"And I like mist; I feel at home in it; I mean, it seems more natural on the hills, and one sees more—it takes one farther," replied Mrs. Trelawney, with that far-away, dreamy look in her eyes, that Annie had often noticed in them when she looked up at the Tors from her window.

"How can you possibly see more in a mist?" she asked, in a provokingly matter-of-fact tone ; "are your eyes made differently from other people's? And what do you mean by its taking you farther? do you feel more inclined to stay out in it? I don't; I like to see every thing clearly, quite plain, without any trouble of looking for it. I wish I could understand you!" she added earnestly, turning and looking her companion full in the face, as she pulled up rather suddenly at a gate which opened upon the moor.

Mrs. Trelawney smiled. "I am afraid I say very foolish things sometimes," she said; "they are not at all worth understanding; I ought to beg your pardon for talking so outrageously *off book.*"

"Off book! for goodness' sake, don't talk *like a book!*" exclaimed Annie; "if you only knew how I hate it! Bother this gate! you stupid old Nabob, you've opened it a hundred times before; come, that's it at last;" and she held it while Mrs. Trelawney rode through. "Now, do tell me what you mean by seeing more in a mist; it must be very convenient,—you would never lose your way."

"Well, I didn't exactly mean *that*, so don't trust to me for a guide; and I don't know how to explain myself; but I always think a mist seems to draw heaven and earth closer together."

If she had spoken Chinese, Annie could not have looked more completely puzzled; she did, however, to a certain extent, follow the idea, for she said:

"Do you expect to be drawn up to heaven in it, like St. Agnes in the poem? is that what you mean by *going farther?* You will think me very wicked, but I may as well say it as think it: when I get up here on the Tors, and look down, the world seems so beautiful, so very beautiful, that I love it with all my heart, and don't want to go to heaven at all—after all, you know, God made the world, and made it beautiful, and said it was very good; so I think one *ought* to love it a little, don't you?"

"I think one ought to love it a great deal;

because He loved it, and came down into it, and fills it now, and speaks through it," replied Mrs. Trelawney, her eye kindling, and the colour mounting to her cheek, as a fresh breeze sprang up, and the ponies tossed their heads and sniffed it with delight.

Spiritus Domini replevit orbem terrarum.

No one spoke the words, but the wind seemed to waft them on its wings as it passed, and to whisper them into the ear of one at least of the two riders.

"Ah!" said Annie; "I see now; you look up from it, and I look down into it: that makes all the difference; but I like to look down, it is so bright down in those sunny valleys; and then it is one's home, and one can't help loving it. Look there; do you see Stinchcombe Manor, just peeping up out of the trees? You have no idea how lovely those woods are. Well, do you know—I may as well tell you—oh, please look at Stinchcombe, not at me—that is to be my home some day, when—when I am Mrs. Arthur Hatton; and now I must have a gallop, for Nabob is pulling my arms off. Do you see that bit of stone wall higher up? I will wait for you there, if you like to come on more slowly. Take care; Jessie will be off, if you haven't got her well in hand;" and without giving her time to answer, Annie shook her rein, and was flying over the soft turf.

Mrs. Trelawney was too good a horsewoman to need the caution, and Jessie, though by birth only a rough Exmoor pony, was too well trained to venture on a start in defiance of the hand which controlled her, though it must be owned

I

her temper was a little ruffled at finding herself turned short round, and made to face the steepest ascent of the Tor, instead of the valley below, which she had been contemplating through half-shut, lazy eyes. But this was all; she was not called upon to grapple with the almost perpendicular ascent, but only to keep her footing steadily, while her rider, leaning forward, and resting one arm on her shaggy mane, gazed upwards at — or was it through? — the mist-wreaths that swept swiftly and silently over the hill, half veiling, half disclosing its rocky summit and stone-crowned head. There was a break in the clouds above, and a gleam of sunlight for a moment transformed the mist into that glory of golden haze which seems the fitting pathway of guardian angels between earth and heaven; that dazzling veil,

"Which the King of kings
As a curtain flings
O'er the dreadfulness of eternal things."

Behind her, far below, lay the Stinchcombe woods, many-coloured with their autumn tints, steadily and gracefully baring their strong arms to meet the coming winter blasts: Annie's future home, the home already of her heart, a home whose beauty might well beguile any human heart, and chain it to earth.

"Poor child!" thought Mrs. Trelawney, "how she loves it!—no wonder. She is right; the world is very beautiful while it lasts; will it last for her?" But she never looked back. What was Stinchcombe Manor, with all its loveliness, to her? She never relaxed the strained, upward gaze of her eyes, and a thought somewhat akin to that of the Syrians of old passed through her mind: "The Lord is God of the hills, but He is not God of the valleys." She had gone forward to meet a bright future herself once, a happy earthly home; and the Lord had not been God of that valley; but what right had she to judge others? Because human love is a curse to some, are none to be safely trusted with it? Might not Annie be happy and holy too? Why could she not bear to think of it? Was there a secret, hidden poison of jealousy in her heart?

"No, not that; God forbid!" she thought; and at that moment her eye caught sight of a white handkerchief which Annie was waving at their appointed meeting-place. How long had she kept her waiting? She had no idea; but gathering up her reins, she turned back to the open part of the moor.

No need of the whip for Jessie; a shake of the bridle and a word of encouragement were enough; and she darted off like an arrow from a bow, eager to rejoin her companion.

"You have had a long talk with the mist, or with the 'Spirit of the Fell,' or something," said Annie; then, noticing Mrs. Trelawney's flushed cheek and bright eye, tokens of the excitement inseparable from a quick gallop over yielding turf on a wild moor, she exclaimed:

"Oh, I am so glad you really do enjoy it!"

"Indeed I do; did I not tell you I should?" was the reply; but even as she spoke, the colour died out of her cheek, and the light faded from her eye; riding was to her what a strong stimulant would be to another person, giving unnatural spirits, and followed by a rapid reaction.

"I ought to congratulate you"—she began, after a moment's pause; but Annie broke in hastily with:

"Oh, please don't; I told you here on purpose because I could run away. Don't even say a word to me about it. I brought you up here to tell you, because I could never have said it any where else; but now I *have* told you, and that's enough about it. Shall we have a canter?"

They started off, this time keeping together, though without speaking. But the canter soon came to an end, for they were now breasting the hill, though not on its steepest side. Annie looked up; a thick mist rested on the summit.

"We shall see nothing from the top," she said; "Hillsborough has put his cap on, as we say. Shall we go on or not? There is no fear of losing our way, the mist is not thick enough for that, and I know every inch of the ground,—so do just as you like; we shall see nothing, that's all: at least, *I* sha'n't; perhaps you and the eagles may."

Mrs. Trelawney hesitated a little, and then said: "I should like to go on, if you really do not mind; but if you would rather wait here, I will go alone, and come back to you."

"No, no, that won't do!" exclaimed Annie; "in the first place, you might leave me here till to-morrow, if you took a fancy for spending a night in cloudland; and in the next, though *I* know my way here, *you* don't; and as you could not see me from the top, you might easily come down the wrong side, and find yourself twenty miles from every where at the bottom. Though they do call me Scatterbrains, I am not quite so bad as all that: I shall take care to bring you safe home; so now for it; follow me, and we shall be at the top in ten minutes."

So they were; but their view extended only to themselves and their ponies. Annie jumped off, slipped her bridle over her arm, and seated herself at the foot of the heap of stones. Mrs. Trelawney followed her example.

"Well! this is lively!" said Annie, after a few moments' silence. "We *ought* to be looking down upon Plymouth Sound, and across the Tamar into Cornwall. Can you see any thing? I can't."

"No," replied Mrs. Trelawney, keeping this time to matter of fact, "I can't say I do; but I think it is very *resting* to see nothing and to feel nothing."

"Very resting!" repeated Annie. "Are you tired? Has it been too far for you?"

"Oh, no, not the least tired; I was not thinking of bodily rest," she replied; "at least, only in the sense that one's eye gets wearied of seeing, and one's ear of hearing. Down below one can only get the relief of darkness; but here, one has the same rest without the nothingness. A mist on a mountain-top always seems to me like being in heaven with one's eyes sealed; like the cloud before the Mercy-seat; like a veiled Exposition. It must have been that to Moses, to Elias, to our Lord Himself, to His Apostles when He was caught up from them in the cloud on the Mount of Olives."

She spoke in hushed tones, as if in an unseen presence; and Annie looked reverently at her as she said,

"You would have liked best to come here alone. I shall go round to the other side of the stones: come when you are ready; I think we ought not to stay more than a few minutes,—it is getting late, and the mist might get thicker."

Mrs. Trelawney made no answer, and indeed Annie was out of sight before she had finished speaking. Intensely grateful for the kind feeling which thus gave her a few moments of loneliness, she yet hardly seemed able to make much use of them. She rose and stood leaning against the stones, with the mist, which happily was only a dry one, sweeping over her. What manner of communion her soul held with the unseen world during those few minutes, she could never have told in any mortal ear; but sooner than Annie had expected her, she appeared at her side, ready mounted. She simply said,

"Thank you: I am quite ready now, if you are."

Annie sprang up, threw the rein over Nabob's neck, and, bringing him close up to a large stone, was on his back in a moment.

"How did you get up?" she said. "I am used to it, but I would have acted groom for you; are you all right?"

Mrs. Trelawney smiled; she had been "used to it" too in days long past; and we never quite lose the influence of an old habit.

"I got up the same way as you did," she said; "Jessie is not very high,—and she seemed quite to understand what was expected of her. I am quite right; I suppose we must pick our way a little, till we get lower down."

"Dear old Jessie! of course she did," cried Annie, putting out her hand to pat her favourite's neck; "she always stands like a lamb for me to get up and down."

They were not long making their way home, for the short November day closed in rapidly, and the mist had turned to rain lower down. As they clattered through the village, they passed Father Wilfrid.

"All safe, you see; no need to search the bogs or the granite-quarry this time!" said Annie, without, however, drawing her rein; it was too late and too wet to stop.

At Mrs. North's door, they found a groom waiting to take Jessie, and Mrs. Trelawney dismounted.

"I hope you won't catch cold," said Annie; "take off your habit as fast as you can. Are you going to practise with the choir to-night?"

"Yes, I think so; at eight o'clock," she replied.

"Then I shall see you again at the church. Good bye now;" and Annie scampered home as fast as Nabob could carry her, utterly regardless of Charley's request that she would "bring him in cool."

CHAPTER XI.

> "Oh, who that in youth's morning light,
> With sails full-set and songs, did ride
> Into love's harbour with the tide,
> Hath dreamed that it would ebb at night?"
>
> F. W. FABER.

STINCHCOMBE MANOR was a long, low, old-fashioned house, nestled deep in its own woods, about two miles from Stonebridge. White jessamine and clematis and honeysuckle crept lovingly up its walls, and peeped in at its windows; the lawn before the house was almost overgrown, except quite in the centre, by the large hydrangers, some pink and some blue, whose luxuriant growth had never been checked; and below it, shutting out from sight a public road, which separated this part of the garden from the park beyond, was a thick myrtle-hedge—such a myrtle-hedge as one only sees in Devonshire; and which, especially in the autumn, when in full blossom, was the admiration and envy of all travellers coming from a less-favoured climate.

Stinchcombe would have fared ill in the hands of a modern millionaire: the trees grew close to the house, and darkened the rooms—he would have marked them at once for execution; the jessamine and clematis harboured insects, and attracted the wasps—he would have stripped them from his walls; the rooms were too low, and the house too insignificant-looking—he would have raised the ceilings, added another story, built a billiard-room among the hydrangers, and swept away the fir-plantation at the back, to make room for his hunting-stables and kennels.

But, happily both for itself and for all who could appreciate it, Stinchcombe had been, from time immemorial, the heritage of a family who loved every tree in its woods, every shrub in its grounds, almost every blade of grass on its banks, with a jealous affection, effectually protecting it from the hands of the spoiler, and the "improvements" of the architect or the landscape-gardener. The axe was never heard in Stinchcombe woods, except under circumstances of the most absolute necessity; and the tree that it felled was mourned over almost like a child: every year the hydrangers grew larger and larger, and the rhododendrons spread farther and farther, so that what had once been an open lawn was fast changing into a shrubbery; and, occasionally, a few shrubs were removed and transplanted, that the centre of the grass-plot might be left free, and the view of Hillsborough not be quite shut out from the windows. Every year the fragrant white jessamine had crept higher and higher, and stretched farther and farther, till now it covered three sides of the house, from ground-floor to roof; and its offshoots were following its example in many a distant home, to which they had been borne by sons and daughters anxious to carry with them some lasting memorial of their childhood. In short, Stinchcombe Manor was not a "place," or a "country-seat," or a "residence," but emphatically a *home;* a home to which its possessors had clung as closely as the creepers to its walls. They had lived, each one, generation after generation, under his vine and under his fig-tree—even literally, for vines and fig-trees flourished at Stinchcombe; and though they generally spent a part of the year in London, and occasionally travelled abroad, or even passed a winter in Rome, the return to the old manor-house was always a "going home," even to married sons and daughters, who had perforce left it for other homes of their own.

The present lord of the manor was the Mr. Hatton whose engagement to Annie had been so bluntly announced by her to Mrs. Trelawney on Hillsborough Tor; he was now five-and-twenty, and had been in possession of the property four years; his father having died when he and his brother Robert were respectively fourteen and fifteen years old, leaving them under the sole guardianship of his widow, who still continued to live with her eldest son at Stinchcombe—for it was not "the way" of the Hattons to break up old family ties, and Arthur's marriage was to make no difference in this respect.

"You will not mind my mother living with us?" he had said to Annie.

"Mind it! why, where on earth *else* should she live?" had been the prompt reply.

Robert was a solicitor, fast rising in his profession, and living in London, though he "ran down to the old house" whenever he could spare time to do so, even if it were only for a Sunday; on which occasions he would beg for Annie to come and sing duets with him—for he was passionately fond of music. Annie, though she had not been far wrong in saying that she played abominably, had a good voice and a good ear; and as Robert undertook the accompaniment, the duets were generally a success. It was in this way that her acquaintance with the Hattons had first begun, when they were all children together; and Annie, in her innocence, had never known that there was any difference in her feelings for the two brothers, till, one day in the spring of the year in which our tale commences, when Arthur had ventured to ask for something more than had hitherto been thought of between them, she suddenly exclaimed, blushing furiously:

"O Arthur, I am so glad it is you, and not Robert!"

He could hardly help laughing at the simplicity of the confession, as he asked:

"Why are you glad, Annie?" to her unspeakable confusion.

"Well," she said, "because—oh, dear, what disagreeable questions you do ask!—because I should not have known how to answer him."

"Then you do know how to answer me?"

She made no reply in words; but when they returned from their ramble in the wood, an hour later, Arthur led her up to his mother, who was sitting in the shade of the hydrangers on the lawn, and said:

"Mother, dear, here is a daughter for you; give her your blessing."

This was on a Saturday; and that same evening, Robert came down for one of his home-Sundays, as he called them. Of course, Annie was there; she looked shy and conscious, which was so unusual with her that he wondered what was the matter, and looked at his brother for an explanation: Arthur drew her towards him, and said,

"You must love her, Robert; she is your sister now."

Robert sprang suddenly backwards, a dizzy faintness came over him, and he sat down on the nearest chair, staring in a sort of absent way at his brother and Annie; but only for a few moments: then he went up to her, and, taking her hand, said:

"God bless you, Annie! I am so glad; you will make us all very happy. I was a little startled at first, that was all."

Yes, that was all—all *they* would ever know. He sang duets with Annie that evening; and they all three walked up to see the sunset from the fir-plantation the next day, after Benediction; "like old times," said Arthur.

"Yes, let it be like old times for to-day," replied Robert, when Annie's little hand rested lightly on his shoulder for support, as she jumped from the low wall skirting the plantation; and there was no sound in his voice to betray that, for him, those old times had passed away for ever, leaving a wound that would never be altogether healed, though no external scar told of its existence.

Arthur had noticed with some surprise, and a little anxiety, the first effect of his announcement to his brother; and when he returned from escorting Annie home that evening, he went to his room, and said:

"Was it news to you, old fellow? I thought you must have seen it a long time. I did not mean to startle you: are you hurt that I did not say any thing to you till it was all settled? Of course I should have done so, if you had been always at home; but, somehow, I never could pull it in head-and-shoulders: and, then, it didn't seem quite fair till I had asked her father's consent—I only got that yesterday, and her own to-day; so you have not been kept long in the dark."

Robert threw his arms round his brother's neck (they were old-fashioned people, those Hattons, and not ashamed of loving each other), as he said, with a smile the cost of which Arthur little knew:

"Well, I suppose I am as blind as a bat, for I certainly *was* surprised; but I am glad with all my heart for you, Arthur; she has always been like one of ourselves, and she will love the old place, too."

"Won't she just! Why, she loves it like a true Hatton already. I asked her to-day if she didn't think the magnolia smelt a little too strong so near the drawing-room windows, and she exclaimed against having it removed as if I had proposed some awful sacrilege. We don't want any changes. Mother will live here always; and you must give us all your spare time, till you set up housekeeping for yourself. Stinchcombe is *home* till then, you know; don't ever forget that."

"Thanks; I am not likely to forget it," was the reply, spoken so gaily, that any shadow of misgiving Arthur may have felt was completely and for ever dispelled.

And, from that time, every thing went on in the old way at Stinchcombe—except that, of course, Annie was there more frequently, and daily felt more and more at home there. Neither she nor Arthur ever perceived any change in Robert; perhaps they were too much preoccupied to have noticed any slight difference of manner; and, as he neither grew thin nor pale, nor threatened to go into a consumption, nor in any way whatever made himself an object of anxiety to his friends, not even by losing his appetite, of course there could be nothing of any kind the matter with him. No doubt he might have secured plenty of sympathy and compassion if he had selfishly made up his mind to suffer and to die; but he chose, on the contrary, to suffer and to live, which is a very different thing: one is nature, the other is grace; and, while one brings human consolation, the other does its best to make us as commonplace and uninteresting as possible to those around us. Few people believe in suffering where they cannot see it; and fewer still believe it possible to suffer with a merry laugh and a sparkling eye, unfailing good temper, and, to all appearance, unimpaired bodily health; scarcely one in a thousand, perhaps, really and honestly believes in the *joy* of self-sacrifice, or understands that a man whose dearest earthly hope has been blasted on the threshold of life can be sincerely happy. And Robert Hatton *was* sincerely happy—happier than if he had himself won the prize which he gave up by an act of perfect renunciation: at what cost, after what struggle, it matters not to inquire. He was young, and impetuous, and warm-hearted, and of a fiery temperament; and it was a stormy sea which had flung him breathless and exhausted on the shore; but he had risen up with a braced mind and a strong heart, and gone forward with the earnest prayer, *Non mori, sed pati.*

For one month after that first announcement of Annie's engagement, he had remained in London. "Too busy to run down just now: got to study a Chancery-suit ten miles long," he wrote to his brother; but, at the end of that time, he reappeared at Stinchcombe one Saturday evening, in excellent spirits, and full of all manner of wise advice about marriage-settlements, greatly to Arthur's amusement, who declared that the only settlement he should make would be to give every thing to Annie, and leave her free to do what she liked with it.

But it is high time to introduce Mrs. Hatton. She was, according to the testimony of every one who knew her, "a dear old lady,"—not so very old, either, though her early widowhood had silvered her hair, and encompassed her with that indescribable look of gentle dignity which is a woman's brevet rank, and entitles her to reverent homage; in fact, she was not yet sixty, and was as active and energetic as she had been twenty years ago, before her great sorrow fell upon her. It had crushed her for a time; for she was a loving, tender-hearted woman; but she was also a devout Catholic,—she could say with her whole heart: "The Lord gave, and the Lord hath taken away; blessed be the name of the Lord." She knew well that, even in the scathing flames of penal fire, the holy souls are unspeakably blessed, because the deadlier flames of sin can no longer touch them; and she also rejoiced in the hope that, through the strong power of prayer, and the still more mighty intercession of the Holy Sacrifice, the soul of her husband had been already released from its prison-house, and had joined the blessed company of purified saints before the Great White Throne. Human love and human sympathy had never been to her as a possession which she could claim for her own, but only as a happiness lent to her for a time, to be rightly used, gratefully enjoyed, and cheerfully renounced whenever the renunciation should be required of her. She had been taught early in life the great lesson of detachment, and it had led her far on in the path of perfection.

Let no one, however, suppose that Mrs. Hatton was cold, or unfeeling, or indifferent; grace does not supersede nature, but purifies and ennobles it. Annie Crofton would have said that she was the most dear, soft, loving, affectionate darling in the world; and she had good reason to say so; for Mrs. Hatton had done her best to supply a mother's place to the wilful, high-spirited child, left so young to the tender mercies of a nurse and a governess. She was no match-maker, and never for a moment *planned* the result which had taken place; but perhaps it would be going beyond the truth to say she had never thought of or wished it; and it certainly would be very far from the truth to deny that it was a source of great happiness to her.

The marriage was to be delayed two years, on

account of Annie's extreme youth: this had been insisted upon by Mr. Crofton, who refused, reasonably enough, to let his daughter run the risk of marrying in haste to repent at leisure, and said he wished to give her full time to know her own mind.

Annie professed herself very glad of the delay: it would take her at least two years, she said, to learn the first rudiments of matronly propriety, and she was in no hurry to begin the lesson; she had only just begun, she declared, to have her own way, and to do as she liked, and it would be too bad to have to give it up again directly; she would be as stiff and as stately as they pleased when she was the lady of the manor; but she was the child of the moor now, and must be left free to run wild.

"I feel like Selim," she said to Mrs. Hatton one day,—Selim was Mr. Crofton's favourite hunter: "I want a good hard gallop, and a few stiff fences to leap, to take the spirit out of me, and then I shall be as quiet as a lamb; I daresay two years will do it."

Mrs. Hatton stooped over the fairy-like figure sitting at her feet, and smoothed back the hair from her brow, as she replied: "I hope not. I don't want to 'take the spirit out of you,' as you call it, only to see you rule it a little more—use it, instead of letting *it* use *you*. You may need a brave heart, one of these days, for other things than leaping fences."

Annie laughed. "Oh, as to that," she said, "if it came to Stinchcombe Manor having to stand a siege, I think I should find courage enough to defend it; I *couldn't* be a coward—no, not if my spirit and my heart were both broken," she exclaimed, raising her head proudly.

"Yes; I think you would fight bravely; but could you suffer bravely?" asked Mrs. Hatton.

"Suffer?" repeated Annie. "I don't know; what must I suffer? Oh, not to lose Arthur—not that—you don't mean that? Oh, God would never be so cruel to me.! I should go mad; I know I should. Oh, what do you mean? Why do you say such dreadful things?"

"My dear child," exclaimed Mrs. Hatton, taking her in her arms and kissing her, "it is you that say them—not I. I never thought of any special trial—only of such sufferings as we must all have, sooner or later, if God calls us to be saints,—at least, if a life without suffering would be a life without sanctity, as Father Wilfrid said in his sermon last Sunday."

"Look here," said Annie, turning back her sleeve, and showing a deep scar on her arm; "I think I can bear pain pretty well; I did this just to try."

"Did what?" exclaimed Mrs. Hatton, looking in some alarm at what had evidently been a really bad cut.

"Oh, not much: just scratched myself with a penknife for an experiment; it is nothing to signify. Don't look so frightened."

"Promise me never to play those tricks again; you might cut a vein, and bleed to death," entreated Mrs. Hatton earnestly.

Annie laughed merrily. "Well, I won't, then," she said; "there, I promise you I won't; don't be frightened any more. You don't suppose I would break a promise, do you?" And, hastily covering her arm, she said she must run home, or she should be late for dinner.

It might have fared ill with Annie in those days if she had not been a good and sound Catholic, and also under wise and safe direction. She had a little *breeze* with Father Wilfrid every now and then; but even in her wildest moments she never dreamed of taking the bit between her teeth, though she did now and then kick over the traces.

The words Mrs. Hatton had repeated rang in her ears, and haunted her all the way home: "A life without suffering would be a life without sanctity." They had haunted her when she first heard them, and had caused her to make the singular experiment recorded above; now they did something more, they troubled her. She did not want suffering; she did not want sanctity; she had the fulness of human happiness both in possession and in prospect; and she told herself honestly she wanted nothing more: and yet the words troubled her. She knew that she *ought* to want something more—that the happiness she felt *ought* not so entirely to fill her whole heart; and yet, as a matter of fact, it did, and she could not help it.

"I do believe I am a downright heathen," she said to herself at last, "and I don't even want to be a Christian. Well, I must try to be one without wanting it, that's all."

The next morning she was in church as soon as the doors were opened; and, going straight up to Father Wilfrid, who was saying his Office, asked him if he could say the Mass that day for a particular intention.

She looked so eager, that he beckoned her into the sacristy, and asked if any thing was the matter.

"Any thing the matter? No, nothing at all; I only want a Mass said for a special intention. Is that any thing so very wonderful?"

"An intention of your own? Can you tell me what it is?"

"No; I can't,—at least, I don't choose. If I ever get it, I will tell you; but you need not be afraid; it is not any thing wrong."

"Or any thing that is not worthy to be offered to God in the Holy Mass, I hope," he replied. Then, as she made no answer, he continued: "Very well, I will do so on the condition that it is according to the will of God."

Nearly six months had passed since then, and her prayer still remained unanswered. She was daily approaching nearer to a future whose happiness was still unclouded; and sometimes she remembered her intention with a slight shudder—a sort of half-formed wish to retract it; but she never did retract it: she was not one to reclaim a gift that had been freely offered. And now she had been reminded of it by those words of Father Wilfrid's: "Don't meddle with sorrow till you know what it is: it is a holy thing;" and during the ride home in the rain from Hillsborough Tor, when talking had been out of the question, she had been speculating as to what had become of her intention, and whether it would ever "recoil upon the heart that was its home" in some unlooked-for and terrible way. She had never told Father Wilfrid of it: it was her one secret, even from him—a secret that she had guarded with jealous vigilance, and, as yet, with perfect success.

CHAPTER XII.

*"For the Mass shall be sung,
And the bells shall be rung,
And the feast, the feast, eat merrily!"*
Red-Cross Knight.

NOVEMBER fog had given way before December frost: the lanes were too hard and too slippery for riding—at least, so said Mr. Crofton—though Annie pleaded, first, that Jessie was sure-footed; then, that she had been rough-shod; next, that she wanted exercise; and, finally, that it couldn't possibly be slippery on the grass, and that she only wanted to canter across the heath-field, and tell some boys who lived on the other side to bring plenty of evergreens for dressing the church.

"And how do you propose to get to the heath-field, my dear, without going over two miles of hard road, including a steep hill, which is now one sheet of ice, first? You are like that Roman count you laughed at so much the other day for saying he had hoped to come to England without crossing the sea."

"O papa, Jessie doesn't mind the ice; she can

slide beautifully," said Annie, hazarding this marvellous assertion on faith in her favourite's power to do any thing, rather than on any absolute knowledge.

"Indeed! A very questionable accomplishment, I should say, for a pony, and one I should be sorry to encourage. If you don't take care, you will break her legs, as well as your own, some day."

"And which should you be most sorry for?" asked Annie, laughing.

"Well, as I don't wish to put that question to a practical issue, you really must content yourself with walking to-day," replied Mr. Crofton. "I am going up to Stinchcombe presently; will you come with me?"

It was not often that Annie got a walk with her father—he was generally too busy; and it was always a great enjoyment to her; but to-day she had set her heart upon a ride, and did not accept the proposal quite so eagerly as usual.

"*Must* you go to Stinchcombe, papa?" she said; "couldn't we walk to the heath-field instead?"

"What! to the heath-field, and across it to the other side? Too far, Annie; and, besides, I really must go to Stinchcombe; Mrs. Hatton wants to see me about something."

Annie sprang up. "Now, that is too bad!" she exclaimed; "I do hate to be talked over and settled about, as if I were a new piece of furniture. Have you decided yet in which part of the drawing-room I should look most ornamental, and whether green or blue hangings would be most appropriate for me?"

"Annie, Annie! when will you learn to be reasonable?" said her father; "my business with Mrs. Hatton to-day does not concern you in the least, as it happens."

"Then I had better not be mixed up with it," she replied, a little crossly. "What could you do with me while you talk to her?"

Mr. Crofton looked surprised. "Arthur and Robert are both at home," he said.

"Are they? Well, I don't see what difference that makes to me; they are sure to be out somewhere in the grounds, and I can't go roaming about to look for them; it wouldn't be respectable."

But at this climax Annie's ill-temper gave way—it never lasted long; and she burst out laughing at the extremely grotesque aspect it had assumed. That she, of all people, should start a scruple on the score of propriety!—she who, six years ago, had scared her governess by roundly declaring that she "hated morality;" and who, not a year ago, had set all conventionality at defiance by coolly asking Mr. Hatton to ride to Abbotsleigh with her, long before there was any engagement between them to justify such a proceeding. It is true he had refused, and thereby offended her for a whole week; but, as far as she was concerned, she would have done it without a moment's hesitation. Not from boldness: Annie was not the very least bold or "fast;" but from sheer childish innocence and gaiety of heart.

And now she was pretending to make a difficulty about walking with him in his own private grounds after a six months' engagement —a thing which the veriest prude in the whole world could not have objected to. It really was too absurd.

"What a fool one makes of oneself when one is cross!" she thought.

Perhaps Mr. Crofton thought so too; for he looked at her in some astonishment as he replied: "Not respectable to go and find them in their own woods? What on earth are you thinking of, child?"

"O papa, I was cross, that's all," cried Annie; "I will be ready in five minutes to go with you;" and she ran up-stairs, presently returning fully equipped for a cold walk, in a beaver hat and sealskin jacket, with her warm linsey skirt looped up just high enough to show a good stout pair of Balmoral boots. She did not care a straw about dress; nor had she any need to do so: she would have looked pretty in a smock-frock and coalheaver's hat; but Mr. Crofton cared about it for her, and spoilt her a little in this, as well as in other respects. His business—that of a banker in Stonebridge—brought him in a very good income; and, as he was not a man of extravagant tastes or habits, he could very well afford to dress his daughter according to his own fancy. When Annie went out alone, she generally put on the oldest and shabbiest things she could find, from the same feeling which, as a child, had led her once to ask, as the greatest birthday treat she could think of, "Please, nurse, may I make myself as dirty as I like?" But, when she went with her father, she "condemned herself to decent clothing," as she expressed it, in deference to his wishes.

They found Mrs. Hatton sitting alone in the drawing-room, over a fire on which a large log of wood was blazing brightly.

"I have come to settle accounts with you," said Mr. Crofton; "I suppose Annie will find Arthur at home somewhere?"

"I think they are both gone down to the lake to skate," she replied; "I saw them pass the window about an hour ago, with Lion and Lufra; and I think they had their skates in their hands."

The lake was little more than a large pool, dignified by that name, and situated about a quarter of a mile from the house, in the wood: the little river Lewin ran through it at one end, and the other was only frozen over in the very hardest frosts. Lion and Lufra were two Newfoundland dogs, great favourites of Annie's.

"Is the ice strong enough to bear yet?" asked Mr. Crofton.

"Yes, I believe so; Mudge said this morning it was quite safe," answered Mrs. Hatton, who was not nervous about imaginary dangers.

"And, if they get in, the dogs can pull them out," said Annie, evidently not at all troubled by the possibility; "I will run down and dance a reel with them on the ice to warm myself; I'm freezing hard now."

"Don't, Annie—don't go on the ice!" called out Mr. Crofton, who was always nervous where Annie was concerned; but she was already out of hearing.

"Don't alarm yourself," said Mrs. Hatton quietly; "Arthur will take good care not to let Annie hurt a hair of her head."

She, meanwhile, walked quickly on through the wood, crushing the dead leaves, crisp with frost, under her feet; but, long before reaching the lake, she fell in with Robert, who was carefully selecting and cutting twigs from a hollybush.

"How you do startle one!" she exclaimed; "I thought you were skating on the lake, and I was on my way to join you. What are you doing here in the cold?"

"Picking out the best berries, to go along the top of the reredos for Christmas; we want to have a row of wax candles there for the midnight Mass, with bunches of red berries between them. Don't you think it will be an improvement on last year?"

"Of course it will—beautiful, delightful! But you have not got leaves enough with your berries; we must have the thorns, you know. Here, lend me your knife a minute, and let me help you;" and she pulled off her gloves in preparation.

"You would only prick your fingers, and tear your clothes," said Robert. "Arthur is down at the lake with the dogs; had not you better go to him?"

"Well, upon my word, you are polite!" exclaimed Annie, "to send me away when I offer to stay with you, and to insult me with personal remarks into the bargain. Arthur has the dogs, and you have no one; so I shall stay with you. Look here; these are the sort of sprigs you ought to get;" and she tore one off, scratching herself unmercifully in the operation, and leaving a large piece of the feather from her hat on a hollybranch.

"There! I told you how it would be," said Robert. "Come, I will go with you to the lake; there is no hurry about this; and, you know," he added, rather gravely, "Arthur will be vexed if you go away without seeing him,—and you would not like to vex him."

"Wouldn't I?" said Annie mischievously. "I rather think I would, though, just to see what it would be like."

"Don't," said Robert,—"don't play with edged tools."

"And end by murdering some one," she replied, laughing,—rather startling Robert, who had never heard the phrenologist's opinion of her organ of destructiveness.

"Well, don't look so frightened; I shall not murder *you*. Oh, dear, how dreadfully good every body is, except me!" she continued, with a half-sigh, though little thinking how fatally she had played with edged tools in the case of poor Robert himself. "But I really will be good now, and come down to the lake with you,—where are your skates? I want you and Arthur to skate a reel with me on the ice."

"I am not sure that the ice is safe for you," he said; "it has been thawing a little since the morning."

"How very unaccommodating you are to-day!" she said, rather pettishly. "If the ice is strong enough for you, I am sure it is for me; I am not so heavy as you are."

"I had no intention of going on it; but we shall see," he said. "My skates are down there; Lufra carried them."

"Nice old dog! I wish he could wear them!" said Annie.

On reaching the lake, they found Arthur wheeling about in circles of a form that Euclid would have been puzzled to classify, and the two dogs jumping merrily round him. On seeing Annie, he made a rapid dash for the shore, nearly losing his balance as he brought himself to a sudden halt in front of her.

"I had no idea you were coming to-day," he said, "or I would have had the sledge ready for you; it is not quite finished yet."

The sledge was a sort of rocking-chair, composed of fir-poles, which the ingenuity of the two brothers had constructed to serve as a sledge for Annie.

"Oh, never mind," she said; "I didn't mean to come to-day, but papa would not let me ride, and brought me here instead; and I don't want the sledge—I want to dance a reel and warm my feet."

"Ride! I should think not, indeed, in this weather!" he exclaimed. "Come, Robert, put on your skates; Lufra has deposited them somewhere on the bank."

"How is the ice?" asked the cautious Robert.

"The ice?—oh, all right; a little weak towards the river-end, safe enough if we keep this side," replied Arthur; and, no further objection seeming possible, the reel began, and was kept up with great spirit for about ten minutes, though the figure was occasionally interfered with by the dogs, who, never having learnt dancing, executed a somewhat disorderly *obligato* accompaniment.

"Keep off, Lion!" exclaimed Annie at last;

"you have spoilt my very best 8;" and she turned round with the intention of chasing him off the ice. He ran towards the river, breaking the thin ice at the edge, and plunging in. Annie could not stop herself, and would have followed him in another moment, if Robert, who was nearest to her, had not seized her arm, and dragged her towards the bank. Only just in time; the ice broke, and she was nearly up to her knees in water,—but no further harm was done; Robert, jumping on shore, though unable to stand with his skates on, succeeded in half pushing, half throwing her on the bank, almost before Arthur had seen what had occurred. She jumped up as he sprang towards her, his skates off already, and looking horribly frightened.

"All right!" she said; "no harm done, except wetting my feet, thanks to you, Robert;" and she gave him a bright smile, which Arthur would have liked for himself, and which Robert turned away from, as he said:

"You'll catch your death of cold; shall I run up to the house, and send my mother's maid down with some dry stockings and so on for you?"

"You dear, foolish old Robert!" exclaimed Annie, laughing heartily, "I should be much more likely to catch cold waiting for them; you may run on, if you like, and ask her to get some ready for me, and I will come as fast as I can. Oh, dear, what a pickle I am in, to be sure! What will papa say? Go in the back way, Robert, and don't tell any one but Janet. I don't see why papa need ever know any thing about it. You stupid Lion, it is all your fault, and I think the least you could do would be to beg pardon,—come here, sir!"

"Nonsense, Annie; come home and change your wet things, as fast as you can. What a mercy Robert was so near you," said Arthur, hurrying her on.

"Yes, indeed, it is no thanks to you if I have escaped drowning," replied Annie; then, seeing that he looked shocked at her levity, she added: "After all, you know, there was no real danger; I could have scrambled up the bank easily if no one had been near me," which no doubt was perfectly true, though Arthur was unwilling to admit it, and insisted on a fervency of gratitude which she thought quite disproportionate to the occasion, though she did at last allow that it would have been just possible for her to have slipped under the ice and been suffocated, and that an act of thanksgiving was not altogether misplaced.

On reaching the house, they found Janet in the housekeeper's room, fully prepared to meet all emergencies, and with an array of blankets and hot-water bottles that would have done honour to the Humane Society's receiving-room.

"Oh, dear!" cried Annie, "what a dreadful fuss about nothing! I only want a pair of clean stockings, and to dry myself a little at the fire."

On examination, however, it turned out that considerably more than this was required, and consequently it was some time before she made her appearance in the drawing-room, where Arthur had preceded her, thinking some sort of explanation of the state of affairs would be desirable: Annie had got her feet wet by the river, he said, and was making free with his mother's clean stockings in consequence.

"Naughty little puss!" said Mr. Crofton; "I'll be bound she came out with thin shoes on. It is very odd that girls never have any common sense,"—a view of the matter which Arthur was content to let pass, though he might with great truth have defended Annie from the imputation in this particular case.

Presently she came in, her long dress let down and sweeping the ground, to conceal a pair of boots of Mrs. Hatton's, considerably too large for her. Her skirt could not be called dry, though it had been long enough by the fire not to look very wet: every thing underneath it she had been obliged to change, but this happily was not apparent, and she flattered herself that she was *quitte pour la peur* this time.

"Why, Annie, what mischief have you been up to now?" exclaimed Mr. Crofton, looking with some dismay at her stained dress. "You really deserve to be called Duchess of Draggletail."

"I have been *down* to it, not *up* to it," she replied, with a mischievous look at Arthur, which quite upset his gravity. "Lion jumped into the water, and gave me a tremendous splashing, and I didn't know I was so near the edge till I had got my feet wet; but Janet has found me some dry stockings; so I am all right now, and ready to go home as soon as you like."

"Well done!" thought Arthur. "Commend me to a woman's wit for getting out of a scrape!"

"I would ask you to stay and dine," said

Mrs. Hatton, "but I am afraid the roads are too slippery for sending you home in the carriage at night."

"Thank you," replied Mr. Crofton; "I dare say Annie would not mind the walk, if we go early."

"Papa," she exclaimed, "I do really believe you are beginning to lose your memory; have you forgotten that Mrs. Trelawney is coming to us this evening to show me how to make white lilies for the church for Christmas?"

"I beg Mrs. Trelawney's pardon. I really had forgotten," he replied. "Come, then; we had better go before it gets darker."

"I hear the church is to be very beautiful this Christmas," said Mrs. Hatton, as they said good bye.

"Yes; we mean to astonish the natives, Father Wilfrid included," answered Annie. "Mrs. Trelawney knows of all sorts of devices for decoration, that will be marvellous to behold, if we can only accomplish them; and there will be something else better even than all the decorations put together: but I am not going to tell you what."

"A beautiful crib, I suppose," suggested Arthur.

"A crib! oh, of course we shall have *that;* it is as much a matter of necessity as the midnight Mass," said Annie; "and it *is* going to be a very beautiful one, for I have a lovely Bambino, and we are going to make it exactly like a real stable, with the ox and ass and every thing,—but that is not what I meant."

"Not a real ox and ass, I hope?" said Mr. Crofton.

"A real ox and ass!" cried Annie. "I didn't say that, did I? How stupid I am! But we really must run away now; I shall have hard work, as it is, to get my lilies done in time: it only wants a week to Christmas, and there are all the wreaths to make, and the crib to arrange, and every thing."

The week passed away; the lilies were finished, the wreaths were made and put up: they were twined round all the pillars, festooned between all the windows, trained over all the arches; "the holly's burnished spray" gleamed in bright circlets on the walls, like so many martyrs' crowns, formed sacred monograms in the spandrils of the arches, and clustered thickly over the Gothic-crested reredos,—its bright red berries gleaming among the wax candles, which had been so arranged as to light up the very roof of the sanctuary. Banners of rich silk were suspended at intervals from the walls on both sides of the church, in token of homage; for the Babe of Bethlehem was also the mighty God, and, even as this world counts greatness, a royal Child, "of the house and lineage of David." With beautiful significance, the pictures of the Stations were decorated with the glittering, frosted leaves of the ice-plant, emblematic of the cold which had been so keen a suffering of the Sacred Infancy. Long, delicate tendrils of ivy and other creepers were twined round the marble pillars of the altars, and the pedestals of the statues; scrolls exquisitely emblazoned with various Christmas antiphons, the work of Mrs. Trelawney, left scarcely an unoccupied space any where: one large one especially, containing the words, *Gloria in excelsis Deo, et in terra pax hominibus bonæ voluntatis*, in brilliantly illuminated letters, shone conspicuous on the sanctuary-wall behind the High Altar. But the best of all, of course, was reserved for the altars themselves; and these it was always Mrs. Hatton's peculiar care to supply with the choicest flowers and plants from the hot-houses which she kept for this sole purpose. Both the High Altar and that of our Blessed Lady were now dressed entirely with white flowers; not a vestige of colour was to be seen, except the green leaves,—for it is the special glory of Christmas that it is all joy; no shadow rests upon it of suffering gone before, as at Easter, or of bereavement, as at Whitsuntide. Christmas and Corpus Christi are each in their different ways emphatically all "joy in Jesus," in the possession of Him as our own; each a mighty intonation, as it were, of the glorious truth first proclaimed by the Apostle of love, *Et Verbum caro factum est;* each a white feast, in the fullest meaning of the words.

And so there were white flowers in vases on the altars, and before the statues; white flowers in pots, covered with soft moss, on the sanctuary-steps; a garland of white camellias encircling the throne; and Annie's white lilies (the only flowers not real in the whole church) peeping out among the evergreens, quite at the back of the sanctuary. The crib, a very small one, for want of room, was at the bottom of the church, and, as Annie had said, arranged to look as like a real stable as possible; the heads only of an ox and an ass were visible over the rack filled with hay at the back of it; they had been beautifully manufactured by Mrs. Trelawney out of real skins.

"But I would not let her make more than the heads," said Annie; "I hate to see things looking as if they had come out of a Noah's Ark, in the crib."

But what was the "something" which Annie had announced as "better than all the decorations put together"? That still remained a mystery; but exactly as the hour of midnight struck on Christmas-eve, and the procession, headed by acolytes with holly-wreathed torches, entered the church, the "Hallelujah Chorus" burst forth in an exultant peal from the harmonium, which seemed suddenly to have developed itself into full organ-power. Every one was taken by surprise; what was going to happen? Surely Mrs. Trelawney was not going to play such a "convert trick" as to introduce English singing at the Mass! They need not have been afraid; Mrs. Trelawney would sooner have cut her hands off. Nothing happened, except that Father Wilfrid, with his attendant servers and acolytes, knelt in silent adoration till the music ceased; and then the solemn Mass began,—a plain Gregorian one, as usual, but fuller, richer, more sustained than Stonebridge had ever heard before, for Mrs. Trelawney had been carefully training some new singers, whose voices were to be heard for the first time that night. The *Adeste Fideles* at the Offertory was sung, according to Novello's arrangement, in four parts, with a chorus.

And now the last Gospel was over, and Father

Wilfrid, taking off his chasuble, and laying it on the Altar, went down to the crib, which was instantly surrounded by devout worshipers of the Infant Jesus. He said the Litany of the Sacred Infancy in English ; and as he finished the prayer at its close, a voice from the other end of the church, which some few recognised as Annie Crofton's, sang out clearly the first four verses of Handel's matchless anthem, "There were shepherds,"—which was followed by the chorus, "Glory to God ;" and then another voice, deep, rich, full, rang out the joyful news, "For unto us a Child is born ;" the magnificent "Wonderful, Counsellor" chorus being given with surprising effect by the village choir, who at least sang it with all their hearts.

Father Wilfrid had given leave for this at Annie's urgent request ; and indeed he did not see any harm in permitting it, or in allowing her and Mrs. Trelawney to sing, when it was not during the Mass or any public function.

"There!" she said, when they all got home (no one ever went to bed on Christmas-eve at Stonebridge, and they were all assembled in Mr. Crofton's house) ; "did not Mrs. Trelawney give us something better than all the decorations?"

CHAPTER XIII.

"Love me, or not at all, or all in all."
TENNYSON'S *Idylls—Vivien.*

MRS. TRELAWNEY herself had gone quietly home to her lodgings after the midnight Mass; and while the rest of the party were discussing her splendid voice, and her extraordinary power of bringing such full tone out of so small an instrument as the harmonium, she was lying down, utterly exhausted, hoping to recruit her strength sufficiently to return to the church for the second Mass, which would be said at five o'clock. The third and last was to be at nine, out of compassion to Father Wilfrid, who had been working hard at the decorations all the preceding day, hearing confessions all the evening, and of course up and fasting all the night. He had protested against any necessity for altering the usual Sunday hour, ten o'clock, but had been with some difficulty persuaded to do so. The five-o'clock Mass was to be a quiet one, without any music, and about thirty of the children were to make their first Communion in it; but that at nine would be a grand *Missa cantata,* and after it the school-children were to sing English hymns at the crib; they had been practising, "At last Thou art come, little Saviour!" and "See amid the winter snow," for the last month; somewhat, it must be owned, to the detriment of their other studies.

Of course every one was always expected to be a little tired on Christmas-day; a Catholic

Christmas must share something of the weariness of our Lady and St. Joseph, as well as the joy of the Angels and the Shepherds; but the joy was not to be set aside or delayed on account of the weariness, though early hours were always kept, to insure a good night's rest after the wakeful Christmas-eve. Consequently, the dinner at Stinchcombe was at one o'clock—none too early, since every one had breakfasted between six and seven, except, of course, Father Wilfrid himself; but his cup of coffee at ten o'clock did not disqualify him for it, and he was always expected to join the party; it was the only day in the year on which (unless in some very exceptional case) he broke through his rule of never dining out. The Croftons, of course, were always there, and this year Mrs. Trelawney also. She had tried hard to escape: it was hard for her, even as a Catholic, to put away the memory of happy Christmas gatherings in bygone days; children clustering round the grandsire's knee, while the fagot and Yule-log blazed in the old ancestral hall, and quaintly dressed mummers played their part, and servants and retainers, many of them playing marvellous-toned fiddles, fifes, and even horns, assembled to sing, " Christmas comes, the time of gladness," " God rest you, merry gentlemen," and other hymns and carols, some sacred, some, it must be admitted, in the most literal sense of the word, profane; and when her own childish voice had often led the song,—for in her early Cornish home Christmas was kept in the hearty old English fashion, which is now almost forgotten, and which we could be content to forget, if it had been replaced by the truer and holier rejoicings of a Catholic Christmas, instead of being only exchanged for a contempt of all old-fashioned observances whatsoever.

But this was not all; Mrs. Trelawney had other Christmas memories, of her early married life, different, but not less happy; and then, again, other sadder ones of Christmas feasts, which only brought home more vividly the pain and sorrow of separation. She did not feel *in tune* for the Stinchcombe Christmas festivity; and excused herself first on the plea of her recent widowhood, then on the score of having no claim as a stranger to a place at a family party, and finally tried to shelter herself under the excuse of fatigue.

Annie tried to argue the matter with her; answering to the first excuse, that she might shut herself up all the rest of the year, if she liked; but that it was simply unchristian to dine by oneself on Christmas-day—even Father Wilfrid evidently thought so, as he never did it;—to the second, that it was "downright heathenism;" there was only one "family party" at Christmas, and all Catholics belonged to it; no one could possibly be a stranger, except Jews and Turks;—"and besides," she added, as a clinching argument, "you *can't* be a stranger, when I love you so much,"— a mode of appeal which seemed to give intense pain to Mrs. Trelawney, for she gently unclasped Annie's arm from her waist, and said:

"You will be wiser some day than to waste your love so easily; Mr. Hatton will be jealous."

" No, I sha'n't. I shall never be wiser, as you

call it," cried Annie, "and I don't see any wisdom in it; and as for Arthur—why, how on earth could he be jealous of *you ?*"

Mrs. Trelawney smiled a little sadly, but she did not think it necessary to explain.

As for fatigue, Annie declared they would all be tired—"all in the same boat, for that matter; but, then, who cares about being tired on Christmas-day? No one with a spark of Christian charity in them would think about it or feel it;" and, besides, there were plenty of comfortable chairs at Stinchcombe, and any one who pleased might go to sleep in them after dinner; "we all do what we like on Christmas-day, for once in our lives," she said.

But the utmost she could obtain from Mrs. Trelawney was a promise to "think about it," and let Mrs. Hatton know in a day or two whether she would come or not. The thinking about it consisted in entreating Father Wilfrid to suggest some excuse to her which would be considered a sufficient one.

With what she thought a gratuitous cruelty, he replied:

"Indeed, I shall do nothing of the kind; there *is* no sufficient excuse, and you must go."

"But, father"—she began.

"Look here, my child," he said; "do you wish to celebrate your Christmas by indulging in an act of pure selfishness? Do you wish to weigh your own private griefs in the scale with the joy of the whole Catholic Church in heaven and on earth? If we are bidden to 'rejoice with those who do rejoice,' even at the cost of our own individual feelings, surely all Christians are bound to rejoice in the good tidings which angels left their bright home in heaven to announce to them. Miss Crofton was right in saying that we are all one family at Christmas; and it is a family whose members have no right to refuse fellowship with each other from any selfish motive. I know," he added, "it will be painful to you in many ways; but offer that to our Lord, and don't think any more of it. After all, it is not a great sacrifice; He has more than that to ask of you; put it down before you, and *step over it.*"

Mrs. Trelawney made no further objection, and, to Annie's great delight, sent a note the next morning, accepting Mrs. Hatton's invitation.

The dinner was like most Christmas dinners, and deserves no particular notice. Every one agreed in admiring the decorations, and in thinking the arrangement of music and singing perfect; Father Wilfrid especially, who had never heard, or even heard of, the *Messiah*, was quite enthusiastic in his praise of the anthem,—only, he said, it struck him that the words in the last chorus were not quite correct.

"Not correct!" exclaimed Annie. "What do you mean?"

"Perhaps I ought to have explained to you before," said Mrs. Trelawney, addressing herself to Father Wilfrid, "that as Handel was a Protestant, he naturally adapted his music to the Protestant translation of the Bible. We altered the words in the other parts of the anthem, as far as we could; but it was impossible to change a single syllable of the "Wonderful, Counsellor," without spoiling it altogether; and I thought that, as no false doctrine was involved, and as probably no one but ourselves would know that they were Scripture words at all, there would not be any harm in singing them as they stood."

"Well," replied Father Wilfrid, after a few moments' hesitation, "it certainly gave no scandal, and it was not in the Mass; and I suppose, under the circumstances, there was no harm in it,—but it is a serious objection to Handel's music. What a pity he was not a Catholic!"

"Yes, very provoking of him. What glorious Masses he would have written! We should have had something then really fit to sing in church, besides those old Gregorians," said Annie, who sometimes got a little tired of the severe style of music in use at Stonebridge, and confessed to enjoying a Farm-Street Mass when in London. "Just fancy, father, a *Gloria in Excelsis* like the 'Hallelujah Chorus!' Wouldn't it be magnificent? and wouldn't you let us have it here on great feasts?"

"I am afraid it would be rather *too* magnificent for us," he replied. "I would rather keep to our plain chant; it is solemn and devotional, and distracts nobody."

"Dear me! I wish people would not be so easily distracted; it is very tiresome of them!" said Annie, who, with all her external levity, was not at all easily distracted herself.

"I believe," said Mrs. Trelawney, "that at Warwick Street they sometimes sing that anthem to the Latin words from the Vulgate, and make them correspond very well with the music. Perhaps you would prefer our doing the same, if we can manage it?"

"Yes, I think I should," answered Father Wilfrid; "it would be easy to explain the meaning to the people."

"Very easy, I should think," she said, "for Handel hardly wants words; his music is a language in itself."

"Beethoven wrote a Mass, and he wasn't a Catholic; he had not any religion at all," said Annie. "Why couldn't Handel do the same?"

"I suppose just because he *had* some religion at all," replied Mrs. Trelawney, "and could not compose what he had no sympathy with. Beethoven forgot himself in his art, Handel threw his whole heart and soul into it; Beethoven had only genius, and, perhaps, a fuller portion of it, but Handel had human feeling besides. It was all the same to Beethoven whether he wrote a Mass, or the 'Men of Prometheus;' he could throw his whole power into either: but he would never have cared to write such a song as 'What though I trace,' or even, 'Lord, remember David.'"

She stopped suddenly, astonished at herself for having spoken so excitedly; but Handel was a subject rather apt to run away with her.

"Is there not some story," asked Mrs. Hatton, "about Handel's insisting on choosing his own words for the *Messiah?*"

"Yes," said Mrs. Trelawney; "but I am not sure if it is authentic: at all events, if it is not *vrai*, it is *vraisemblable*. It is said that when he first proposed to compose a sacred oratorio on the life of our Lord, the king—George III.—

suggested that the Anglican Bishops should select the words; to which Handel replied, that he was much obliged to his majesty, but he could read his Bible for himself."

"Bravo, for a good Protestant!" exclaimed Arthur Hatton; "*se non è vero è ben trovato.* But do you believe the story, Mrs. Trelawney?"

"I think it a very probable one," she replied: "Handel had a good deal of pride, and would resent the imputation of incapacity; and of course any composer would prefer being free to choose his own words."

Soon after this, the ladies adjourned to the drawing-room; and Annie, putting her arm round Mrs. Trelawney, quietly deposited her in a corner of the sofa, near the fire, on which a huge "Yule-log" was blazing.

"There!" she said; "now go to sleep and rest yourself; you must be tired to death. Why on earth did you wear yourself out by putting on the steam so tremendously about Handel, at dinner-time?"

Mrs. Trelawney laughed.

"I don't know, indeed," she said; "one must talk about something."

"Talk! yes, of course," said Annie, "but—"

"But I *ranted*, you mean, I suppose?"

"No, I don't. How can you say such horrid things? I only mean that you excited yourself quite unnecessarily. I don't suppose any body half understood you; I'm sure *I* didn't. Does music get into your head, like wine into other people's?"

"My dear Annie," exclaimed Mrs. Hatton, "I

shall think something has got into *your* head, if you talk such nonsense."

"No, it hasn't, dear mother," said Annie, giving her a good, hearty kiss and hug,—she had always called Mrs. Hatton *mother*, since her engagement to Arthur,—"but I always feel so happy at Christmas, I can't help being a little wild."

Mrs. Hatton and Mrs. Trelawney looked at each other and smiled; the reflection of Annie's happiness fell upon them, and they rejoiced in it for her; neither of them had that morose and selfish temper which is distressed by the sight of a gladness it cannot share.

"Yes," said she, going back to Mrs. Trelawney, and speaking more quietly; "I think one should *always* be happy at Christmas—*quand méme;*" and as she slid her hand quietly into Mrs. Trelawney's, the untranslatable French expression spoke volumes.

"*Quand méme!*" The poor widow repeated the words dreamily, as she sat looking into the fire, and perhaps drawing *mind-pictures* in the red embers; then, turning round, she said:

"Yes, we must not be sad to-day; but one is tempted to feel one's loneliness more at Christmas. Maude will be with me, I hope, for the New Year."

"Maude! oh, is she really coming? I am so glad! But I beg your pardon; I have no business to call her Maude. I wonder if I shall ever learn how to behave properly,—I am sure the extra penny was never paid for teaching me manners."

"You need not beg *my* pardon," replied Mrs. Trelawney, smiling, but with an emphasis on the pronoun which Annie understood well enough to imply that Maude herself was not a person whom it would be safe to take liberties with,—as, indeed, she had already experienced.

"How long will she stay? what would she like? what can we do to amuse her?" she asked, and would have run on with a string of other questions, had not Mrs. Trelawney gently stopped her by saying:

"I am afraid she will not stay very long; and I think she will like best to be alone with me; she does not care for amusement, and"— but the tears rose to her eyes, and she could not go on.

Annie kissed her softly. "And she does not like Catholics, I know," she said. "But can we not find some way to make her like them? not by pushing them down her throat, of course—I know that well enough; I believe I should have hated *you*, if I had been *told* to *like* you; but could we not find out any thing that would give her pleasure, and do it for her?"

Mrs. Trelawney shook her head sadly.

"Well, at least I may come and see her while she is with you, may I not?"

Mrs. Trelawney hesitated a moment, and then said, "Yes, dear, if you like; but you must try not to be offended if Maude should be a little stiff with you; poor child, she can hardly bear to see me care for any one but herself." She checked herself suddenly. Annie looked surprised; she could not understand.

"But if I love any one," she said, "I always want every body else to love them too."

"What's that, Annie?" said a voice close behind, which startled her; and looking round, she saw Arthur Hatton leaning over the back of the sofa.

"Are you in training for a spy, or a detective policeman?" she exclaimed. "Pray, how long have you been listening to our private conversation?"

"Only long enough to hear your last words," he replied, "and I want to know what they mean."

"What they mean? why, dear me, how you do snap one up! What were they, to begin with? I have quite forgotten."

But Arthur, apparently, had thought better of it, for he said, "Oh, never mind, then; they are not worth remembering;" but Mrs. Trelawney noticed a shadow on his face, if Annie did not, and said, rather quickly:

"Annie was only speaking of friendship, Mr. Hatton, and saying that it ought not to be a monopoly; don't you agree with her?"

"I don't know," said Arthur, rather gravely; "I don't think I do quite wish my friends to be every body else's friends too; but perhaps that is not quite a Christian feeling."

"Christian!" exclaimed Annie; "I should think not, indeed; and on Christmas-day, too! I wonder you are not ashamed of yourself. Robert! just listen to Arthur's new act of charity; no one is to love his friends but himself: you must take care not to love any one he chooses to set his heart upon. Do you hear, Robert ?" for Robert had turned away, and was diligently contemplating the snow-flakes, which had begun to fall within the last few minutes.

"Yes, I hear," he said.

"To hear is to obey, you know," said Annie. "I advise you to cut all Arthur's friends as fast as you can, beginning with me—at least, if he honours me with his friendship."

Would she never learn the danger of playing with edged tools till she had cut her hands with them ?

"Very well," Robert answered quietly, and without looking round. "Good bye, then ;" and he walked out of the room.

"Poor Robert !" said Annie, laughing; "I do believe he took me at my word. He is marvellously simple for a lawyer ! He looked vexed, too ; and I hate to vex any one on Christmas-day, though I do tease them all the year round besides. I shall go after him, and smoke the peace-pipe."

And she was suiting the action to the words, when Arthur detained her and said :

"Can you come into the library for a few minutes first ?"

"No, not first ; I will come to you there presently, if you like," she replied, and darted quickly out of the room.

She did not see, and if she had seen she would not have understood, an expression on Arthur Hatton's face, which Mrs. Trelawney did see, and did understand ; for she had learnt its meaning by bitter experience. She looked up at him and said :

" Annie seems quite to belong to Christmas, she is so childlike herself; don't you think so ?"

Arthur Hatton was not a man to wear his heart upon his sleeve; and shaking off the little cloud which had gathered on his brow, he replied :

" Yes, yes, indeed she is, like the angels she sang of this morning; but I think she must be waiting for me now; I will go and bring her back to you. I am afraid I interrupted your conversation just now ;" and he proceeded towards the library. Annie was there, but not alone; she was talking eagerly to Robert, who stood in a deep-set oriel window (for Stinchcombe had good old-fashioned walls, two feet thick), still looking at those everlasting snow-flakes. Arthur could not see his brother's face, but there came over him an involuntary feeling that Robert, at least, was not a child.

" But do tell me," Annie was saying,—" do you really think it wrong to tease people ? you look as grave as a judge about it ; can't you give a verdict without a jury to help you ?"

Arthur stood still for a moment, unperceived, waiting with some curiosity to hear his brother's answer ; he gave it without looking round.

" No, not wrong, certainly, Annie," he said ; " but a thoughtless person might easily hurt other people's feelings, without meaning it."

" Most just judge !" replied Annie, with mock

M

gravity. "A thoughtless person!—that means me, I suppose—most delicately suggested, I am sure; and hurting people's feelings means, in the vulgar tongue, treading on their corns. Have *you* got corns to be trodden on, Robert? I am very sorry, but, you see, I could not possibly know it; come, say you forgive me, and be friends again; never mind Arthur's nonsense."

Robert turned to speak; and at the same moment Arthur came forward.

"What, again!" exclaimed Annie, laughing. "Well, you are rightly punished this time, at all events; listeners never hear any good of themselves, you know. Robert and I have been quarrelling; but I think we have done now; haven't we, Robert?"

But Robert was gone.

"Do you want me for any thing?" she asked, subdued, in spite of herself, by something in Arthur's face.

But, as he looked into those clear, pure, truthful eyes, and saw the bright smile of unmistakable affection which greeted him, he felt ashamed of his gloomy thoughts and jealous suspicions, and said: "Nothing, really, darling; only just to have you all to myself for a few minutes."

Annie opened her eyes very wide as she cried: "All to yourself, indeed! How selfish men are! Don't be shocked, or angry, or any thing, please, Arthur," she added, going up to him, and looking half shyly into his face, as she laid her hand in his; "but, do you know, I sometimes think no one has a right to want any one else *all to themselves.*"

"What!" exclaimed Arthur, starting back; "what have you been reading, Annie? some of those disgusting American books I begged you not to touch?"

Annie raised her head, and looked straight at him with quiet dignity. "I don't know what is the matter with you to-day," she said; "you seem to misunderstand me very strangely. You know, you know quite well, Arthur, I would sooner cut my hands off than touch such books, or any like them, even if you had never said a word to me about them. I meant, that it seems hardly right for any one to belong entirely—hardly safe, I mean, to give *all* one's heart away, except to our Lord."

"Annie," he said gravely, "do you want to be a nun? is that what you mean?" and he dropped her hand, and waited her answer with blanched cheeks and quivering lips.

"No," she replied decisively, "oh, no, Arthur; how could I? Don't you know—?" She could not finish the sentence; but her hand found its way back to his in a sufficiently expressive manner.

"But you are afraid we shall love each other too much?" he said, feeling quite reassured; "well, dear, we must pray that may not be; there ought not ever to be any danger of it for Catholics. Come, now, I must not keep you selfishly here any longer; our mother and Mrs. Trelawney will wonder what has become of us."

But they were hardly in a condition to wonder, being both fast asleep, one on each side of the fire; as they had both been awake all night, it was quite allowable. Mrs. Hatton, however, was at no time much given to sleep; and, as the door opened, her eyes did the same.

"My dears," she said, "what time is it?"

"Time for coffee, mother dear, and then for Benediction," said her son, stooping to kiss her brow.

Mrs. Trelawney, now thoroughly awake too, apologised for her seeming rudeness; whereat Annie laughed, saying: "Didn't I tell you we all did what we liked on Christmas-day? I mean to go home and go to bed directly after Benediction; and I strongly suspect, if every one else spoke the truth, they would say the same. Are you too tired to play for Benediction to-night? Very few people come, I am sorry to say; but Father Wilfrid does not like to give up having it, and surrender at discretion to the world; however, it is always early, at five o'clock, so as to leave the evening free afterwards."

"Playing never tires me the least," she answered; "but I certainly don't think I shall be inclined to burn much candle after I go home this evening."

They had coffee; and then a sort of covered car took the whole party into Stonebridge for Benediction, through the thickly falling snow, which threatened to make the roads impassable by the next day. Father Wilfrid looked out at it, thinking of the saint who saw souls falling into hell like flakes of snow, and said his Rosary; Annie looked out at it, thinking it would spoil the ice for skating, and said so; Mrs. Hatton looked out at it, thinking of the poor people, and said:

"Annie, you must give out some warm blankets to-morrow."

Mrs. Trelawney looked out at it, thinking of Maude, and said nothing.

CHAPTER XIV.

*"I remember, I remember,
How my childhood fleeted by,
The mirth of each December,
And the warmth of each July."*

Old Song.

IN spite of appearances, fears, and prognostications, the snow-storm was not a very enduring one this time; the ice was not spoilt for more than a few hours; the roads were not blocked up; and Maude Trelawney made her appearance at Stonebridge on New-Year's Day,—at least, so Annie concluded, as she saw a fly with luggage on it pass on its way from the station late that evening, too late and too dark to see any thing inside. She was right: it contained Maude and her mother.

Annie would have *liked* to rush off to Mrs. North's lodgings at once; but, in the first place, she was in the act of dressing for dinner; and, in the next, she was beginning to learn the first rudiments of self-control with regard to her intercourse with Mrs. Trelawney.

"I will *bide my time,*" she said to herself; "Miss Maude cannot very well help being civil to me here; and if I don't somehow contrive to shake a little of the nonsense out of her, I'll be—*whipped!* There! that really is *not* a naughty word," she concluded, conscious that she did now and then indulge in "naughty words" privately.

"I beg your pardon, ma'am; what did you please to say?" inquired the maid, entering the room at this moment to give a finishing touch to Annie's toilette.

"To say? I did not speak to you at all, Jane," replied Annie demurely, much to the amusement of her abigail, who had heard every word distinctly enough outside the door.

"There's a chance for you now, Charley," said Annie at dinner-time; "you had better begin and make love to your grandmother like a house on fire; for I daresay she will not stay very long. I should recommend an early visit to-morrow, with a bouquet of hot-house flowers, as the best mode of entering the lists at once; though where on earth you are to get them, without going to Stinchcombe, I don't know."

"Eh! Charley, my boy, what's all this about?" said Mr. Crofton, looking up. "Who is your grandmother, if I may venture to ask?"

"No one, sir, that I know of," replied Charley, looking remarkably foolish; "it's only some of Annie's nonsense."

"It was no nonsense at Carew Castle, I assure you, papa," said Annie, glancing mischievously across at her brother; "Charley was raving about Miss Trelawney's great, glorious eyes, and all the rest of it."

"Miss Trelawney!" exclaimed Mr. Crofton,

with an expression of such unmitigated astonishment, that both his children burst out laughing; but Charley presently recovered himself, and turned the tables by saying:

"The fact is, papa, I believe Annie is jealous. Miss Trelawney takes the wind out of her sails; she is handsome enough for an empress."

"And proud enough too!" added Annie.

"Oh, of course!" said Charley, laughing; "beautiful women are always proud, and every thing else bad, are they not? If she were ugly and deformed, you would not grudge her every virtue under the sun."

"I'm sure I only wish she had!" exclaimed Annie, with a reckless contempt of Lindley Murray.

"Had what? It's a pity you girls don't learn Latin grammar; there would be some chance of understanding what you say."

"But I do,—I mean, I have learnt Latin grammar," replied Annie; "and I'm sure what I said was plain enough. You boys muddle your heads with Euclid's problems, till plain English is too straightforward for you."

"A splendid *tu quoque*, Scatterbrains!" said Mr. Crofton; "bad grammar defended by bad logic! Who is this wonderful Miss Trelawney, whose beauty has swamped all her virtues?"

"O papa! I didn't say that!" exclaimed Annie.

"Something uncommonly like it," said Charley; "what was it you *only wished she had?*"

"Well, I daresay she has; I never said she hadn't," blundered out poor Annie.

"Has what? hadn't what?" persisted Charley remorselessly.

"She may have all the seven contrary virtues, for any thing I know," said Annie, quietly settling down on one of the horns of her dilemma, or at least trying to do so, for Charley was inexorable.

"Contrary to what?—to each other?" he asked demurely.

"Oh, don't bother me any more!" she pleaded; "you've teased me till—"

"Till you've 'put on your cloak inside out,' and every thing else outside in; isn't that about it? Come, you know it was all fair play; who began the teasing?"

"Well," said Mr. Crofton, "when you have settled that between you, perhaps you will answer my question,—who is Miss Trelawney?"

"O papa! surely you know: Maude, Mrs. Trelawney's daughter, poor Maggie Vivian's companion."

"Oh! *that* Miss Trelawney, is it? I remember, now, you said the other day her mother was expecting her. I thought she was a rabid Protestant; how came she and Charley to hit it off together?"

"They didn't hit it off," said Annie, laughing; "it was a case of Irish reciprocity. I don't think Miss Trelawney would speak a civil word to any Catholic, if she could help it."

"Indeed! then pray don't invite her here," said Mr. Crofton. "I am sorry for you, Charley; but I daresay you'll get over it."

"Get over Annie's nonsense? Well, if she'll be a good girl, and come for a ride to-morrow morning, perhaps I may."

"A ride!" exclaimed Annie; "of course I

will. The roads are in a nice state of slush since the thaw; but no matter: it will only take James a little longer to clean my habit. Where shall we go?"

"The Tavistock road is the cleanest, I think," he said, "and I want just to leave a message at Abbotsleigh, if you don't mind."

The Tavistock road! They would have to pass under Mrs. Trelawney's windows; Annie revolved in her mind the possibility of leaving a message there too, as an excuse for seeing Maude; only she had not the very remotest idea what message to invent for the occasion. Reckless as ever, however, she said:

"Very well, that will be just right; I want to leave a message too."

"What! at Abbotsleigh? Is it a message to young Ellicombe? I shall tell Arthur to look out for squalls. He is going off to Rome next week, to join the Zouaves; so you must make haste, if you have any little game on hand there."

"There, sir, take that for your impertinence," said Annie, giving him a box on the ears and a kiss both together.

"I want to leave a message for Mrs. Trelawney."

"All right," was the reply. "Mrs. Trelawney's star is in the ascendant nowadays; I wonder whose turn it will be next." Annie vouchsafed no reply to this, being, to own the truth, occupied in devising some subject-matter for the message to be left the next morning.

"Now, then, Annie, what's your message?" asked Charley, as he dismounted to ring the bell at Mrs. North's private door.

"I shall run up and give it myself," she replied, springing from her pony, and knotting the reins to a railing in front of the house.

"Oh! something mysterious, I suppose," thought Charley.

Mrs. Trelawney and Maude were sitting over the fire, both pretending to work, but neither of them actually doing it, and both looking very cold. Annie hardly waited to be announced, and Maude looked round with a start, as her clear, merry voice rang out:

"How do you do, Miss Trelawney?"

It was not in Maude's nature to "welcome the coming guest," however well-disposed she might be to fulfil the latter part of that wise injunction; and she rose slowly and stiffly from her chair, as she replied coldly:

"I am quite well, thank you, Miss Crofton."

Feeling chilled to her very heart's core, Annie turned to Mrs. Trelawney, and, throwing her arms round her neck, said low and softly:

"And you,—are you quite well, really well?"

Gently disengaging herself, and with a little reproach in her eyes, which was meant kindly, but which wounded poor Annie, Mrs. Trelawney replied, in rather a constrained tone:

"Yes, indeed, really quite well; but what brings you here in your habit?—is your pony waiting for you?"

"Jessie brought me here, I believe," said Annie, feeling a little embarrassed; for, to say the truth, she had trusted to "the chapter of accidents" for an excuse for her visit; "and she and Charley and Nabob are all waiting for me outside. I ran up to ask if you want any thing not procurable in Stonebridge; we are going to Abbotsleigh, and shall pass through Ringwood."

Mrs. Trelawney smiled; the excuse was too transparent for her, though Maude, unknowing in the ways and means of the place, might perhaps be blinded by it.

"Thank you, no," she said; "I don't think I have any wants at present."

"Except to get rid of me, I suppose; so good bye," cried Annie, with a wave of her hand to Mrs. Trelawney, and a sweeping courtesy to Maude. The next moment she was out at the door, and, resting her foot on Charley's hand, she vaulted lightly into her saddle, saying:

"Now let us have a good gallop; I am all frozen up."

"Frozen!" said Charley; "why, you said you were quite warm a few minutes ago. Were they sitting without a fire up there?"

"Oh, there was fire enough to *look at*," she replied; "but Maude would freeze all the heat out of a furnace; I think she must be cold-blooded, like a fish."

"Cold-blooded!" exclaimed Charley, "with those"—but he suddenly checked himself; he was not going to "rave" about "great, glorious eyes" to Annie any more; her teasing had taken effect in a direction she would neither have desired nor understood.

Annie laughed.

"Those great, staring eyes, you mean," she said. "Yes; a great many fishes have big eyes, and can stare out of them; do you remember that great cod's head we had for dinner last Friday?"

Now, if one does chance to have any romantic feeling in connection with another person, the suggestion of a fish's head is not just precisely what would occur to one as the most appropriate comparison. Charley's only reply was to bestow so vigorous an application of the spur upon Nabob, that he began to cut the most extraordinary capers, much to Jessie's inconvenience, who kicked out lustily at him,—a misdemeanour which Annie punished by a sharp cut of the whip across her shoulders, starting her off at full gallop—an example soon followed by Nabob.

Little did they think that the very eyes they were discussing had watched the whole scene,—that the cold, stately girl, who would barely condescend to rise from her chair to show common politeness to a visitor, had stood at the window, with eyes distended in their brilliant scorn, and lips compressed with jealous hate, as she gazed down upon the pure-minded, innocent creature who thought *her* "cold-blooded."

She gazed steadily and intently till they were out of sight; but though her eye was haughty, a tear glistened in it. Maude Trelawney was but a girl, after all; and no one is wholly given up to bad passions at eighteen. A kind of pity mingled with her contempt for Annie; and the fierce jealousy that had been excited by the kiss her mother had bestowed on that fair young brow, clashed with an intense yearning for the love that seemed to her thus wastefully lavished on a stranger, "a mealy-faced chit of a girl, who has not two ideas in her head."

But in this Maude was unjust, as jealous people generally are. Annie's worst enemies could not honestly have looked at those bright cheeks, glowing with health, and called her "mealy-faced," and, as for having not two ideas in her head, it was her misfortune rather than her fault, that she constantly had about two hundred there all at once, to their own mutual embarrassment and confusion.

"Maude, dear, what are you looking at out there in the cold?" asked Mrs. Trelawney at last.

"At your friend Miss Crofton," was the reply, spoken in a bitter tone; "she seems to make herself quite at home here."

"She would make herself at home any where," answered Mrs. Trelawney; "it is her nature; she can't help it."

"Can't help her nature!" repeated Maude. "I thought it was the great boast of Catholics, that they were superior to all little weaknesses of that kind; natural affection amongst the rest."

"Maude! Maude!" exclaimed her mother, bursting into tears as she clasped her in her arms.

It was perhaps just as well that natural feeling had vented itself a little on both sides; though Maude's bitter speech had been provoked against her will, by an impulse of resentment too strong for her,—for she was ordinarily self-contained in no common degree; and, moreover, the whole subject of religion had long ago come to be tacitly ignored between her and her mother.

"You don't deny it! you can't deny it!"

she said; and, tearing herself violently away, she rushed into her own room, and locked the door.

Poor Mrs. Trelawney! how could she deny it? how could she speak any words of denial, when her voice was choked, and her heart bursting? She thought she had sufficiently denied it in act; but what were acts to Maude, who looked upon them simply as *acting*, and believed that Catholics systematically employed them for the same purpose that Talleyrand ascribed to the power of speech? It was perhaps the most hopeless complication of the whole difficulty, that Mrs. Trelawney did not, in any adequate degree, realise the strength or depths of her daughter's prejudices; she thought they were hopelessly insurmountable, indeed, but she believed them to be against the faith and supposed doctrines of Catholics only,—doctrines mostly of Maude's own invention, it is true; but she had no conception of the contempt in which Maude held the moral character of Catholics, of the utter degradation into which she supposed them to have fallen. Where or how Maude had imbibed this feeling, she herself even scarcely knew; it was partly founded upon her father's stern disapproval of every thing "Popish," partly on deductions drawn from such vile books as *La Religieuse* and *Le Maudit*, though even Maude had strong common sense enough to see that these were the ungenerous revenge taken by personal pique and wounded dignity; and partly, perhaps chiefly, on what would seem at first sight to have nothing whatever to do with it, a passion for hero-worship. Quite at the very farthest back of her mind, Maude had a feeling that if Catholics

were right, the Saints were not only the greatest
heroes, but the only heroes in the world; and this
was so insufferable to her, that rather than admit
it, she was resolved to strip them of their heroism
by turning it into something even worse than
ridicule or contempt; and just as some people
try to excite hatred for sin, by imagining the
devil to be a huge black monster, with a disgusting tail and hideous claws, so Maude conjured up
imaginations about Catholics in general, and the
Saints in particular, which would be quite unfit
for "ears polite" to hear, or eyes polite to read.
But of all this Mrs. Trelawney knew nothing. She
remembered well enough, indeed, that once, when
Maude was only ten years old, she had gone off
into an ecstasy of hero-worship over Mrs. Hemans's
beautiful ballad, "Casabianca," succeeded by a reaction of strongly expressed disgust on discover-
ing that her hero was "a French boy, and the
French are all Papists;" but she did not know
that thenceforward Maude had revenged herself
by investing poor Casabianca with every vice
and meanness which she was able at that early
age to imagine.

Mrs. Trelawney laboured under a double mistake. She thought she had lost her daughter's
affections by becoming a Catholic, which was not
true: Maude's love was not a thing to be up-
rooted by any mortal power or force whatsoever;
but she did not think that all respect for her
mother was utterly eradicated in Maude's heart,
which would have been true.

Was this double misunderstanding ever to be
set right?

Not yet! not yet!

Let us follow Maude to her room for a few moments, though, if she knew of our impertinence, she would take somewhat strong measures to show her sense thereof.

Her window, like her mother's, looks out over the Dartmoor Tors, and, like her mother, she is straining her eyes towards them; for she too has memories and associations connected with the wild moorlands. She too spent a part of her childhood by the wooded banks of the Tamar, and on the breezy Bodmin moors. How long ago it seemed! and yet—yet, was it possible? Could it be only six years since she had herself one day caught her pony in the field, and, without waiting for the ceremony of a saddle, ridden it bare-backed, and with only a halter for bridle, across a two miles' stretch of heath? She had been scolded when she came home for her "tom-boy ways," and for tearing her frock: she, Maude Trelawney, had actually been *a child* only six years ago! Six short years—no, six long years, six centuries, it seemed to the girl of eighteen, who stood leaning against the wall, and looking out upon Hillsborough Tor. Involuntarily she turned towards the looking-glass; yes, she had not been mistaken the other day: there were two or three not gray, but white hairs shining out conspicuously on the glossy black braids swept back from her brow; there were two deep furrows, too, on that brow: what business had such things there?

CHAPTER XV.

> "Lest when our latest hope is fled, ye taste of our despair;
> And learn by proof, in some dark hour, how much the wretched dare."
> MACAULAY'S *Lays of Ancient Rome.*

Two days passed, and still Annie had not called on Miss Trelawney; not, certainly, from any abatement of her desire to do so, but because, as she expressed it, she really could not get up courage to go through a shivering-fit in such very cold weather. Perhaps, also, Father Wilfrid's absolute prohibition of the very slightest reference to religious subjects may have had something to do with the matter, for Annie was decidedly *not* self-contained; and having once set her heart on effecting Maude's conversion, and thereby her reconciliation with her mother, she was full of eagerness to plunge head-foremost into the troubled waters, and felt by no means sure that the trial of sitting quietly on the brink would not prove beyond the limits of her power of endurance.

"May I not say even the least little word?—not even ask if I may bring you to see her?" she pleaded.

Father Wilfrid laughed heartily. "Not *even* throw a Catholic priest at her head?" he said. "My dear child, you might as well offer to introduce her to his Satanic Majesty at once."

"But she could never possibly dislike *you*, if she saw you; and you would be sure to find out just the right way to do her good."

Father Wilfrid laughed again, as he said :
"Well, as I don't either work miracles or deal in magic, I don't quite see how it can benefit her to look at me; depend upon it, the right way to do her good is to leave her alone; leave her to God, and trust her to our Lady's prayers. Remember, *Nisi Dominus ædificaverit domum, in vanum laboraverunt qui ædificant eam.*"

"Are we to do *nothing*, then ?—not even when it seems as if she were sent here on purpose ?" replied Annie.

"Never mind what *it seems*," answered Father Wilfrid. "You may besiege heaven with prayers for her as much as you like; and do you call that doing nothing ?"

"Not exactly, of course ; only one can do *that* when she is at Stretton, or any where ; one longs to do more than that now that she is actually here."

"*Less* than that, you mean,—you cannot do *more;* all the books that ever were written, all the arguments that ever were invented, all the persuasions that ever were used, all the explanations that ever were made, never kindled one spark of light or grace in a soul ; that is the work of the Holy Ghost, not ours."

"But," said Annie, " I thought Protestants always wanted to argue things out, and have them explained."

"They want the gift of faith, and nothing else," replied Father Wilfrid, more bluntly than Annie had ever heard him speak before : but she would not take the hint, and said :

"Then you don't believe in controversy ?"

"Believe in controversy! well, I don't remember ever having been taught that it was an article of faith," he replied, in a tone which clearly signified, even to Annie, that the conversation was at an end.

She went away with a very dissatisfied feeling; with that sort of *heart-chill* which all enthusiastic persons experience from the slightest check to their eagerness; and which causes a suffering quite inappreciable by the so-called "good sound common sense" which generally inflicts it.

Father Wilfrid, however, was not one of those distressingly sensible persons who think it unreasonable to undertake any thing without a tolerably certain prospect of success, and he understood well enough the mortification he was giving; but he had his own reasons for the line he was taking, and he was not bound to explain them to Annie: a little touch of the curb would do her no harm.

The immediate result, however, was a piece of rash judgment, in good keeping with the reckless part of her nature.

"I don't believe he cares a straw whether Maude is a Catholic or not! So much for fine preaching about the love of souls! What a humbug every body is!" she exclaimed out loud to herself, in her own room, that evening, by way of a vent to her feelings.

And no sooner were the words so spoken, than she was heartily ashamed of them. There is nothing like speaking one's thoughts out loud, for showing one their folly or wickedness, as the case may be; and in certain cases, nothing so surely puts the devil to flight, as answering his suggestions out loud to his face.

But all this time, what of Maude herself? What, for instance, had she been doing that very morning, while her mother was at Mass? Mrs. Trelawney never for a moment doubted that she was sleeping, or, at all events, resting quietly in her bed; for who would get up in the dark, on a winter morning, with nothing to do, and no fire to warm themselves by? But Father Wilfrid, when he turned round to say the *Orate, fratres*, in his Mass, was conscious of a slight distraction arising from a glimpse of a tall black figure, closely veiled, standing in the doorway at the bottom of the church; when he came down from the altar, it had disappeared. It was no Stonebridge figure—that he knew well enough; but surely he had somewhere seen that strangely fashioned crape veil, so arranged as not only to cover the face of its wearer, but to fall from the back of her hat in heavy folds, like a mourner's scarf. Yes, he had seen (and studiously avoided meeting) Mrs. and Miss Trelawney the evening before, walking through the village. But what was Maude doing there? What had brought her there? Was not the Mass a greater abomination in her eyes than the worship of Buddha? Had not the trailing skirts, which now swept the floor of a Catholic church, been jealously guarded from contact with even the dress of a Papist? Had she merely looked in by accident, in the course of her morning's walk? or had she come to satiate a morbid curiosity, by gazing on one of those monsters in human form, so pleasantly described by a very "careful" public speaker as murderers, liars, cannibals, and pickpockets? Let no one, however, suppose that all this, or any of it, disturbed Father Wilfrid's devotion, or interfered with his recollection, during his Mass; his momentary glimpse of Maude had been a wholly involuntary one, for he had not even raised his eyes. He had learnt that very difficult lesson, which enables some men to combine the vigilance of a priest with the asceticism of a religious, viz. to *see every thing*, and *look at nothing*.

Annie used often to say that she was sure Father Wilfrid had eyes at the back of his head, like a fly; for that he always knew if she went to sleep in the sermon, though she was quite sure he had never once looked towards her.

Like most priests, he had seen and known many a strange freak of human nature; but he certainly did wonder a little over his breakfast that morning what could have brought Maude Trelawney to Mass. That she had come secretly, and without her mother's knowledge, was evident; and Father Wilfrid, in his charity, thought it a good sign, a proof *presumptive* that she had some idea of investigating the truth for herself: and remembering that wise counsel of the wisest of men, " Force not the course of the river," he resolved that, as far as he had any voice in the matter, Maude should be let alone, or, as he had said to Annie, " left to God, and trusted to our Lady's prayers," which with him meant practically the offering of constant prayers and severe mortifications for her conversion; he laboured for the salvation of souls much after the same manner as the saintly *curé* of Ars.

What would he have thought, what would he have done, if he had only known her real motive that morning? But he was destined to learn it a little sooner than he had expected.

Maude went home wholly unconscious that she had been discovered, and was seated quietly at the breakfast-table, reading a letter, when her mother came in.

"You are up early this morning, dear," said Mrs. Trelawney; "I hope you have not waited long for me."

"Oh, no, not long," said Maude; "I have only been here a few minutes."

Fie, fie, Maude! have *you* been consulting that very immoral Popish casuist, St. Alphonsus? What business have *you* with one of those "myths" of superstition, a modern Saint?

During breakfast, Maude electrified her mother by asking, in a perfectly matter-of-fact tone, what sort of person the priest at Stonebridge was, and if he ever called upon her.

What sort of person was Father Wilfrid? it was really a most embarrassing way of putting the question: do we, any of us, ever know "what sort of person" our nearest relative or our most intimate friend is? And to be asked "what sort of person" one's director is! If she had only asked whether he were young or old, tall or short, fat or thin, or even if he were an eloquent preacher, or had a good voice, or if he were clever, or learned, or intellectual, or if he were kind to the poor, or took an interest in his schools,—to any or all of these questions, it would have been possible to give a definite answer; but "what sort of person" was he? In sober earnest, Mrs. Trelawney did not the least know. What he was *to her*, indeed, she knew well enough, and had good cause to be thankful that she knew it; but what Father Wilfrid was *in himself*, not even his most intimate friend knew: he did not even know it himself, for his humility was too deep for self-consciousness.

Mrs. Trelawney ignored the first part of the question, and only replied:

"He comes to see me sometimes; but you need not be afraid of meeting him,—he is not at all likely to intrude himself upon you."

"Afraid of meeting him!" repeated Maude, drawing herself up proudly; "on the contrary, I should be glad to see him, or any of your friends."

Mrs. Trelawney looked keenly at her. What was the meaning of this entirely new phase in her character? There was a sort of patronising air about it, which she felt boded no good, and inspired no hope; or was it really, as Father Wilfrid had often told her, that she had allowed herself to be too obstinately persuaded that Maude's was a hopeless case? At all events, she should see Father Wilfrid, and find out for herself "what sort of person" he was, if such a discovery were possible to her; and she should be introduced to Mrs. Hatton, and be compelled to acknowledge that she was the very pattern of an English gentlewoman; and she should see Robert Hatton, and perhaps—but no; that would be a dangerous game to play, in more senses than one.

To say the truth, Mrs. Trelawney thought Mrs. Hatton far more likely to be of use to Maude than Father Wilfrid. In the first place, on the principle that one fact is worth a thousand arguments, it would be quite impossible for Maude to pay even half an hour's visit at Stinchcombe, and not come away convinced that Catholics could have quite as much "natural affection" as Protestants; and, in the next place, Mrs. Hatton was at all points so perfectly a lady, that Maude's fastidious taste would run no risk of being offended: there was no fear of any thing to jar upon either her nerves or her feelings,—no chance of either a thoughtless remark, or any hesitation about the letter H. For the latter, indeed, Annie Crofton might be trusted, but not always for the former.

Mrs. Trelawney accordingly proposed a walk to Stinchcombe for that afternoon, if Maude would not find it too far, or dislike accompanying her to call on Mrs. Hatton; and as she made no objection on either score, the visit was paid.

It was rather a silent one at first on Maude's part, for she left the conversation chiefly to the two elder ladies; and, in consequence of her presence, they talked only on ordinary topics for some time; but presently, to their mutual astonishment, she asked what kind of music was used in the church, and if Mozart's Masses were sung.

As this question was put to Mrs. Hatton, she replied:

"No; Father Wilfrid thinks them too dramatic; we have only Gregorian Masses."

"Then you ought to have a first-rate choir,"

said Maude; "Gregorian music requires perfect singing."

"I am afraid we cannot boast of perfection," replied Mrs. Hatton, smiling; "but Mrs. Trelawney has done marvels with the choir since she came here; I should like you to hear them sing."

"Maude shall come to the practising, if she likes, to-morrow evening," said Mrs. Trelawney, —not, however, without some misgiving as to whither all this was tending.

"Does Miss Crofton sing in the choir?" asked Maude, by way of reply to this proposal.

"Oh, no; we have only men and boys; I play the harmonium for them, but that is all," said Mrs. Trelawney.

"I see," answered Maude; "as you used to do in St. James's Church, at Warwick."

It was said so quietly, that it seemed a mere casual remark, and as such Mrs. Hatton understood it; but Mrs. Trelawney had need of all her self-possession not to betray the sting of this bitter taunt, for *she* understood its full meaning. During the four years when she had been a Catholic in disguise, she had compromised the Sunday difficulty by playing the organ in the Protestant church, thus avoiding the necessity for taking any other part in the service; and verily her cowardice had had its reward: from the moment when Maude had discovered it, she had utterly refused to believe in the sincerity of a conversion which was afraid or ashamed to declare itself. For what purpose or motive her mother had "gone over to Rome," she could not imagine (perhaps she had thrown some one over a cliff, like

Ellen Middleton, or done something else very dreadful, and wanted to confess it); but that she could be a Catholic in her heart, and keep it all to herself for four years, Maude would not for a moment believe; for is it not written, "Out of the abundance of the heart, the mouth speaketh"?

And now she openly accused her of a like hypocrisy in her new religion to that which she had been guilty of in her old one,—openly, and yet secretly, with a refinement of cruelty that would have revolted a savage, for it compelled her to bear the wound, and "make no sign" of having received it. Had Maude no pity, no compassion? Had *she* lost all natural affection? Far from it; but our affections are said to be the horses that draw the chariot of our will; and if we let them take their own course, they are apt to become the most unmanageable brutes in the world. Maude did not *want* to hurt her mother, but her mind was off its balance; the horses had upset the chariot, and were dragging it hither and thither as they would.

On their way back, Mrs. Trelawney stopped at the church, leaving Maude to go home by herself. She spent a quarter of an hour there, and then asked to see Father Wilfrid. But she said not one word to him of that taunting speech— she *could* not betray her own child; she only told him that Maude had expressed a wish to see him, and said how much it had surprised her, as at Warwick she had always shut herself up in her room when the priest came to the house, and would not even walk through the street where the Catholic church was, unless absolutely obliged to do so.

Father Wilfrid smiled as he thought of what he had witnessed that morning, but he knew better than to betray Maude; he only said:

"Well, I suppose, then, I ought to feel flattered; but I never am much inclined to gratify idle curiosity, and it is not very pleasant to be looked at as if one were the last new arrival in a menagerie."

"O father," began Mrs. Trelawney, "you surely don't suppose—"

"No, no," he interrupted; "I quite understand. But I cannot very well call on Miss Trelawney; nor could I talk freely to you in her presence. However, if you really wish it, I will come and see you to-morrow, and bring those books I promised you."

When Mrs. Trelawney came in, she ordered the five-o'clock tea in which she and Maude indulged now, during her holidays.

"Please, ma'am, Miss Trelawney beant at home," said Hannah.

"Not at home!—you must be mistaken, I think," she replied; "I left her nearly an hour ago, on her way home."

"Her did come in, ma'am," said Hannah; "but, sure enough, her went out again."

"Did she leave any message?" asked Mrs. Trelawney.

"No, sure, ma'am, her didn't say nothing; leastways, not as I knows of," was the unsatisfactory answer.

"Very well," said Mrs. Trelawney quietly; "I will wait for tea till she comes in."

She did not, however, *feel* very quiet as she

sat in the shadowy firelight, waiting and listening for the door-bell. Where could Maude have gone? It was possible, certainly, that she might have wanted something, and gone out into the village to buy it; for though Stonebridge had no shops to speak of, such trifles as a bit of ribbon or a reel of cotton could be obtained there: but, in that case, why had she not made her purchase on her way home, instead of going out again? Had she gone to see Annie?

Very unlikely; for Maude was the last person in the world to do an unconventional thing, or to intrude herself unceremoniously even on people that she liked—and it was a very clear case that she did not like Annie. Still, she had already said and done so many unlikely things that day (more, by a good deal, too, than her mother knew of), and seemed altogether in such an unnatural state, that it was impossible to say what she might or might not have done.

Mrs. Trelawney waited, more or less quietly, till nearly six o'clock, almost two hours after she had parted from Maude in the village; and then she began to be seriously anxious. It never, for a moment, occurred to her that Maude could have come to any real harm; but she did conceive it possible that the poor girl might have taken some sudden freak into her head—some offence or alarm; perhaps, after all, she *was* afraid of meeting Father Wilfrid, and had run away lest he should be brought down upon her that very evening. Run away! Yes; but in what direction? It was a long journey, of some hours, to Stretton; and she had no other home.

Mrs. Trelawney did not choose to betray her anxiety to her landlady by asking any questions; but she went quietly up to Maude's room, to try if she could discover any clue to the mystery.

The bonnet and velvet jacket she had worn for the visit to Stinchcombe lay on the bed; she had evidently gone out in her hat and travelling-cloak,—but there was no appearance of her having taken any thing with her; nothing was disarranged or displaced about the room or in the drawers, and both her carpet-bag and small travelling-bag were there: she had not gone out, then, with the intention of being long absent.

Mrs. Trelawney went into her own room, and lighted a candle; Maude might, perhaps, have left some written explanation or message there for her. No; not a word, not a sign—stay, what book was that on the floor? She picked it up; it was her own *Golden Manual;* and as she opened it, there dropped out from between the leaves a slip of paper, which Father Wilfrid had put into her hands one evening in the church, and on which he had written in a bold hand, and with a very black pencil, so that the words could scarcely fail to catch the eye of any one who saw them: "You know I cannot say a black Mass for a Protestant; but I will offer mine to-morrow for the soul of your husband: we have every reason to believe he died in good faith."

Was it possible, was it conceivable, that Maude had read that note? Was her own child capable of such a dishonourable action? Mrs. Trelawney felt "shamed through all her being," for she instinctively *knew* that Maude had read it. But how came she to find it? What could she have been doing with that book?—she, who used to fling Catholic books from her with a passionate hate, if she ever chanced accidentally to touch them.

It was this, then, that had driven her out of the house; but why? What was there in it to offend or excite her? Enough, and more than enough, as Mrs. Trelawney well knew, to excite such a temperament as hers; though she understood her too little to know exactly what form of excitement it was likely to produce. Had Maude rushed madly off somewhere by the first train she could find? or by the Tavistock coach, which passed through the village about five o'clock? or had she wandered out on the moor, and lost her way? or what?

CHAPTER XVI.

"I can no more: for now it comes again,
That sense of ruin which is worse than pain;
That masterful negation and collapse
Of all that makes me man."
Dream of Gerontius.

As soon as Mrs. Trelawney left him, Father Wilfrid had started on a sick call to a man named John Luscombe, who lived about three miles off, in a lonely cottage on the moor, a portion of which he had enclosed and turned into a small farm; by no means, however, binding his flocks and herds to keep the enclosure, for his red Devonshire cows might often be seen refreshing themselves in a deep pool of the Lewin, some two miles distant from their home; and his coolies were trained to pick out and fetch back any individual sheep from the very top of Hillsborough Tor. Occasionally, a cow would be found half buried in a bog; or a sheep would stray into Fairleigh Wood, and be never heard of more; or a young colt would be missing when the eldest boy, Bill, went out to drive the horses home at night, and would be reported by that young hopeful as spirited away by the *pixies*, for their own particular use and benefit: but, on the whole, John Luscombe's farm was a thriving affair, and his ducks and chickens fetched a good price in Tavistock Market, to which he and his wife rode "jollifant," Devonshire fashion, every Wednesday, unless the amount of their "cargo" made a cart necessary.

The more "civilised" townsfolk of Tavistock laughed at Betty Luscombe, and asked her " why she didn't have her own horse, and ride by the side of her husband, like a respectable farmer's wife, instead of behind him, like a saucy wench with her sweetheart?" But she laughed at them in return, and said, "it was too much trouble to manage her own horse; and if it wasn't respectable to ride behind her own husband, as her mother and grandmother had done before her, she would like to know what *was*, that was all."

But just now good John Luscombe was laid up with "the roomatics, uncommon bad;" and

Betty had walked in to Mass herself that morning, and asked, would his reverence be so good as to go and see him, which "his reverence" had promised to do that very evening: and, though he had been detained by Mrs. Trelawney till nearly dark, he was not a man to break his word for so small a matter as a twenty-minutes' ride after sundown.

"A ride, indeed! very pretty extravagance and self-indulgence for a priest! could he not use his own legs?"

Yes, gentle reader, right well and right willingly, when it so pleased him; but his parish extended to places ten miles distant, and sick calls were frequent, and time was valuable in such cases; many a poor soul would have passed to its eternal account unconfessed and unanointed, had Father Wilfrid preferred the mock humility of walking, to the Gospel charity of hastening to its succour; and even for so short a distance as three miles of rough moorland, a twenty-minutes' ride or an hour's walk might often be a question of eternal life or death. Nor did he even so far study appearances as to ride a sober, jog-trotting mule or pony, such as would be the ideal "mount" for a priest; he was not the kind of man to do any thing "for an idea;" and he rode a strong, well-bred cob, a little over fourteen hands high, and a match in speed for any horse, not a trained racer, in the county. Nevertheless, lest his reputation should suffer through this fact, let it be clearly understood how he came to possess this valuable steed.

When he first realised the truth that a horse

was a necessity for him, he went straight to a dealer in those animals, for the purpose of buying one; the man looked shrewdly at him from top to toe, and, having sufficiently taken the measure of his customer, asked him in what manner he could serve him.

Father Wilfrid explained that he wanted a good-sized pony, fit for hard work, and fast in its paces.

"Just so, sir," said the man; "I think we have just the hanimal for you here; a splendid little black mare, nearly thorough-bred, goes like the wind;" and he was proceeding to descant on the nobility of her race, as exemplified in the "cleanness" of her fetlocks, when Father Wilfrid interrupted him with:

"My good man, this won't do for me; I want a stout, strong horse, that can trot twelve miles an hour, and won't be likely to stumble or fall lame. If you can supply me with such a beast, you need not trouble yourself as to his pedigree, as I do not care the least about it."

Which speech sent him down to zero in the other's estimation; but of course he bowed politely as he gave orders to a groom to bring out "Spotted Bob," and there presently appeared a small but strongly built gray horse, marked with those peculiar large dark blots which are seen more frequently in a circus than any where else. This animal, the man assured him, was both stout and strong, unlikely to stumble or otherwise misconduct himself, and warranted to trot fourteen miles an hour, if necessary. The creature laid back its ears and showed the whites of

o

suspiciously; but on being assured that this was only "playfulness," and having also ridden it a few times round the paddock, and discovered nothing to its disadvantage, Father Wilfrid, who always trusted every one till they had once deceived him, —but let them beware of doing that!—bought it.

Soon, however, he repented of his bargain, though he could not accuse the man of having absolutely deceived him,—"Spotted Bob" undoubtedly *was* stout and strong; he had never once stumbled or gone lame, and he certainly *could* with ease trot fourteen miles an hour; but then he could also occasionally gallop at the rate of twenty miles an hour, and had an inveterate habit of catching the bit between his teeth, for the purpose of so disporting himself. Also, he had an unpleasant trick of rearing bolt upright, and falling backwards on his rider; and was of so impatient a disposition, that, if left for a few minutes tied up to a gate or tethered with a heavy stone, he would invariably break his bridle and scamper home, leaving the good priest to follow as he best might.

All this was, to say the least of it, inconvenient; and Father Wilfrid one day confided his troubles on the subject to Mr. Crofton, who very soon settled the matter by giving him a useful and valuable cob of his own in exchange for Spotted Bob, who, after a few months of severe discipline under a groom, had turned out the very Nabob now ridden daily by Charley, and occasionally also by Annie.

Father Wilfrid was trotting quickly along,—for, though John Luscombe's case was not a serious one, his own time was too valuable to be wasted,—when he overtook a young man, also on horseback, and mounted on a tall, well-formed hunter, with a large cloak strapped behind his saddle, and a handsome black retriever running by his side.

"Good evening, father," said he. "I hope you are not going far; it will be a very dark night, no moon till quite late in the morning."

"Only to Helstone Farm," was the reply. "Does your road lie that way?"

"I can easily make it do so, and I shall be glad of a chat with you," answered the horseman, who was no other than young Ellicombe, of Abbotsleigh; at that time on the eve of his departure for Rome, to enrol himself as a private among the Papal Zouaves.

They rode on together, talking gravely and anxiously of the future prospects of Italy; for at that time all the powers of the world seemed leagued together against Holy Church, whilst her "eldest son" stood aloof, and seemed to have abandoned her to the spoiler and the blasphemer,—for the Antibes Legion was yet in its infancy, and any prophet who had predicted the glorious victory of Mentana would have been treated as a visionary.

And yet neither Father Wilfrid nor his companion were disposed to take a gloomy view: faith is not given to nice calculations; and they both firmly believed that, in His own time and way, God would prosper His own cause. As to his personal prospects, Herbert Ellicombe troubled himself not a whit; he had devoted himself body and soul, and with his whole heart, to the cause of the Holy Father, and it was his

III.

...but on being assured that this w...
...ness," and having also ridden it a...
...and the paddock, and discovered noth...
...dness, Father Wilfrid, who alw...
...every one till they had once deceived...
...them beware of doing that"—bough...

Soon, however, he repented of his barg...
though he could not accuse the man of ha...
suddenly learned him — "Spotted Boy"...
...was sound and strong; he had...
...stumbled or gone lame, and he cer...
...with ease twelve miles an hour...
...he would also occasionally gallop at the...
...of twenty miles an hour, and had an invet...
...of catching the bit between his tee...
...of disporting himself. Also...
...trick of rearing bolt uprig...
...backwards on his rider; and was of a...
...disposition, that, if left for a few m...
...on a stop or tethered with a heavy...
...peacefully break his bridle and a...
...leaving the good priest to follow as...

All this was, to say the least of it, incon...
and Father Wilfrid one day confided his t...
on the subject to Mr. Crofton, who v...
...the matter by giving him a use...
...nag of his own in exchange for S...
Boy, who after a few months of severe d...
under a groom, had turned out the ver...
...ridden daily by Charley, and occa...
...him...

Father Wilfrid was moving quickly along...
though John Luscombe's case was not d...

the
two
icles
the
him
one
ever,
she
own

and
was
ready
fol-
far
dog
rks, as

ur way,
ome to

of the
riously,
rolonged
aken the
nted Prin-

id Herbert
ke that for
heir horses'
the sound
ith one ac-
. planted
olutely

highest ambition to be permitted to give his life for it: "Only," he said, involuntarily tightening his hand on the rein as he spoke, "I *should* like to give one good sword-thrust first, and sell my life dearly."

To say the truth, Father Wilfrid felt little inclination to reprove the words; he only said: "It must be a terrible thing to send the soul of a fellow-creature straight to judgment. May God forgive those who compel us to such acts! Never forget, Herbert, that you are a Christian soldier, and fight in a holy cause: be brave in the battle, and merciful to the wounded, and don't expose your life rashly for pride or bravado. Your death can profit the Holy Father little; but your good arm and sword may avail him much: keep both for him as long as you can."

"And after all," said Herbert, a little sadly, "your prayers will avail him more than either; and we can only get the 'barren honour' of a victory that your Masses have won. I am half inclined to be jealous of you."

"Come, come," said the priest, with a smile, "that is not fair; we have each our own work to do: and there would have been no victory, mind you, at Amalec, if Josue had left off fighting when Moses lifted up his hands."

They were now about half a mile from Helstone Farm, which lay sheltered in a hollow, the descent into which was somewhat steep. Perhaps the dampness of this situation had something to do with poor John Luscombe's rheumatism, but it would have been high treason to hint such a thing to him; had not his great-grand-father built the farm-house, and was not the unfailing health as well as prosperity of the two succeeding generations written in the chronicles of the house of Luscombe? This was about the only point of dispute that ever arose between him and Betty, who occasionally "minded" that one of his uncles had died there of rheumatic fever, for which inconvenient exercise of memory she was always promptly bidden to "mind" her own business.

The two riders were proceeding slowly and carefully down the rugged sheep-track, which was the shortest way to the house,—for it was already dark, and a false step might easily have been followed by a roll over into the boggy morass far down on their left,—when Mr. Ellicombe's dog suddenly set up a series of short, sharp barks, as if in perplexity or distress.

"Here, Rover! where are you? lost your way, you simpleton, eh? Come back, sir! come to heel!" shouted his master.

But the dog took no further heed of the command than by barking still more furiously, presently changing this into a loud and prolonged howl, which might have sufficed to awaken the Seven Sleepers, or the celebrated Enchanted Princess of the fairy tale.

"There's something the matter," said Herbert Ellicombe; "Rover does not howl like that for nothing;" and they both turned their horses' heads in the direction from whence the sound proceeded. But the two animals, with one accord, after taking about a dozen steps, planted their fore-feet firmly in the ground, and resolutely refused to stir another inch. Both riders knew well enough what this meant; they were on the edge of a large peat-bog. Both also jumped to the same conclusion; it was not altogether an unheard-of thing, though of very rare occurrence, that a child should sink into one of these peat-bogs, and be lost.

"Rover will save it, whatever it is," said Herbert; "let me go and see, while you hold my horse; I have strong boots and leather gaiters on, and shall not hurt; I have a light, too;" and, dismounting, he took a small lantern and a match-box from his pocket, and struck a light, by the help of which he picked his way, treading on the firmest pieces of turf, till he reached the place where Rover was howling piteously, and scratching away the wet earth with all his might.

The next moment a shout reached Father Wilfrid's ear:

"Unstrap the cloak, and spread it on my saddle; it's a woman;" and in less than ten minutes Herbert reappeared, carrying what looked more like a bundle of wet clothes than a human form.

"She was up to her knees in the bog," said Herbert, "and couldn't move; and she is as cold as a stone. What shall we do?—have you got a brandy-flask?"

No; unfortunately neither of them was so provided. But, with the quick instinct of one experienced in such matters, Father Wilfrid, after one earnest gaze into the woman's face, said:

"She has only fainted;" and, hastily wrapping the warm, dry cloak round her, he laid her gently down on the ground, and began chafing her stone-cold feet, desiring Herbert to do the like office for her hands.

The face was wholly unknown to him, and yet it was strangely like another that he knew well; and surely he had somewhere seen that broad-brimmed black hat, with its long crape streamers, though it was all crushed and disfigured, and the veil was torn into shreds? Was it possible? could it be the same that he had seen, for the first time, two days ago in Stonebridge, and for the second time that very morning at the bottom of the church? One more glance, and that but a momentary one, sufficed; it *was* Miss Trelawney. But what could she be doing here at this hour, all alone? Was she out of her mind? Was she a somnambulist? Was she—no, no; how dared such a thought suggest itself?

One thing, at all events, she very certainly was, viz. in danger of being frozen to death, if further assistance were not presently forthcoming; for their united efforts failed to produce the slightest warmth in her numbed limbs.

Finding it utterly impossible to support her on the horse, it was agreed that Father Wilfrid should ride on as fast as possible with the two steeds to the farm, and bid good Dame Luscombe prepare a bed with all speed; while Herbert should follow, carrying in his arms the insensible form of the girl.

Who or what she was, he had of course no idea, nor did Father Wilfrid think fit to enlighten him, merely saying:

"I think I know who it is ;" and Herbert, being a discreet youth, asked no further question.

They were both far too much taken up with the grave reality of their adventure for any thing in the shape of a ludicrous side to occur to either of them, though Herbert did say :

"I suppose this is to be my first lesson in marching with the ambulance."

It was a pity there was no eye-witness to carry the tale to Mr. Whalley's ears, or to send off a sensational paragraph to the newspapers, which might serve as a text from which that doughty champion of Protestantism could easily have proved to the "common sense of the House" that an organised system of plunder and rapine was being carried on in this realm of England by the soldiers of the Pope, and at his own personal instigation, aided and abetted by those cruel and rapacious tyrants, the Jesuits.

Mr. Ellicombe was not yet a soldier of the Pope, and Father Wilfrid was not a Jesuit ; but those little inaccuracies are of no importance whatever, when speaking of such cheats and liars as the Papists ; and if it all turns out a mistake or a mare's-nest,—well, no matter, some people will believe it: paint the picture with the very deepest lamp-black; while one is about it, one may as well be hung for a sheep as a lamb.

Happily, honest John Luscombe's case was not so urgent but that it could well give way before the more pressing necessity Father Wilfrid came to announce ; and by the time Herbert Ellicombe arrived with his burden, a bed was prepared, and Betty's very best night-gear (part of her wedding-outfit, carefully hoarded up) was warming at the fire.

The sudden change from the cold night-air into the heated atmosphere of the farm-house parlour, where a large peat-fire burnt on the bare hearth, did what all the previous chafing had failed to do; with a start and a gasp, Maude opened her eyes, just at the very moment when Father Wilfrid came forward to assist in carrying her up-stairs. Before he had time to draw back, she had fixed them upon his face with that scared look which so often precedes a full return to consciousness.

"That's right, deary; bless your pretty face!" said Betty, bending over her. But the benediction did not appear to have a very soothing effect; the scared expression of Maude's eyes changed into one of horror and disgust, and Father Wilfrid made a sign to Betty to take his place in supporting her head, while Herbert carried her up the steep and narrow staircase. It did not much matter, for she had fainted again immediately; but Father Wilfrid would not risk another recognition.

Telling John that he would come back the next morning to see him, and Betty that he would send a doctor from Stonebridge, and tell the lady's friends that she was safe, he was about to mount his horse, when Herbert came out.

"Father," he said, "I spoke rudely to you just now; I beg your pardon."

The good priest looked at him in unfeigned astonishment. "I have not the least idea what you mean," he said; "I never heard you speak rudely in my life."

"What!" exclaimed Herbert, laughing in spite of himself; "not when I ordered you so cavalierly to unstrap my cloak, as if, for all the world, I had been a belted knight, and you my humble esquire?"

"Oh, you call that rude, do you?" said Father Wilfrid; "I think it was the most sensible thing you could do, under the circumstances; and now I must congratulate you on the success of your first adventure in knight-errantry, though you fell in with it more by good luck than by good management."

"Good luck, do you call it, father, to find a woman half dead?" said Herbert, in no way disposed to look at the matter from a romantic point of view; moreover, as Father Wilfrid knew well enough, the young Zouave was under a vow to espouse no cause save that of the Holy Father, so long as it needed a defender.

"Nay, I hope not half dead," was the reply; "I hope the case is not so serious as it seemed at first; but that is thanks to your timely aid. Another hour in that bog might have been fatal; you have saved her life, and may thank God for it."

"I think Rover ought to get the credit," said Herbert, who appeared singularly unwilling to appropriate any to himself. "Nice old dog!" he continued, stooping down, and patting him; "you deserve a silver medal for to-night's work; and you shall have one, and wear it round your neck. Can I be of any further use ?" he added, as he sprang lightly into his saddle.

"No, I think not, thank you," was the reply. "I shall send back all that is needed, from Stonebridge, in half an hour;" and they started on their separate ways.

In another quarter of an hour Father Wilfrid rang the surgery-bell at Dr. Wilson's house in Stonebridge, which was answered promptly by the worthy doctor himself.

On hearing the service required of him, he said:

"Found in Helstone bog, did you say, sir? Ah! very sad, very sad; poor thing! These cases are really very distressing. I will do my best for her, but maybe she won't thank me much for sparing her life; these poor girls, you know—"

"It is nothing of that kind," said the priest sternly; "I know who it is, and will send her own friends to remove her to her home as soon as you consider it prudent for them to do so. She is a stranger here, and must have lost her way." And, without further parley, he rode on to the only inn the little village could boast, where he ordered its only available fly to be got ready as soon as possible, and sent to Mrs. North's lodgings.

"Take a strong horse, as you will have a rough road to drive," he said to the hostler, and galloped quickly on to Mrs. Trelawney's.

There he found all in consternation, but no one at home except Mrs. North and her household. The young lady had come in, they told him, soon after four o'clock, and gone out again about half an hour afterwards, leaving no message, and apparently under no excitement or agitation of any kind ; her mother, after waiting till six o'clock for her, had also gone out again, merely saying that probably Miss Trelawney had gone to call upon Miss Crofton, and she would follow her ; but Mrs. North happened to know that Miss Crofton was away from home that day. What *could* be the matter ?

CHAPTER XVII.

" *Ursula (despairing).* Then Elsie, my poor child, is dead ?
Forester. That, my good woman, I have not said."
LONGFELLOW'S *Golden Legend.*

THOUGH Mrs. Trelawney had not chosen to betray any anxiety to her landlady, it was not with the very smallest expectation of finding Maude at Mr. Crofton's house that she went out that evening in search of her. With all a mother's knowledge of her child's character, she knew that, whatever impulse had tempted Maude to read words never intended for her eyes, the act would be immediately followed by a sense of shame and degradation, which probably had goaded her into flight or temporary concealment, even independently of the effect produced by the note itself. But whither could she have fled ? Where could she hide herself ?

Instead of seeking her first at Mr. Crofton's,

Mrs. Trelawney bent her steps towards the railway-station, calling on her way through the village at the coach-office, and ascertaining that no passenger had left Stonebridge that evening for Tavistock. Not that this was by any means a satisfactory *quietus* on the point, for Maude was as likely as not—nay, a good deal *more* likely than not—to have walked on, and let the coach overtake her on the road; still, it was the utmost that could be obtained.

At the station the evidence was more decisive —no young lady in deep mourning had left by any of the evening trains, or been seen near the station; and a train cannot very well be stopped and entered on its road, like a coach. Hitherto Mrs. Trelawney had been so fully possessed by the idea that Maude would take either the coach or the train, that no other had occurred to her; and now, for the first time, a terror seized upon her that perhaps the poor child had wandered up to the moor, and lost her way—a misadventure that might have no very serious consequences in the summer, but which, on a cold, dark January night, was quite another matter; and the moment such a possibility entered her mind, she started off at her utmost speed, by a short cut through some fields leading from the station to Mr. Crofton's. He had hunters and grooms; he could send men to scour the country for miles round,—and any kind of whistle, or horn, or huntsman's bugle, would be heard for a long distance over the moor.

Fancy a huntsman's horn on Dartmoor at eight o'clock on a winter's night! Who would thenceforward dare to question the grim legends of the "Wilde Jagd" or the "Erl-King"? Would even the audacious Bill Luscombe dare any more laugh to scorn Johnny Barton's tales about pixie-hunts and stolen horses?

But little did the thought of any such consequences trouble poor Mrs. Trelawney's mind, as, after a mile's weary tramp over rough ground, quite unfit for winter walking, she rang the bell at the Cedars, Mr. Crofton's house. She had left home at six; it was now after seven. To her anxious inquiry for Mr. Crofton, the servant replied that "Master had gone out to dinner with Miss Crofton."

"Where—where is he gone?" she demanded, with a frantic vehemence which greatly astonished the quiet old butler.

"To Mr. Elmore's, ma'am," he replied respectfully; for Mrs. Trelawney was well known at the Cedars.

Now, Mr. Elmore was the squire of the next parish, and lived at Yatton Hall, some four miles distant.

"Master Charles is at home, ma'am," he added, moved to compassion by her evident distress. "Would you like to see him?"

"If you please," she said, with a not very successful effort to speak calmly; and she was ushered into the library, where Charley came to her immediately.

"What is it, Mrs. Trelawney?" he said; "Jones tells me—" He stopped suddenly, startled by her pale lips and scared eyes.

It was a hard task for the poor widow to own

to a boy like that, that her child had fled from her; and yet, if any good was to be done, the truth must be told. She softened it as much as possible; clasping her hands tightly together in her agony, she said:

"Maude went out alone this evening, more than two hours ago. She is fond of wandering about by herself, and I am afraid she may have lost her way on the moor. Could you spare a man and horse—"

Without waiting for another word, Charley rang the bell so violently that the whole household rushed to the door, thinking that at least some one must have had a fit. Seeing, however, nothing to alarm them, they slunk back, rather ashamed of themselves, as Charley, addressing the butler, said:

"Tell Dick to saddle my pony directly, and to get Selim ready for himself; I must take him with me."

"Selim, did you say, sir?" asked Jones, unwilling, evidently, that a raw groom should be mounted for a night-ride on his master's best hunter; but Selim was the fastest horse in the stable, the only one faster than Nabob, and Nabob was capricious, and would not put out his speed for any one but his own master,—else Charley would certainly have taken Selim for himself, and left the pony for the groom.

"Yes, I did," replied Charley, disdaining, with boyish arrogance, to explain himself further to a servant; "and tell him to make haste about it, and let me know as soon as he is ready, and to take a lantern with him, and to buckle on a pillion behind each saddle, and these"—tossing two thick railway-wrappers to Jones, to that functionary's extreme amazement. Perhaps something in the expression of his face struck Charley, for he added, with a delicacy which Mrs. Trelawney little expected, and gratefully appreciated,

"I hear one of our people is lost on the moor; I am going to look for her. One life is as much worth saving as another; and if Miss Crofton were in danger, the whole village would be off to the rescue."

Jones bowed respectfully, and withdrew to give the necessary orders, albeit he greatly misdoubted how far Mr. Crofton would approve of his favourite Selim being taken out on such an errand, or, for the matter of that, of Master Charley being employed in it either; for did it not stand to reason and common sense, that a Stonebridge girl who could go and lose herself on the moors she had been familiar with all her life, must be "lost" in more ways than one?

With more consideration than she would have given him credit for, Charley then fetched wine and biscuits, and compelled Mrs. Trelawney, sorely against her will, to partake of them, while he exchanged his coat for a rough pea-jacket, and his slippers for stout boots.

"We will each take a different road," he said, "and ride till we find her: she cannot have wandered far; don't be uneasy,—it is a fine night, and not freezing very hard. By the by, she can sit on a pillion, I suppose?—I don't know how else to bring her; I'll take the greatest care of her, if I find her;" and a flush, which he could not altogether suppress, mantled in his cheeks; "and Dick, though he is a rough fellow, would sooner cut both his hands off than let a hair of her head be hurt. I will send him by the quarry-road, and strike up Hillsborough myself. Stay," he added, as if a sudden thought occurred to him: "have you any thing here belonging to her, any thing she has ever worn?"

By the merest accident, as we should say, Mrs Trelawney had put on a pair of Maude's gloves in mistake for her own; she took them off, and gave them to him, in utter bewilderment as to what he could possibly want with them.

"Thanks," he said; "the horses must be ready now—good bye; you will go home now, won't you? I hope you will not have long to wait."

She tried to thank him, but he stopped her quickly:

"It is nothing," he said; "I shall enjoy the ride."

"But your father?" she said.

Charley laughed. "Oh, papa will be glad enough to find me doing any thing half so sensible," he said. "I believe he thinks me the idlest dog in the world."

The horses stood ready at the door, with Dick at their heads, looking, if truth must be owned, not best pleased at the prospect before him; but Charley had a way of making himself loved by his inferiors, and the man's sullen countenance brightened as his young master accosted him:

"Where's Floss?" he asked.

Now, Floss was a pointer of great reputation for sagacity; but Dick marvelled much of what

P

use she could be in the present instance; he unchained her, however, as desired, and she came bounding up to Charley, who held one of Maude's gloves to her nose.

"*Find,*" he said; and the creature, with a look of intelligence, seized the glove in its teeth, and started off towards the village, Charley and Dick following.

"Now, look here," said the former, as they went along, throwing off all mystery; "Miss Trelawney lost her way on the moor this afternoon; she may have slipped on the edge of a quarry, or a bog, or something. You turn down the quarry-road when we get out on the heath, and I will make tracks for Hillsborough, unless Floss shows us any thing better; don't keep straight on, but ride round and round in circles from time to time, and shout, or whistle. If you find the lady, take her up behind you on the pillion, and carry her safely home; if you don't find her, meet me at Helstone Farm in two hours. If you are not there, I shall know it's all right; and if you don't find me there, you may conclude the same, and ride home as fast as you can."

Probably Charley had never used his brains to so much purpose in his life, as in devising this scheme; but its wisdom was quite lost upon Dick, who replied, with matter-of-fact stolidity:

"But suppose, sir, she don't choose to come with me, what be I to do?"

This was a "combination" that had never occurred to Charley, and at first it seemed to him supremely absurd; but after a moment's reflection, he admitted to himself that there was some sense in honest Dick's question; and that it was just possible that a lady might scruple to allow herself to be seized and carried off by an unknown rider, even with the alternative of being left to die of cold on the moor. Annie, who trusted every body, and, like the young Nelson, "never saw Mr. Fear," would not have hesitated a moment; but he was not so sure about Maude: she might think it was some plot to carry her off to a convent, or "Goodness knows what!" thought Charley. He felt in his pockets, and luckily found an old letter,—and he was never without a pencil,—but it was quite dark; presently, however, they passed a cottage, where a bright light was burning in the window: he drew up for a moment close to it, and, taking the envelope, which of course was directed to himself, wrote in the inside—"You may trust this man.—C. CROFTON."

"Give her this," he said to Dick, "and you will have no difficulty."

To say the truth, he spoke more certainly than he felt; for the doubt having been once put into his head, he could not help feeling uneasy. Maude was so unlike any other girl he had ever seen, it was impossible to judge of her by the same rules; still, surely no one would refuse to be brought home when they had lost their way; and, at all events, he had done all he could; but more earnestly than ever he hoped that her discovery might fall to his own lot rather than to Dick's.

On turning out of the sunk fence upon the open moor, Floss careered round and round, barking and sniffing the ground, but evidently uncertain what course to take: she tried two or three, but came back, apparently dissatisfied, and looked up with a vexed, disappointed expression in her master's face. Presently, however, she trotted off, but not with much alacrity, in the direction of Hillsborough, looking back rather wistfully in the direction of the quarries, which she had already tried and abandoned.

"Maybe," said Dick, "the lady crossed the stream down below; the dog has lost the scent."

But Charley thought otherwise, for Floss seemed in better spirits now; however, he could not be certain, and judged it best to adhere to the original plan. Accordingly, Dick turned off down the quarry-road, muttering to himself:

"Well, sure, if this here ain't the queerest start as ever I seed! Holloa! you brute! hold up, can't you!" as Selim's foot slipped over a large, loose stone. "I sim master won't thank me for laming of *you;* so look sharp, and mind your own legs."

Thus admonished, Selim took more heed to his steps, and accomplished the descent to the edge of the large quarry safely. There Dick dismounted, and, tethering the noble hunter firmly by means of a large piece of rock, lighted his lantern, and commenced a careful search all around and within the quarry; if he misliked his night's work, at all events, he was not the man to do it negligently; and, "sure enough, too, Miss Trelawney is a mighty fine-looking young woman," he said to himself,—for which free-spoken opinion, Charley would have liked to knock him down, if he had heard it.

But Charley was tearing round and round

in wide circles on Hillsborough Tor, greatly to Spotted Bob's delight, who perhaps was visited by distant memories of his youthful days in connection with certain circus-riders, and who put forth his speed to so magnificent an extent, that at last Charley was obliged to pull up and rest for a moment, from sheer giddiness. He called, he shouted, he whistled, and Floss ran up and down, and round and round, barking with all her might; then he rode on half a mile or so farther, and began wheeling round again in circles,—in short, by the time the two hours were over, he had scarcely left a spot untraversed on nearly four square miles of moor,—and not only was the brave pony's strength well-nigh exhausted, but his own too; and he turned his steps towards Helstone Farm, earnestly hoping that Dick's absence from the trysting-place might give token that he had been more successful than his master. But a deep groan of anguish escaped him as, on approaching the outbuildings of the farm, he heard the clatter of a horse's hoofs behind him, and, looking round, recognised Selim's graceful head and neck, and saw that the pillion on his back was empty.

"A pretty wild-goose chase this for a winter's night, Master Charles!" began the groom, in a tone of sullen discontent. "I've been a-crawling about in them confounded quarries, and a-floundering in filthy bogs all the time,—pitch-dark they was, too,—but never a sign of any living being did I see; maybe the lady is enjoying a dance with the pixies to-night; I've heerd they're rare good company, when they takes to a body."

"Hold your fool's tongue!" exclaimed Charley angrily; "you, a Catholic too, to talk about pixies! haven't you learnt your catechism yet?"

Perhaps his frequent gyrations in the saddle that evening had slightly confused his ideas, for he would have been rather puzzled if called upon to say what part of the catechism repudiated pixies, though assuredly they would find no place among those "things which every Christian is bound to believe."

"Maybe I have, and maybe I haven't," was the somewhat gruff reply, for Dick did not relish being taken to task in this way by a mere boy; "but be us to go on to Helstone, sir? A drop o' beer 'ud be uncommon handy; my throat's as dry as a ditch in June with hollering."

Of this original comparison Dick was so proud, that he was in the habit of trotting it out on all suitable or unsuitable occasions.

Charley had never thought of himself; but now that the subject was brought perforce before him, he was fain to admit to himself that a cup of milk or a "dish o' tay" would be far from unpleasant to his own throat; the horses, too, would be grateful for refreshment; and Floss—

Ay, where was Floss? Charley whistled, but with no result; he whistled again, and she came bounding towards them straight from the farm, with a joyous bark, quite different from the howl she had indulged in on the moor.

"Hurrah!" exclaimed Charley; "Floss has found her!—I'm sure she has; taken refuge at Helstone, of course: what a fool I was not to think of that before;" and he dashed on at full speed through the farm-yard, and up to the door of the house, on which he rattled with the handle of his whip.

"Holy Virgin!" exclaimed Betty, "here's more on 'em! Beant a body to get no sleep tonight!"

But after a rapid glance from her window to ascertain who were her visitors, she came down in a state of high good humour, and asked what Master Crofton pleased to want.

"Is there a lady here?" asked Charley unceremoniously.

"There has been two ladies here to-night, sir, but they're both gone home," replied Betty, with studied brevity; she was somehow under the impression that she was the *confidante* of some mysterious secret.

"Two ladies! what ladies, and where are they gone? Was one of them Miss Trelawney?" pursued Charley, who had no idea, now that things had gone so far, of making a needless mystery about them.

"Well, I suppose it ain't no harm to tell you," replied Betty, as if speaking under protest; "they was Mrs. and Miss Trelawney, and they're gone back to Stonebridge in a *shay*, a fly they calls it now."

"Mrs. Trelawney!" exclaimed Charley, in astonishment. "But how—how did every thing happen, I mean?"

Having once broken the ice, Betty gave full license to her tongue, explaining circumstantially, and with as much of interpolation as Charley did not cut short, how Father Wilfrid and Mr. Ellicombe ("him as is to be captain of the Pope's army—God bless him!") brought in a young lady they had just dug out of the bog, in a dead faint; how she had fainted again on being carried upstairs, and never "come to" till she, Betty, had applied burnt feathers to her nose, when she started up, and screamed out, quite wild-like, "What's a black Mass?" to the extreme terror of all the inmates of the farm; how, without waiting for any answer ("and sure enough we was all too frightened to speak"), she had gone "right off" again, and so continued, "on and off like," till Dr. Wilson came, who gave her "a lot o' brandy and such-like, till she com'd round a bit, and went off to sleep so *quite* as a child;" how the said doctor had sat watching her till Mrs. Trelawney drove up in a fly, when, after a brief consultation, the young lady was wrapped up warm in blankets, and put into the carriage, "and went along home with her mother; and the doctor, he took his horse and went after 'em; and they'll be all in Stonebridge half an hour agone, sir."

"Was the young lady better when she went?" asked Charley.

"Lord save us!—yes, sir; or else she hadn't a-been let to go. I heer'd the doctor a-telling of Mrs. Trelawney, says he, 'Keep her quiet for a bit, very quiet, and she'll be all right in a week or so.' Will you take a drop o' summat, sir, to keep the cold out?"

Charley only accepted a draught of milk for himself, and a pint of beer for his companion, and then they too "went along home."

They had reached the farm by a very circuitous route, and on quite a different side from the Tavistock road, which accounted for their having seen nothing of either the fly or the doctor.

Mrs. Trelawney, on reaching home, had found Father Wilfrid waiting for her, and the fly at the door; and but few words passed between them before she started for Helstone. Dr. Wilson had some difficulty at first in convincing her that Maude was not either dead or dying; but happily she opened her eyes before she was put into the fly, and evidently recognised her mother, which somewhat reassured her.

CHAPTER XVIII

"Knowing that none of the words that were spoken
Would ever mend one of the eggs that were broken."
                                        SOUTHEY.

SQUIRE ELMORE's guests were all assembled in the large drawing-room at Yatton Hall—no, not quite all: there was one guest still missing; and some of the others began to wax impatient, as half-past seven struck, and the dinner was still delayed,—for old-fashioned Devonshire folk have hardly even yet accustomed themselves to London hours and ways. Squire Elmore himself stood on the rug with his gold hunting-watch in his hand, and as the pointers reached the half-hour he said:

"Five minutes more, ladies and gentlemen, by your good leave, and no longer; we will grant him no further grace, the young rascal! If he dallies in this way with parade and roll-call, he'll find himself the wrong side of the hedge before long; Pio Nono will pardon much to his trusty Zouaves, but I doubt if he will put up with lack of discipline in his army."

"Indeed, I am quite distressed at Herbert's rudeness," said Mr. Ellicombe, *père*; "he is generally so very punctual, too: I can't account for it. He had business in Ringwood this evening, and said he should ride on here, and beg the use of a dressing-room; we brought his dinner-gear in the carriage with us."

"Oh, dear! perhaps he has been robbed and murdered by highwaymen on that dreadful moor!" exclaimed a young lady fresh from London, who seriously believed Dartmoor to be infested by robbers and brigands.

Not exactly a cheerful suggestion, considering that his father and mother were present; but no one seemed in the least disturbed by it, not even Mrs. Ellicombe, who positively was heartless enough to laugh, as she said

"No fear of that, I hope, Miss Maxwell; we have no *brigandage* down here; I would as soon cross Dartmoor alone by night as in broad daylight."

So, perhaps, would Miss Maxwell, inasmuch as she would never have dared to set foot upon it in the broadest daylight that ever existed.

But the five minutes' grace was over by this time, and dinner was announced. It was supposed, or politely understood to be supposed, that young Mr. Ellicombe's business at Ringwood had detained him till too late to keep his dinner-engagement, and that he had returned to Abbotsleigh instead, though even in that case he might easily have found a boy at the inn to ride over with his excuses; it certainly was a most lamentable want of good manners.

About the middle of dinner, however, the clatter of a horse's hoofs was heard, and presently the door-bell rang out loud and long.

"Here comes the gallant captain, after all; better late than never," exclaimed Mr. Elmore. "Excuse me for a moment; I will just go out and hear what he has to say for himself."

In a few minutes the Squire returned, laughing heartily; for Herbert had not chosen to represent Maude's case as a serious one—nor, indeed, did he imagine it to be so.

"Master Herbert seems to have ridden out in search of adventure, like a knight of the olden time," he said; "and has been chivalrously employed in rescuing a noble damsel out of the Erl-King's hands."

"What? what? Oh, do tell us all about it," was the general exclamation.

"Come, come; don't press me too hard," said the Squire. "You know the old riddle about majesty deprived of its externals?—well, our gallant captain's adventure, stripped of its gloss, comes to about this: he fell in with Father Wilfrid on the moor, and went a mile out of his way to keep him company. When near Helstone, Rover's barking attracted their attention to the great bog down in that hollow—Luscombe ought to have that bog drained; it's a scandal to the whole country—and there they found a woman, stuck fast and half frozen; so what does this gallant squire of dames do, but take up the woman or girl, or whatever she was, in his arms, and carry her to the farm-house, where he and Father Wilfrid gave her into old Betty's charge! It seems the father knows her belongings, and will give notice of her whereabouts to them at Stonebridge."

Thus related, certainly the tale had little enough of any romantic element about it, as possibly Herbert himself had taken good care to secure; but the word *Stonebridge* struck upon Annie's ear, for she knew almost every one in the village, and she asked with some anxiety if Mr. Ellicombe knew the girl's name, or who her friends were.

"I don't know indeed—he didn't say; but you can ask himself presently; he is having some dinner now in the library, and will join us later."

He did not, however, make his appearance in the dining-room till after the ladies had left it, and it was quite late in the evening before Annie could find an opportunity for her question, for poor Herbert had to run the gauntlet of all manner of jokes and innuendoes about the "fair lady," in whose behalf he had kept seventeen hungry persons waiting more than half an hour for their dinner. He took it all very good-humouredly, but professed himself quite unable to satisfy any one's curiosity as to who or what the "fair lady" might be, or even whether she were either "fair" or a "lady" at all.

But Annie had no mind to be so easily put off. Taking advantage of a quiet moment just before the party separated, she asked him if Father Wilfrid had given him any idea who the girl was, or what was her station.

"Don't think me inquisitive, Mr. Ellicombe," she said; "I only ask because, if it is one of our people, I should like to go and see her to-morrow, or send her any help that may be useful."

Herbert glanced round for a moment, and, seeing that every one else was otherwise occupied, said very quietly:

"Father Wilfrid told me nothing, Miss Crofton; but I could easily see for myself that she was a lady. He only said that he knew her friends, and would send them to her."

"A lady!"—but Annie's exclamation was stifled by a warning gesture from Mr. Ellicombe; and even she had prudence enough to understand that it was best to let the subject drop.

"Thank you," she said aloud; "I suppose we must be content to let it remain a mystery."

On her way home, however, while her father thought she was sound asleep in a corner of the carriage, her imagination ran riot in every direction on the subject of this mysterious lady,—in every direction, that is to say, except the right one, for not even the wildest flight of her imagination wandered into *that*. Who could ever suppose for a moment that the cold, proud, statuesque Miss Trelawney would be guilty of the impropriety of a solitary night-ramble on Dartmoor! Why, even Annie herself, who had pluck enough for almost any thing, would have shrunk from it,

except in a case of obvious duty. It was much
more likely even for Mrs. Trelawney to do such a
thing, than her daughter; and, to own the truth,
Annie's thoughts did for a moment revert to *her*,
for there was that about Margaret Trelawney
which betokened a latent capability for almost
any thing in the way of wildness or passion; perhaps some persons might have discovered the
same inheritance in Maude, but not Annie, to
whom all such signs were as a sealed book, and
who only thought of Mrs. Trelawney that she was
"the kind of woman to leap a five-barred gate if
it came in her way." But what manner of five-
barred gate could possibly have come in her way
to-day? Besides, Mr. Ellicombe had distinctly
said that it was *a girl* whom he had saved, and
surely no one would be so blind as to speak of a
woman in widow's weeds as *a girl*. She looked
out as they passed through Stonebridge, with a
vague idea that she might see *something;* but it
was nearly midnight, and the good people were all
safe in their beds. There was a light in Mrs.
Trelawney's window, certainly (Maude's shutters
were too tightly closed for any to be visible there);
but that did not strike Annie as any thing out of
the common, or more than the ordinary night-light.

She was, however, destined to receive information from a very unexpected quarter. Old
Jones, when he opened the hall-door on the
arrival of the carriage, thought fit to relieve his
conscience and "lift up his testimony" after the
following manner:

"Please, sir, can I speak with you before you
go up-stairs?"

"What, now, Jones—to-night?" said his master; "won't it do in the morning?"

"O Jones, for goodness' sake, what's the matter? Is Master Charles ill?" demanded Annie anxiously.

"No, miss, he is not ill, that I knows of; though riding about on Dartmoor all night is enough to make him so."

"Riding about on Dartmoor all night! What on earth do you mean? Come in here," said Mr. Crofton, entering the library, followed by Annie and Jones. "Now, then, tell me the meaning of all this."

But that was precisely what Jones could not do, for the very excellent reason that he did not know it himself. To the best of his ability, however, he delivered himself as follows:

"Well, sir, about half an hour after you was gone, Mrs. Trelawney called here, and asked to see you most partikler; I told her as you and Miss Crofton was gone out to dinner, and then she asked to see Mr. Charles,—leastways, I told her as he was at home, because, you see, sir—"

"Yes, yes, never mind that; well, she saw Master Charles, I suppose?—go on," interrupted Mr. Crofton.

Annie had started from her chair at Mrs. Trelawney's name, but on second thoughts she sat down again.

"Yes, sure, sir," resumed the butler; "he saw her in this here very room, and a few minutes after he rings the bell so sharp as we all thought the lady must have been took'd ill sudden, or summat,—but it were nothink o' that sort; only when I answers the bell, 'Jones,' says he, 'tell Dick to saddle my pony, and to take Selim for himself, and to strap on a pillion behind both of them as quick as possible, and to come with me; there's been a woman lost on the moor,' says he, 'and I am a-going out to look for her;' and him and Dick went off, sir, and never come back till past ten o'clock; and Dick do say, sir, as they 'ad a *hawful* ride, and as how it was Miss Trelawney as was lost."

Annie waited for no more, but rushed up to Charley's room, which she burst into without further ceremony, after receiving no answer to her knock,—for his violent exercise in the cold wind had acted like an opiate on Charley, in spite of his anxiety about Maude.

Annie shook him rather roughly by the shoulder, whereupon he growled out in a sleepy tone:

"Get off, Floss—down, I say!"

"Charley!" said a voice close at his ear, which certainly was not that of Floss.

"Eh! what! oh! you, Annie, is it? What's the matter now?"

He was evidently still only half awake.

"I think that question is for me to ask," she said. "What have you been doing? What has been the matter? Where is Maude?"

Charley rubbed his eyes, and sat up in bed, looking rather bewildered.

"Maude?" he repeated; "Miss Trelawney? She is safe at home, I hope. Why? What have you heard?"

"Jones says you and Dick have been scouring

Dartmoor in search of her all night. What does it mean? how came she there at all? I am determined to know; so you may as well make full and true confession at once."

By this time Charley was quite awake, and gave Annie as full and circumstantial an account as she could desire of all that had occurred,—only, of course, he was no more able than Jones to explain what it all meant, or how Maude came to be on Dartmoor that evening at all.

"It's very strange," said Annie thoughtfully; "something dreadful must have happened. But it is too late to do any thing to-night. I must go down the first thing in the morning, or perhaps I had better ask Father Wilfrid after Mass. And you took Selim, Charley!—how could you? Papa will be in a fine way. I hope he isn't lamed, or any thing?"

"I don't know, I'm sure, and I don't care," said Charley; "I would have lamed twenty Selims, to save Miss Trelawney. Why, Annie," he went on, rather ashamed of his vehemence, as he saw her look of amazement, "you don't mean to say you would set an immortal soul against the legs of a horse!"

Annie fairly burst out laughing—she really couldn't help it; the proposition, true and serious as it was, sounded so irresistibly ludicrous in Charley's way of putting it.

"Why, of course not," she said, as soon as she could recover herself; "but you might have taken some other horse."

"No, I mightn't," was the prompt answer; "old Douglas crawls like a snail, and Merlin has

Q

cast a shoe, and the carriage-horses were out; so there was no other to take."

"You could have taken Jessie."

"What! your own special pony, that you will never even allow a groom to exercise for you, and that you would not let me ride into Ringwood on Thursday, when Nabob was out of sorts! Suppose *she* had been 'lamed, or any thing;' shouldn't I have caught it, just! I wonder what you would have said then!"

Annie saw that *she* was caught; but instead of trying to back out, she said honestly:

"Well, perhaps *I* should have said that a Christian soul was worth more than my pony's legs."

"Bravo, Annie! But is the *pater* really angry about Selim? I'll tell him all about it in the morning; and the beast is *not* lame, or any thing else wrong, that I know of; so you needn't look so grave about it. But I say, Annie, I'm really awfully tired; it's no joke, I can tell you, describing circles for two hours on Nabob's back: I never knew before what a life those circus fellows have of it. Can't you let me have a snatch of sleep before it's time to get up to breakfast?"

"Poor boy!" said Annie; "there, go to sleep, then, and dream that you are carrying off Miss Trelawney from an enchanted castle, pursued by two fiery dragons. Oh, dear, though, I wish I knew what is the matter; poor Maude! You are sure, Charley, that woman heard the doctor say she would be all right in a week?"

"Quite sure; you may depend upon that;" and Charley turned round, by way of conveying a gentle hint that he wished to be left to his slumbers.

Annie rushed back to Mr. Crofton, who was still in the library, but had dismissed Jones. He certainly was rather angry about Selim, though Dick had left a special assurance with the old butler that the "hanimal" was all right; for even the most easy-tempered man (and Mr. Crofton was often characterised as "amiable to a fault") feels aggrieved at his favourite hunter being treated as unceremoniously as if it were a common hack.

But Annie smoothed down both his brow and his temper very speedily, for, as he said presently:

"It's no use crying over spilt milk."

"But, papa, no milk has been spilt," urged Annie; "they all say Selim is none the worse; and I am sure, if you had been at home, you would have done the same yourself: now, you know very well you would."

Yes, Mr. Crofton did know very well he should; so, kissing Annie, he said:

"Well, well, all's well that ends well; go along to bed with you, now. Fine stories there'll be all over Stonebridge to-morrow; we must try and get at the rights of it, somehow. Good night, birdie."

Yes, that was just the worst of it; there would be no end of tales and reports in the village: the Luscombes and Dr. Wilson were sure to tell, if no one else did,—and Annie fully expected to hear the next morning that Maude had eloped with Herbert Ellicombe, and been discovered and brought home by Father Wilfrid; or, perhaps, that "the captain of the Pope's army" and her brother had fought a duel on Dartmoor, and been interrupted by Maude; who, after stopping the combat, had rushed to commit suicide in Helstone marsh, to avoid being the cause of any further quarrel. Nothing was too wild or improbable for the credulousness of Stonebridge gossips, and Protestants might even devise worse tales where a priest and a runaway girl were concerned. "Not in Stonebridge, though," thought Annie; "no one would dare to breathe a word against Father Wilfrid there."

Still, there was no denying that the facts themselves were of an unpleasant character; and though Annie felt no shadow of doubt that every thing would be explained satisfactorily, she did not sleep much that night.

CHAPTER XIX.

"I stand
Upon my strength; I do defy, deny,
Spurn back, and scorn ye!"
Manfred.

OTHERS were sleepless, too, that night, besides Annie Crofton; but Maude Trelawney was not of the number. Before leaving Helstone Farm, the strong soporific administered by Dr. Wilson had done its work well; and neither the jolting of the carriage, nor the subsequent undressing (or, rather, unwrapping) and putting to bed, had really roused her, though more than once she had opened her eyes with a sort of vacant, sleepy stare: but from the time when she was fairly "settled" in her bed about ten o'clock, till nearly the same hour the next morning, she had never shown the slightest sign of consciousness; and poor Mrs. Trelawney, who had been watching by her bedside the whole night, began to be alarmed at this continued sound sleep, though Maude's breathing was easy and regular; and though Dr. Wilson had said that if she could only sleep for twenty-four hours, there need be no further serious anxiety.

He pronounced the case to be one of "strong excitement acting on a nervous temperament," and suggested that probably the young lady had been frightened by something or some one on the moor—"mistook some honest farmer riding home for Dick Turpin, or thought she saw a ghost, or heard a scream, or—dear me, ma'am, there are ten thousand things that might have frightened a timid young lady, especially if she had lost her way; and then, you see, she would run as fast as she could, without looking before her, and so get knee-deep in the bog before she knew where she was: the whole thing is easily accounted for."

Mrs. Trelawney did not think it necessary to inform him that the young lady in question was neither "timid," nor "of a nervous temperament;" and, indeed, if she had done so, she would not have spoken quite the truth: Maude was certainly not nervous, in the ordinary sense of the word,— nor, in *any* sense of the word, *timid;* but her nerves were too highly strung not to be keenly sensitive to every strain upon them; and any severe, long-continued strain must at last, according to nature, end in a collapse. Such a strain Maude had endured for the last ten months, and now "the last straw" had come, that was to "break the camel's back." It was a very light straw in itself, but it was enough; and Mrs. Trelawney knew it, and understood it, as she sat through the watches of that long, lonely night. She could understand—for she possessed that wide power of sympathy which is the birthright of all vivid imaginations—very much, though not quite all, that her child must have gone through since that long night during which they had watched together by her father's dying bed; and had not her own trial, too, been a still longer one, and, oh, how unspeakably more bitter! Maude had *only* bereavement and loneliness to bear; she had *only* lost her father, and been estranged from her mother (though how much was involved in that last pang, Mrs. Trelawney did not know): while *she*—God help her!—she had not only a double portion of this same misery to endure, but she had been the origin and the cause of all. It was she who had broken her husband's heart, she whose conduct had sown the seeds of the disease which had gradually wasted his strength and undermined his health; yes, she thought with a shudder, Maude might well look upon her as his murderer! And she had done all this, she who loved him almost (but for a miracle of divine grace, it would have been quite) better than her own soul; she who had been again and again on the point of seeking to win him back to life at the cost of that soul; who, perhaps, would have done it, if God had not at length mercifully interposed, and taken into His own hands the earthly love which was so sore a temptation to her. It was her own conduct, too, which had estranged her child from her; no shadow had crossed their perfect love, till that terrible day when Mr. Trelawney had come in with blanched lips and dilated eyes, and, taking his wife into his study, had asked her sternly:

"Margaret, is this true that I have heard? Hartley tells me he saw you take the Sacrament one day last week in the Roman-Catholic church at Birmingham."

Mr. Hartley was a Catholic client of Mr. Trelawney's, who ought to have known better than to make such a remark; but he was a man wholly devoid of tact, and he had, moreover, no reason to suppose that there were any secrets between Mr. Trelawney and his wife.

Bitterly had he reproached her in the first moment of his anguish, not for being a Catholic, but for her want of confidence in him,—for the shallowness of the love that could bear to live on day after day, for four long years, with this concealment; and though afterwards he had seen and acknowledged the injustice of his accusation, the iron had entered into her soul, there to remain to the end of her life; for, after all, was it not true that, if she had loved him more, she would have feared him less? And her strong love for him was just the one thing she could not bear him to doubt: she could have borne to give him any amount of pain, if only he would have acknowledged *that* through it all; but that doubt, once expressed, always haunted her, and was her "sorrow's crown of sorrow."

From that day, too, Maude had shrunk from her as from one plague-stricken, and, as far as lay in her power, interposed herself as a barrier between her and her father.

And all this she had had to endure, for what? For being a Catholic, for having dared to follow the voice of conscience, and the light of faith, and the teaching of the Holy Ghost, in preference to mere human guides. She had risen up and left them, and turned her back upon the "City of Destruction," when so plainly called that she could not choose but hear; but she had shrunk from the dreary wilderness, and taken refuge in the Zoar of human love; and when that, too, was threatened with destruction, she felt as if nought remained to her but to lie down and be crushed under its ruins. Nay, there were wild hours in which she cursed the very light and truth that had brought all this suffering upon her, and would have returned of her own free will into the darkness, if only it had been possible for her to do so—if God were not more merciful than at such a time to "take us at our own vain word."

Once, about this time, a priest who had been trying to rouse her to gratitude for the great grace of her conversion, said,

"Surely you would not refuse to give our Lord any thing He can ask in return?"

"I don't give it, He takes it," was the fierce reply.

And it was the truth—she not only did not give it, but she wrestled long and hard before she would let Him take it, till at last He had arisen to judge His own cause, and compelled her, as sooner or later all His enemies will be compelled, to surrender before the banner first unfurled by the glorious St. Michael in heaven, *Quis ut Deus!*

But the surrender was far from being complete. Even now, as she sat silent and watchful by Maude's bedside, there was ever and anon fierce rebellion in her heart, though its only outward signs were clinched hands and compressed lips; only, happily, she had the grace to complain, not *of* God, but *to* Him : and are not " His ears always open" even to our discontent and murmurings?

To what end, she asked, like the Jews of old, had she afflicted her soul, and offered sacrifice which He regarded not, nor accepted, since His hand was still so heavy upon her? Had she not given Him enough? What did He want more from her? Was she to sacrifice her child to Him : the fruit of her body for the sin of her soul? Would He take all, every thing, and leave her utterly desolate? What had she done, that He should chastise and scourge her so cruelly, so vindictively? Let Him take her life, if He would : she was weary of it; only let Him take it at once, not crush it out piecemeal. Oh, why had she ever brought all this misery upon herself? Why had she ever become a Catholic? Ay, why, indeed? Was it that she might have rest, and ease, and peace, and happiness in this world? Was it that she might sit quietly all her life under her vine and under her fig-tree, basking in the deceitful sunshine of human love and earthly affection? Was it that she might go softly all her days, leaning on her husband for support, and on her child for tender care? Was this what she had meant, when, in the first fervour of her conversion, she had replied to one who tried to frighten her back by drawing a vivid picture of the supposed loneliness of her position, and represented the living Church of God as a barren and dry land,—"Is not the gleaning of the grapes of Ephraim better than the vintage of Abiezer?" Was this what she had *felt*, when her thanksgiving after her first Communion had been a never-ending repetition of that touching outburst of gratitude, *Quid retribuam Domino pro omnibus quæ retribuit mihi?* Were these the real thoughts of her heart even in that hour of weakness and heart-faintness? No, a thousand times no; for even in the midst of that terrible struggle, there came a still, small voice, low and sweet, "Whom hast thou in heaven but Me, and who is there upon earth that thou canst desire in comparison of Me? Wouldst thou make thyself unworthy of Me by preferring thy poor, finite human loves to My love, which is infinite, unchangeable, eternal? Have I not given thee, of My own free grace, that priceless treasure, the gift of faith? and what wilt thou give Me in return?—nay, rather, what canst thou refuse Me? What is worthy to be compared with it?"

"Nothing! oh, nothing! Not for father, or mother, or husband, or child, would I lose that precious gift; not for all the joys of earthly affection, ten thousand times multiplied, would I exchange it," was the heart's response, even in that dark hour of sorrow and temptation.

Even then, too, she felt—with a vague, half-shrinking fear of the deep waters on whose brink she stood—that there would come a time when this sort of *negative* self-sacrifice would disgust her by its lukewarmness and half-heartedness, when even counsels of perfection would hardly satisfy the energy of her love, and when she would exclaim with the Psalmist, *Viam mandatorum Tuorum cucurri, cum dilatasti cor meum.*

Yes, that time would come sooner, perhaps, than she would have thought possible; but it had not come yet.

There was also another solitary watcher that night—Father Wilfrid.

But why should he watch? What care, what anxiety, had he, on that particular night, that should cause him to spend it in earnest pleading at the foot of the Altar, instead of in sleep or rest? Surely he had already done all he could for Maude, —far more, indeed, than, had she known it, she would ever have accepted at his hands,—and he had every reason to believe her quite safe now. He had called on Dr. Wilson late that evening, and asked for his honest opinion on the subject, and the worthy doctor had assured him that, with Miss Trelawney's apparently vigorous constitution, no worse consequences were to be apprehended than a severe cold, and a temporary "shock to the nervous system," which might require change of air and scene for a time to perfect her recovery. Change of air and scene! Why, she had come to Stonebridge for that, and had only been there a few days as yet. "Yes, yes, my dear sir," said the doctor, "all very well; but in these cases" ("What cases?" thought the priest, but he kept his question to himself) "it is always advisable to remove a person from all unpleasant associations; it insures greater tranquillity. I shall recommend Mrs. Trelawney to take her daughter to Dawlish, or Torquay, for a fortnight or so, as soon as she is equal to the journey."

With this *dictum* Father Wilfrid was obliged to content himself, for not a word more could he get out of the doctor; but it supplied him with matter for reflection as he walked home, for it went far to corroborate his own impression about Maude.

When Mrs. Trelawney had found him waiting for her, on her return from Mr. Crofton's, there had been little time for any thing but giving and receiving the necessary information, and preparing to start off to Helstone; but he had asked her if she knew of any thing that could account for Maude's strange conduct, and she had replied that she could not tell, but Maude had been looking at some of her books, and perhaps had read something that had startled or shocked her. *What* she supposed her to have read, she did not say; it was, certainly, no part of her duty to confess Maude's sins.

This information, however,—such as it was, —Father Wilfrid put together with what he had seen himself only that morning, and drew his own conclusions, which were somewhat complicated by the recollection of the single glance Maude had bestowed upon him at the farm-house, and the expression of which it was impossible to mistake.

But what was there in all this to excite so deep an interest? What was Maude Trelawney to him? Surely *he* was not her keeper?

No; but, then, it never occurred to him to ask or think what she was to *him*. He only knew that she had a soul, which Jesus had loved enough to die for it; and after what he had seen and heard, he could not doubt that that soul was in great peril; and such knowledge, in one who had a real thirst for souls, was quite enough to account for any effort he might make in its behalf.

Mrs. Trelawney was not at Mass the next morning; but he had not expected to see her there; of course she could not leave Maude. Annie, however, was; and she pursued him into the sacristy afterwards, full of eager questions about Maude; but he could tell her little more than she knew already, except the fact of her having been brought safely home.

"But how very strange! What can have induced her to go there at all? Haven't you the least idea?" persisted Annie.

"That, I suppose, no one will know, till she is able to speak for herself," replied Father Wilfrid quietly.

"Do you think I might see her?" was the next question; but neither to that could she get any satisfactory answer; and at last she went away with a permission, not very willingly given, to go after her breakfast, and ask to see Mrs. Trelawney.

He did not, himself, wait for much ceremony of breakfast, beyond his cup of coffee, before going on the same errand. He would not go up-stairs, lest Maude should hear and be disturbed by the sound of his voice; but sent up a message, to ask if Mrs. Trelawney could come to him in the dining-room. He was not kept long waiting; but there was little to hear, beyond that Maude was still sleeping, and that Dr. Wilson was expected every moment. Evidently, too, Mrs. Trelawney was nervous at Maude being left alone; so Father Wilfrid took his leave, saying he would call again in the afternoon.

On his way home, he met Annie, told her all that there was to hear, and advised her to delay her visit for a few hours, as she would then have a better chance of seeing her friend; the reasonableness of which advice she was fain to admit, though she declared it was "too bad that she might not even go in and look at Maude; that could not possibly hurt her."

In the afternoon, Father Wilfrid called again, as he had promised. The report of Maude was decidedly favourable; she had roused up out of her sleep about eleven o'clock, and taken some food; and had begged so hard to be allowed to get up, that Dr. Wilson, seeing really no objection to it, had given leave; and she was now sitting, warmly wrapped up, by the fire in the drawing-room. She had been very quiet ever since; speaking little, as though still partially under the influence of the opiate. "But," said Mrs. Trelawney, "one of the few things she has said, was a request to see you if you should call."

Whatever Father Wilfrid may have felt, he expressed no surprise, but only said he should be very glad to see her.

Mrs. Trelawney accordingly went to prepare her for his visit, and almost immediately returned to fetch him.

Maude was sitting on a low chair, drawn close to the fire; and though the heat of the room was stifling, her fingers were numbed and her lips blue with cold; and a violent shivering-fit shook her from head to foot, as her mother entered the room, followed by Father Wilfrid. She tried to stand up to receive him, but utterly failed in the attempt.

"Pray do not move," he said kindly; "I am very thankful to see that you are able to sit up at all. You must take care of yourself now, till you are stronger."

She kept her eyes fixed on him while he spoke, with a cold, stony look in them; and as soon as he stopped, she said slowly,

"I suppose you saved my life last night. I am very grateful to you for taking so much trouble for any one you could not possibly have known."

Her eyes grew keen and searching, as she said the last words.

His conveyed no meaning whatever, as he replied :

"Indeed, Miss Trelawney, you have very little to thank me for; it was Mr. Ellicombe who found you and brought you to Helstone; or rather, if every one is to have his due, you owe your rescue to his dog Rover, who first discovered you. It was by mere accident that I was there at all; and I did nothing but call on Dr. Wilson and your mother, on my way home."

She still continued to look at him fixedly, as she said:

"I should like to say a word to you alone, if you will allow me."

Mrs. Trelawney vanished in a moment, and Father Wilfrid very quietly seated himself near enough to Maude to hear her easily; for her voice seemed very weak.

She turned upon him like a creature standing at bay, and determined not to yield an inch.

"What is a black Mass?" she asked, in the tone which had so startled and scared all the inmates of Helstone Farm the night before.

But Father Wilfrid was neither startled nor scared. He answered her as quietly as if she had merely asked what o'clock it was.

"It is a Mass offered for the souls of the departed."

"What does it mean?"

"That would take a long time to explain," he replied, "longer than you could bear now; but, briefly, it means a sacrifice and prayer offered for the deliverance of souls, or any particular soul, out of purgatory, that it may the sooner go to heaven."

Fire flashed from her eyes, and the wild strength of excitement was in her voice, as she exclaimed:

"And you can't do that for a Protestant! You won't pray that *they* may go to heaven! You give them up to hell for all eternity! They are not even worth praying for! If that is your religion, it is fit only for devils!"

"Stay a moment," said Father Wilfrid, very

gently; "you have quite mistaken me, though I do not understand how. What makes you suppose that we think so harshly of Protestants, or that we do not pray for them?"

Maude hesitated a moment; she was not going so far to humble herself as to acknowledge that she had read his note to her mother. But it was only for a moment; she could not restrain herself longer.

"You will say a black Mass for a Protestant?" she said, with a fixed look, which seemed to say, "Deceive me if you dare!"

He began to feel the ground under his feet now, and tried to explain that the Mass could be said, though the black vestment could not be worn; but this only seemed to enrage Maude the more, though her anger took a different line.

"Then you are ashamed of praying for them; you dare not let people know you do it! Well, it's a good thing they don't want your prayers; thank God, my dear father is safe in heaven now, out of your reach: I suppose you and my mother think he is in hell?"

"God forbid!" said Father Wilfrid fervently, "and forbid that you should think so hardly of us: you will understand us better some day. Purgatory is not hell, but the resting-place of holy souls."

"I don't understand, and I don't want to understand," said Maude; "I beg your pardon, if I have been rude,—I couldn't help it. But now" (her strength was evidently nearly exhausted, and she spoke with an effort), "if it is true, as people say, that priests can keep secrets well, I will ask you not to repeat what I have said to my mother."

For the first time during their interview, he returned her fixed look, as he said simply:

"You may trust me."

CHAPTER XX.

> "Though thy slumber may be deep,
> Yet thy spirit shall not sleep;
> There are shades which will not vanish,
> There are thoughts thou canst not banish;
> By a power to thee unknown,
> Thou canst never be alone;
> Thou art wrapped as with a shroud,
> Thou art gathered in a cloud,
> And for ever shalt thou dwell
> In the spirit of this spell."
>
> BYRON.

"TRUST *him!*" thought Maude, curling her lip scornfully as he left her; for, seeing that she was in no state either to hear or speak more at that time, he went away, hoping that some other and better opportunity might arise for correcting the literally "*onconscaivable* ignorance" which seemed to have so wofully distorted her ideas, and almost distraught her brain. Some allowance, he felt, was to be made for what Dr. Wilson had called "the shock to the nervous system" which she had sustained the night before, and some allowance also for the *confusing* effects of the opiate, which evidently had not altogether passed away; but still there remained the broad fact, as yet unexplained and unaccounted for in either of these ways, of her having wandered out alone, nearly three miles from home, on a desolate moor, after dusk.

Mrs. Trelawney had seemed to be almost as much in the dark as himself; she only supposed Maude must have read something in one of her books that had disturbed her. But what could she have read, that was likely to throw her mind so completely off its balance? He did not know that its burden had been gradually heaping up, till a feather's weight was enough to turn the scale.

Something about Masses or prayers for the dead it must have been, and he would have given a great deal to know what, that he might understand better how to meet it; that in her present mood she would not be at all likely to tell him, he felt very certain, and also that she was still less likely to tell her mother.

Mrs. Trelawney looked anxiously at him when he rejoined her in the dining-room; but she knew better than to venture upon any question. He only said:

"I think you had better go back to her presently; talking seems to have exhausted her very much. You must try to keep her as quiet as you can; Dr. Wilson said so, did he not?"

"Yes; but, O father, what does it all mean? is he going out of her mind?"

"I trust not," he said; "but indeed I understand it as little as you do. You spoke of her having looked at some of your books yesterday,—have you any idea what book, or what she is likely to have read?"

Though he could give no hint of what Maude had said, it was not a confession, and he was under no obligation not to make use of it.

Mrs. Trelawney hesitated; she did not know of what importance the information might be, and was afraid to incur the responsibility of withholding it; while, on the other hand, she instinctively shrunk from giving it.

After a few moments' pause, which he did not interrupt, she said:

"I will fetch the book I found lying on the floor, and you can see for yourself."

On her way up, she looked into the drawing-room; Maude seemed to be asleep, but started up as the door creaked (all lodging-house doors invariably do), and said sharply, though hardly above a whisper:

"Is he gone?"

Mrs. Trelawney heartily wished she could have said "Yes," instead of "No;" but even if her conscience had been sufficiently elastic, it would have been worse than useless, for Maude was sure to find out sooner or later that she had been deceived,—for she had a special talent that way: once, as a child, she had heard the proverb, that truth lies at the bottom of a well, and had forthwith exclaimed indignantly:

"Then show me where the well is, and I'll go down in a bucket and fetch her up!"

And from that day forward she had been perpetually, in a metaphorical sense, going down wells in buckets; but, unfortunately, many of the seeming truths that she discovered were not the pure gold itself, but base metal which she mistook for it.

Had Father Wilfrid known of this propensity, he might have been less puzzled to account for her appearance in the church the previous morning.

Maude turned away her head wearily, but made no reply, as she received her mother's answer; but as the door closed behind her, she again repeated to herself:

"Trust *him!* trust a priest! did he think I was such a fool? He may say what he likes; I only wanted to try how long his promise would last: he is breaking it already, I suppose."

In happy ignorance of the rash judgment passed upon him, Father Wilfrid awaited Mrs. Trelawney's return. She was not long, and she came holding open in her hand the *Golden Manual,* which she quietly held towards him.

"I found it," she said, "lying open on the floor at this place, and this paper had dropped out of it."

She spoke in the stiff, mechanical tone that had belonged to the first days of his acquaintance with her, and which he had begun to hope was entirely discarded; but he understood it the moment his eye fell upon the little slip of paper, which contained his own handwriting. The book was open at one of Mrs. Trelawney's favourite devotions, the "Litany of the Holy Name." *That* could have had no connection with Maude's strange excitement; it contained nothing to startle or shock the most bigoted Protestant in the world.

He took the paper, looked straight at Mrs. Trelawney, and said:

"She has read this."

"I suppose so," was the reply,—and for a moment neither spoke.

Then he said:

"It is always best not to leave these things lying about; you should have destroyed it."

"But I never thought"—she began; and the colour mounted to her temples, as if she had herself been caught in a dishonourable action.

"Don't let it trouble you," he said kindly; "we must make some allowance always for peculiar circumstances and temptations. Remember *all* that your daughter thinks, or may think, of Catholics, and then imagine the curiosity, the suspicion perhaps, that would be suddenly excited by the unexpected appearance of that slip of paper; after all, one must take people a little on their own ground, meet them half-way, as the saying is. You remember those lines of Burns's,

'What's *done*, you partly may compute,
But know not what's *resisted*.'"

Mrs. Trelawney looked up with an expression of relief; she could not have borne that *he* should judge Maude hardly; but she only said:

"I did not know you had so much imagination."

"Imagination!" he repeated. "I don't think I have any; but, you see, it is often a part of my duty to study characters and motives, and I am afraid I am sometimes apt to do it when it is a mere idle speculation."

"Is *this* an idle speculation?" she said; "is it useless to try and discover what could have so terribly excited Maude in those few words,—what she could have meant to do when she started on that wild walk?"

"There is only one way to do that," he said; "try to win her confidence, and she will perhaps one day tell you herself; meanwhile, you can only pray for her. Don't harass her with questions."

Mrs. Trelawney did not need that caution; she knew very well that *asking* for confidence is very seldom the way to win it, and, in the few cases when it is so won, it is not worth the having. To be of any value, it must be freely and spontaneously given.

"When will you come and see Maude again?" she asked.

"Whenever she wishes it, but not unless she expresses some such wish. I should be very sorry to annoy her in any way."

"Annoy her! what, after saving her life! Besides, she did express a wish to see you before all this happened; you remember what I told you yesterday?"

"Perfectly," he replied; "but now she has seen me; and perhaps, like some other wonderful sights, she may think once seeing is enough; however, you know I am always ready to come if I am wanted." And with these words he took his leave.

Mrs. Trelawney returned to Maude, who had apparently fallen asleep, for her head rested on her hand, and she did not make the slightest movement as her mother made up the fire, which was getting low, and then took up a book, intending to read; but after about a quarter of an hour, she was startled by Maude saying suddenly:

"Mamma, your book must be very interesting; you have been holding it upside down for the last ten minutes at least."

It was an undeniable fact; but Mrs. Trelawney was too glad to hear Maude speak so quietly and naturally, to trouble herself much about what had called forth the remark.

"Have I?" she said; "well, I am afraid I must plead guilty; but I thought you were asleep, Maude."

"Asleep? I think I slept enough last night to do for all the rest of my life: it seemed like a hundred years; I only wish I might never go to sleep again."

"How could it seem long, while you knew nothing about it, dear?"

"I knew all about it," said Maude; "only I could not speak or move: I suppose the cold had paralysed me. I heard the doctor talking nonsense about pressure on the brain; and I felt the jolting of the carriage; and then, for hours and hours, I heard people walking up and down, and round and round, in the room. Who were they?—what did they do it for? They were talking all the time, too—a horrid jargon of bad Latin. Why couldn't they be quiet? Why did you let people come and mutter spells over me? Did you think I was bewitched?"

"My poor child," said Mrs. Trelawney, "you

were dreaming. There was no one in your room all night but myself, and I never spoke a word; no one else came near you till Dr. Wilson called this morning."

If she had not known something, by former experience in her husband's sick-room, of the strange effects sometimes produced by strong opiates, she would have been frightened; as it was, she only resolved to avoid, if possible, any recurrence to such remedies for the future.

"Dreaming, was I?" said Maude. "Then perhaps I am dreaming now. Tell me what happened last night."

She spoke peremptorily, and was evidently determined to have an answer of some kind; but it was not so easy to find one.

Mrs. Trelawney said: "When I came home yesterday evening, I found you had gone out again; and I suppose you must have lost your way on the moor."

"Yes, yes, I remember now," broke in Maude. "I will tell you how it was."

Was the explanation really coming quite spontaneously, after all? Mrs. Trelawney waited eagerly for it. She did not know that for the last four hours Maude's brain had been hard at work, first, in trying to recollect all that had happened—in which, of course, she was completely baffled, as she had been unconscious the greater part of the time; and, next, in putting together some tolerably reasonable way of accounting to others for as much as she could remember of the preceding night's *escapade*. She could do wild things; but there was "a method in her madness;" and she was much too clever to let herself be made "a nine days' wonder" of.

"I recollect now," she repeated. "You went to the chapel" (Maude would not call it a church) "on our way home from Stinchcombe, and left me to come on alone. I thought you would be a long time; and you know how I love the moors" (yes, Mrs. Trelawney did know that); "so I changed my dress, and found my way up there. I thought I could get across somehow to the other side of the village, but I suppose I took a wrong turn; and then it got dark; and then I followed a woman, thinking she was sure to be going there; and then my foot slipped, and I rolled down into a bog, and couldn't get out again: and that is all I know about it. Were you frightened? What did you do?"

Mrs. Trelawney did not think it necessary to say exactly what she had done; that she was frightened nearly out of her senses she acknowledged readily; for the rest, she only said that she had gone to Mr. Crofton's in search of Maude, and that, on her return, she found Father Wilfrid, and heard from him what had happened.

"You went to look for me at Mr. Crofton's? What on earth made you suppose I should go there?"

"I did not really suppose it; I could only take the chance."

Maude looked up at her mother, and started as she saw the anxious, haggard expression of her face. She stretched out her arm, drew Mrs. Trelawney's head down towards her, and kissed her tenderly.

"Poor, dear mother!" she said; "don't fret about me; I shall be all right again very soon. I wonder Miss Crofton's brother did not offer to go out in search of me. Do you know that he is desperately in love with me? Is not it ridiculous?" and Maude laughed, but not exactly a hearty laugh.

"Well, he did go out to look for you; but I didn't know he had any personal interest in the matter. Did he tell you he was in love with you?"

"No, of course not; he is not altogether a born idiot," said Maude, with another little constrained laugh. "But tell me all that happened last night. Who did find me, after all? Mr. Wilfrid told me the name; but I forget it. I want to know all about it."

She spoke eagerly; and Mrs. Trelawney did her best to stifle the laugh she could hardly repress: it sounded so very odd to hear any one talk of *Mr.* Wilfrid. She told Maude all particulars—as far as she knew them herself—of the events of the preceding night. Maude listened attentively, but made no remark till she had heard all; then she said:

"If Mr. Ellicombe calls, let me see him, please; I should like to thank him myself."

"He can hardly call; for he does not even know who you are, or where you came from," said Mrs. Trelawney; "Father Wilfrid did not tell him."

If she thought that this proof of delicacy of feeling would be a point in Father Wilfrid's favour, she was greatly mistaken. Maude drew herself up proudly, and said:

"Oh, I suppose he thought I was doing something I ought to be ashamed of. I am much obliged to him for his consideration and regard for my reputation. By the by, how came he to know me himself? He had never seen me before, had he?"

Her eyes glistened with feverish excitement, to Mrs. Trelawney's surprise, who was quite ignorant of its cause.

"I don't know, indeed," she said; "I did not ask him; but he may have seen us walking together, or may have been struck by some likeness to me."

"Oh, well, it does not matter; but I wish you would ask him to tell Mr. Ellicombe the truth when he has an opportunity. I don't want to be made a mystery of."

She was evidently bent upon having every thing clearly accounted for; and, after all, Mrs. Trelawney could not but acknowledge that it was the wisest course; but she only gave a brief assent, for Maude seemed tired, and closed her eyes wearily.

They had both been silent, and perhaps dozing, for nearly an hour, when a ring at the bell roused them; and Hannah presently came up to say that Miss Crofton was down-stairs, and would like to see Mrs. Trelawney.

"Let her come up, please," said Maude,—"at least, unless you want to talk secrets."

"Certainly not that, dear; but you have had so much talking already; and Dr. Wilson said you must keep quiet. Are you not too tired?"

"No," replied Maude; "sleeping tires me

much more than talking—I dream so fast; and, besides"—but, apparently, she had no intention of finishing her sentence. Have we not often a *besides* which means far more than all the reasons we choose to *give* for a thing put together?

Hannah was dismissed, therefore, with orders to show Miss Crofton up-stairs.

Annie would have preferred seeing Mrs. Trelawney alone for a few moments first, but she had, of course, no choice; she, however, asked Hannah privately if Maude seemed very ill.

"Well, her do look uncommon bad, sure, miss," replied that damsel, "and her ha'n't made use of nothink but a dish o' tay since morning, and her do groan awful, times, and speak strange-like in her sleep."

"How do you do, Miss Crofton?" said Maude, putting out her hand, and speaking in such a natural tone that Annie, for a moment, was deceived by it.

"I came to ask how *you* do," she said; "how is she now, Mrs. Trelawney?"

But Maude answered for herself:

"I am only a little tired, thank you, and very cold; all the bog seems to have got inside me. I hear your brother was good enough to trouble himself for me last night: it was very kind of him."

"Not at all," said Annie; "I assure you he felt himself highly honoured in serving you; not that he did serve you, by the way,—he was too late to be of any use: he is jealous enough of the young Zouave, I can tell you."

"Of what? of whom?" exclaimed Maude, with

dilated eyes and flushed cheeks; and Mrs. Trelawney gave Annie a look—half warning, half reproachful: all which together frightened her a little.

"There I go again!" she thought to herself, "always putting my foot into it somehow or other!"

"Oh, only Mr. Ellicombe," she said; "he is just going into the army."

Maude had heard and understood perfectly, but she made no further remark; and Annie, by way of changing the subject of conversation, said:

"You must let me take you for a drive when you are strong enough, Miss Trelawney; you will find the country much prettier here than about Stretton: I do hate those flat, tame Midland Counties."

"Thank you," said Maude; but she sighed wearily; and Annie remembered, to her dismay, that Warwick had been Maude's home. Feeling herself at desperation-point, she turned to Mrs. Trelawney, and said:

"I am afraid papa is waiting for me; I really only just called to inquire, not to trouble you: I will come again another day."

And mother and daughter were left alone again.

CHAPTER XXI.

> "For Romans, in Rome's quarrel,
> Spared neither land nor gold,
> Nor son, nor wife, nor limb, nor life,
> In the brave days of old."
> MACAULAY'S *Lays of Ancient Rome.*

"WHAT an uncomfortable person Miss Crofton is, mamma," said Maude; "she always contrives to set all one's teeth on edge."

"She is young and happy," was the reply, spoken with a half-suppressed sigh, as Mrs. Trelawney contrasted Annie's bright, joyous face with the worn and haggard-looking one of her own child; "and has had nothing yet to make her thoughtful, either for herself or others; I am sure she did not mean to hurt you."

"Happy, is she?" said Maude, not taking any notice of these last words; "ah, yes! I forgot: she has her father;" and she turned her head away to conceal the tears she was too weak now to control.

Mrs. Trelawney knew it would be worse than useless to attempt consolation, but she tried to turn the current of Maude's thoughts by saying:

"And she is engaged to Mrs. Hatton's eldest son."

But Maude took no heed of the words; nor did she speak again for the rest of the evening, except to beg, about an hour later, that her bed might be got ready, as she felt too tired to sit up longer,—and to refuse Mrs. Trelawney's offer of sleeping in her room; she would burn a light, she said, and, as their rooms were close together, if she wanted any thing, she could knock against the wall. Mrs. Trelawney tried to contest the point, for she did not think Maude in a fit state to be trusted alone, but without success; and, finally, a compromise was agreed upon, to the effect that she should look in about midnight, and again towards four o'clock in the morning, to see if Maude wanted any thing, and to give her her medicine if she were awake.

"It's just the most effectual way of keeping me awake all night, mamma," said Maude; "but, of course, if you will not be satisfied without, you must do it: 'He who will to Cupar, maun to Cupar.'" But Mrs. Trelawney trusted to the potency of the sleeping-draught which Dr. Wilson had persuaded her was absolutely necessary for that night, at all events.

And she did not trust in vain: Maude slept, to all appearance tranquilly, for several hours; and at four o'clock she was still asleep, but there was a disturbed, distressed expression on her face, her lips twitched convulsively from time to time, and she muttered something which Mrs. Trelawney could not distinctly catch, but which sounded something like, "Go away, go away."

She raised her head a little on the pillow, and stooped and kissed her; but Maude put up her hand and pushed her roughly away. She was asleep, unconscious; she could not know what she was doing; she was probably only trying to shake off some painful dream; but love is unreasoning and unreasonable, and the poor.

mother sank down on the floor, and wept passionately. What more was God going to require of her? He had taken her husband from her, He had turned her child's heart against her; was she even to be denied a mother's right to watch over and care for her? Words that she had been familiar with from her childhood flashed across her mind: "To whom much is given, of him shall much be required;" and she knew that "much," inestimably much, had been given to her.

"O Lord, give less, and require less," was the cry of her poor, weak human heart; but the very words themselves, as they took form and substance, startled her by their ingratitude and want of generosity, and the courageous prayer of the large-hearted St. Augustine took their place: "Give what Thou commandest, and command what Thou wilt."

If even then there was a lingering afterthought of "but not yet," surely it was forgiven by Him who granted in all its fulness to the great Saint the grace he had demanded with so seemingly insincere a reserve. Yes, she was right—God did require something more of her: He required a fuller realisation of the truth, that they who love son or daughter more than Him, are not worthy of Him; but if she would only acknowledge this, and take her child's love from Him, and not as her own by right, He would perhaps give her even the very consolation that He seemed to take away.

Two hours later she went in again, thinking that, if Maude were tolerably quiet, she might venture to go out to Mass, leaving Susan Blackmore in charge—one of her pupil-teachers, whom she had engaged the day before to attend upon Maude during her illness, and who had slept on a sofa in the dining-room, as Maude resolutely refused to have any one in her own room.

Mrs. Trelawney felt now the inconvenience of having no servants of her own, and yet she did not really wish to change her present mode of life; it was much less trouble; she hated housekeeping, and servants were always more or less of a plague; and, besides—yes, there was a very extensive *besides* in this case, so extensive that she did not understand it herself, beyond what she had long ago told Father Wilfrid, viz. that she had answered his advertisement under a vague sort of impression that, as her husband had been taken from her, and her child had forsaken her, she must be intended to give herself up in some way entirely to God; and not knowing in what way, she had caught eagerly at the first opportunity which presented itself of devoting herself and her money to His service; and not being the kind of person to do any thing by halves, she had resolved to live in such a manner as to spend the least amount possible upon herself, especially as she had only a life-interest in her husband's fortune—at her death it all reverted to Maude; so that, as she said, whatever good she was to do with it, must be done during her lifetime. Moreover, if Maude were to marry, half of the whole fortune was to be settled upon her at once.

"So that, you see," Mrs. Trelawney had said, "you had better take all you can of my money whilst you can get it."

When Father Wilfrid heard all this, he no longer wondered that no separate provision had been made for Maude. Mr. Trelawney would naturally suppose that his wife and daughter would live together till the marriage of the latter; and it must also be remembered that, at the time he made his will, there was no difference of religion to suggest the possibility of a separation.

But we must come back from our long digression.

Maude opened her eyes as her mother bent over her, stared at her for a moment, and then closed them again.

"Maude, dear child," said Mrs. Trelawney, "are you awake?"

If she had not been before, she was now; the well-known voice had completely roused her.

"Is it you, mamma?" she said; "is it really you?—not any thing, any one else?" Then raising herself up, and looking round, she continued, "I see now, I was dreaming before. Have you been here long, mamma? Did I talk in my sleep?"

"No, dear, not a single word, that I heard; but I have only just come in twice to look at you, as I said I should; you seemed once to say something, but I could not distinguish any words. Do you feel rested after your long sleep?"

"No," said Maude, "I feel very tired; dreaming tires me so. I don't want to go to sleep any more. What o'clock is it?"

"About half-past six. I am going to dress now; and then Susan shall bring you some breakfast: you had better stay quiet till then."

"Very well," replied Maude; "it is too cold to get up. Are you going to church? Susan can do all I want. Don't mind leaving me, if you wish to go."

Mrs. Trelawney did wish to go, almost more than she had ever wished it in her life; she wanted the refreshment and the strength that she was certain to find there, and there seemed really no reason why she should not go; Susan was a thoroughly trustworthy girl, and Maude would not get up for some hours yet, so there was not much that could be wanted during her absence.

Father Wilfrid came back into the church after Mass, and beckoned her into the sacristy.

"I need hardly ask you," he said; "you would not be here, if you could not leave her comfortably."

"I almost think I should have been here in any case this morning," she answered; "yesterday was such a long, dreary day, I could not have borne such another without the Mass to support it,—but I hope Maude *is* better; she slept tolerably quietly all night, and had not been long awake when I came out. It was her own suggestion that I should come, too, but only out of consideration for me. She seemed more bitter than ever, yesterday, after you were gone. O father, I feel more hopeless than ever about her."

To her astonishment, Father Wilfrid replied, with a radiant smile:

"Ah! well, never mind; I should not think

it a bad sign if she were very much more bitter than she is; she will fight hard with the truth before she surrenders to it,—and as long as the battle rages, there is hope of victory."

"But I see no sign of any battle," said Mrs. Trelawney; "she doesn't fight with the truth, she simply hates it."

"You have no right to say that of any one," he said, a little sternly; "you cannot see into their hearts; and to resist truth, is not necessarily to hate it. And now take courage; you may not see any ground for hope, but I am quite sure there is none for despair."

He spoke as if *he* saw some ground for hope; where had he found it? Could he not tell her? Had he received some secret answer to his long prayer for that poor wandering soul? If so, he would have been the last person in the world to speak of it.

Finding that she did not speak, and looked a little hurt, as if he had been wanting in sympathy, he said cheerfully:

"Come, don't be discouraged, and don't let yourself be too easily vexed or worried. Give that poor child a little time to get over the shock to her Protestant nerves of being picked up by a priest and a Zouave. I daresay she dreams all sorts of horrors about both of us; never mind that: dreams don't last for ever, and can't hurt any one very much, after all. Don't reason with her or contradict her now; pray for her, and leave the rest to God."

The mention of "a Zouave" reminded Mrs. Trelawney of Maude's message about Mr. Ellicombe, which she immediately proceeded to deliver, without, however, adding Maude's further remark on the subject. He seemed rather amused.

"I will tell him, by all means, and send him to call, if you like," he said; "but I cannot promise that he will do it. Herbert has sent off his heart to Rome before him, and takes no interest in any thing else."

Annie followed Mrs. Trelawney out of church, and entreated to be allowed to walk home with her; she had so many things to say, and it was the only chance of seeing her alone.

"I dare not come and see you with Maude again," she said; "I am sure to make some more stupid, blundering speeches. Has she forgiven me yet for what I said yesterday?"

Mrs. Trelawney was quite of opinion that it was better for Annie to keep away from Maude for the present; so she only said, that she thought Maude was hardly strong enough yet to receive visitors.

"Very well; I shall not come," said Annie, feeling the repulse instantly; "but you know it was her own doing, not mine, that I saw her yesterday."

"I know it was," said Mrs. Trelawney; "I never meant to blame you for it, dear; but invalids are not always the best judges of what is good for them, and I think the quieter Maude is kept just now, the better."

"Yes, I daresay," said Annie, rather shortly; then, with sudden penitence for her little fit of temper, she exclaimed:

"What a brute I am to be cross with you, you

dear old thing! Now, look here; you want to take Maude to Torquay, or Teignmouth, or somewhere, when she is well enough to move, don't you?"

"Dr. Wilson recommends it; but the school begins again next week, so I cannot."

"*Je ne vois pas la nécessité*—I mean, *l'impossibilité*," said Annie; "let me take the school for you, while you are away; I will try and not get it into dreadful disorder: at all events, it will be no worse than it was for the two months before you came here, probably not so bad,—for the children can hardly forget the excellent training you have got them into, in so short a time; will you trust me with them?"

"Trust you, Miss Crofton!" but before Mrs. Trelawney could say another word, Annie had come to a sudden halt, and stood straight in front of her; luckily they were in a narrow lane, and no one was in sight.

"How dare you call me Miss Crofton?" she exclaimed. "Now, then, not one step farther shall you go till you say Annie, like a Christian."

Mrs. Trelawney laughed in spite of herself.

"Well, then, *Annie*," she said, "you surely don't suppose I would ask you to make such a slave of yourself?"

"No, I don't suppose you would ask me," she replied; "that is just why I ask you. Come, don't let us waste time in discussing such a very simple matter; will you trust the school to me for a few weeks?"

"How can you ask such a question?" said Mrs. Trelawney; "you know I would; but, indeed, I cannot take advantage of your kindness in that way. It is not the least necessary for Maude to go to the seaside; Dartmoor air will do her quite as much good."

"H'm! well, it is rude to contradict; but the logic of facts is against you; she had plenty of Dartmoor air the other evening, and it does not seem to have had a very beneficial effect: seriously, now,"—and Annie really did speak seriously this time,—"you know she ought to go away, and that you ought to go with her; and it won't be the least bit of trouble to me to take the school. I shall quite enjoy having something to do; and it will help to break away a host of scruples about the idle life I am leading, which I sometimes torment Father Wilfrid with, and he always says: 'Then why don't you find something to do?' So I am sure he will be pleased. Now, don't make any more objections or compliments, but just let us consider it settled."

"I cannot quite do that without Father Wilfrid's sanction," replied Mrs. Trelawney; "you know it is his school, not mine."

"Oh, dear! how dreadfully punctilious you are! You know very well he lets you do just what you like about the school; when father does trust people, he trusts them thoroughly, and you know he trusts you."

"All the more reason for not abusing his confidence; but have you proposed the plan to him?"

"I?—oh, dear, no. When I really want to do a thing, I do it first, and tell him afterwards. He can't forbid me then, you know; and I get my own way without being tempted to disobedience."

Mrs. Trelawney laughed at this ingenious way of avoiding occasions of sin; though, to own the truth, she felt a little shocked: but she had been a Catholic long enough to know that it is a greater fault to take scandal easily than to give it.

It was finally settled, greatly to Annie's satisfaction, that her proposal should be accepted, subject to Father Wilfrid's approval.

She then started off on another subject, telling Mrs. Trelawney that an old aunt of her father's, "having taken it into her tiresome old head" to think that young people ought to see a little of the world, especially young people who have been foolish enough to entangle themselves in an engagement before they had any opportunity of knowing their own minds, had prevailed upon her father to promise that he would take her to London for a few weeks during the season.

"Won't it be horrid?" she said; "they will drag me about to balls, and operas, and concerts, and *déjeûners*, and introduce me to all the best matches of the season, as they call it; for, of course, Aunt Hanmer's real object is to get rid of Arthur. She hates him, first, because he is a Catholic; next, because he is Devonshire, which she thinks low and vulgar; and last, not least, because he has no title, and can't trace his ancestors very much further back than the Deluge. It never seems to occur to her, that on all three grounds she ought to hate me at least equally."

"But"—said Mrs. Trelawney, opening her eyes wide with astonishment.

Annie laughed merrily.

"But I am engaged to him, you mean, and it

would be so dishonourable, &c. &c.! Don't you know me better than that yet? Do you suppose all the aunts in the world, or all the rank and riches in the world put together, could make me give up Arthur? They may persecute me as much as they please, but they can't do *that;* and, happily, papa would no more do it than I would. He only wants to pacify Aunt Hanmer a little. But I mean to revenge myself in my own way, and play them some nice tricks. Arthur must be punished a little, too, for he is beginning to be horribly jealous already, in anticipation." She looked mischievously up in Mrs. Trelawney's face, as she added, "Do you think it is very wicked to flirt—just a little, you know? it would be such fun! I wouldn't do any thing very bad; I wouldn't really hurt any body for the world: so don't be frightened. I won't break any one's heart,—but so few people have hearts to break! There are plenty without the article, and I know I could make fools of them gloriously!"

Annie's eyes danced and sparkled with sheer merriment,—there was not the faintest gleam of passion or malice in them,—but she gave Mrs. Trelawney no time for her intended warning.

"I thought once," she said, "of trying experiments on Herbert Ellicombe; I don't think his heart would have suffered much. It is packed up in a box, and ticketed, 'Rome, with care.'"

"Annie!" exclaimed Mrs. Trelawney, quite aghast; but Annie was in wild spirits, and shook her head wilfully.

"Well, don't be shocked," she said; "I didn't do it, in the first place, heart or no heart. Her-

bert Ellicombe is rather too good to be trifled
with; and really, since he has put on armour, in
good earnest, for the Pope, I respect him too much
to play with him; besides, he rides such a tremendously high horse now, I can't reach up to
him. He seems to think himself a Crusader, or
a Knight of St. John, at the very least; and that
we, poor women, are not to be looked at, much
less spoken to. I wonder if he has made a vow
not to sheathe his sword till all the States of the
Church are restored to the Holy See, or not to
marry till he can offer Garibaldi's head as a *gage
d'amour* to his wife! It would be just like him;
he is terribly quixotic."

Mrs. Trelawney saw plainly that words would
be wasted on Annie just then, so she merely
said:

"Is he? He seemed to me, the only time I
ever saw him, to be just simply in earnest."

"Ah!" said Annie, rather suddenly sobering
down; "yes, I suppose he is. I wonder what
being just simply in earnest feels like; if *I* were
in earnest, I don't think it would be simply, but
furiously."

But here their roads parted, and they both
went their separate ways.

CHAPTER XXII.

*"For why? because the ancient rule
Sufficeth them: the simple plan,
That they should take who have the power,
And they should keep who can."*
Rob Roy.

IT so happened that Father Wilfrid had an opportunity that very day of enlightening Mr. Ellicombe with regard to the heroine of Helstone bog, for the embryo Zouave came to him for a little final direction before leaving England.

"Do you think I ought to call and inquire?" he asked, on hearing Maude's name and condition.

"Pray don't come to me for advice about etiquette and politeness," replied Father Wilfrid, laughing; "you ought to know the rules of society better than I do; but I certainly think it would be kind and neighbourly of you to call."

"And I think it would be quite proper, besides being kind and neighbourly; so I will do it. It looks detestably like asking to be thanked, but I suppose one must put up with the mortification."

"Take Rover with you, and turn the thanks over to him; he certainly deserves the lion's share, for having made the first discovery," said Father Wilfrid; "though, after all, the person who really took most trouble was Charley Crofton."

"Charley Crofton! why, what had he to do with it?" asked Mr. Ellicombe; and thereupon he was told the history of Charley's night-ride—told in a very matter-of-fact way—for Father Wilfrid, though he might be given to pointing morals, was by no means an adept at adorning tales. He never could understand what amusement people found in reading novels, and had actually once been heard to say that he didn't care about Shakespeare,—which candid expression of opinion earned him the unmitigated contempt of a devoted admirer of the great English dramatist, to whom it happened, unfortunately, to be addressed.

"Just like those Catholics!" he remarked afterwards at home to his family; "they are the most stupid, ignorant, ill-educated set of people on the face of the earth!"

Perhaps it did not occur to him that a priest had experience enough among real living characters, not to have much sympathy left for fictitious ones.

Mr. Ellicombe looked rather grave, as he listened; and said, when the story was ended:

"Then I suppose there is plenty of gossip rife in Stonebridge? Charley might as well have had the wits to leave his groom at home; those fellows never hold their tongues."

Father Wilfrid laughed, as he said:

"Yes, but I suppose we mustn't expect an old head on young shoulders. Master Charley's wits seem to have been concentrated on the idea of beating the whole of Dartmoor; and, on the supposition that there was any one to find, it was not such a bad idea, after all. As for gossip, I don't come in the way of hearing much of it; but I daresay there is, as you say, plenty. One old woman asked me, yesterday, if it was true that

Miss Trelawney had been riding late at night on the moor with Captain Ellicombe, and been run away with by her horse, instead of by him, and deposited in Helstone bog. But I soon set the old goody right. Very likely there may be other stories afloat; but, with nothing to support them, they will soon die a natural death."

But "Captain" Ellicombe did not seem inclined to take matters so quietly.

"How very disgusting!" he exclaimed. "What lie will they invent next! I never set up to be a model of perfection, but I don't know what I ever did to justify any one in thinking me a blackguard."

"Come, come; don't make mountains of molehills," said Father Wilfrid. "Your reputation is not so bad as to be injured by an old woman's tale; and I assure you Miss Trelawney is not the sort of person to care two straws about it: so it won't hurt her. For the rest, I expect most of us get credited some time or other with more than we ever gave any one reason to lay to our charge. I am not aware of having a particularly tyrannical disposition; but I should not be at all surprised to hear that Miss Trelawney had run away from her mother, because I was trying to force her into a convent against her will."

"And you would not care about it?"

"No more than if they said I had two heads or six legs, or any other palpable absurdity. Why should we care? Either what people say is true, or it isn't; if it is, we deserve it, and have no right to complain; if it isn't, it can't do us any harm."

"I don't know that," was the reply; "a calumny may do a great deal of harm."

"Yes, to those who invent and spread it; not to those who suffer it," answered Father Wilfrid quietly.

Possibly, something that had transpired in the earlier and more confidential part of their conversation gave a point to this remark, for it silenced Herbert Ellicombe at once; and he soon after took his departure.

As he rode through Stonebridge, closely followed by Rover, he noticed that many curious eyes were upon him; and he felt as if he would rather charge a whole regiment single-handed, than ring the bell at Mrs. North's private door, at that particular moment. But, perhaps, reflecting that cowardice, in any form, is disgraceful to a soldier, he jumped off his horse, and rang the bell with an energy that startled Mrs. Trelawney and Maude, as they sat pretending to sleep by the fire, "in the dimmets," between daylight and candle-light; and elicited a vigorous "Lawk a mussey!" from Hannah, who rushed to the door with a toasting-fork in her hand, by the help of which she was preparing the ladies' tea.

Wholly unconscious of the commotion he had excited, Mr. Ellicombe sent up his card to Mrs. Trelawney, with a polite message of inquiry for her and Maude, to which the reply was a request that he would come in, as the ladies would be very happy to see him. Consigning his horse, therefore, to the charge of a stray boy, and bidding Rover "wait,"—a word of command the animal perfectly understood,—he followed Hannah up-stairs; not, it must be confessed, wholly devoid of curiosity in respect of the woman whom he had carried for half a mile in his arms, but of whose personal appearance—except that she was a lady—he had very little idea.

Maude was a little stronger to-day, and succeeded, though with some difficulty, in standing up for a moment, as she put out her hand to him, and raised her eyes to his face. Perhaps she too was not altogether free from the weakness of curiosity in respect of her deliverer; but her voice failed her, and she left all verbal expression of gratitude to her mother.

But he quickly interrupted her thanks by disclaiming any credit for an act of ordinary humanity which he could not have left undone without being a brute, and which he would equally have performed for any old woman in the village; "though," he added, with a chivalrous impulse, which was a part of his nature, "I assure you I am most grateful myself to have had an opportunity of doing you any service. I only wish I had known better what to do. I am afraid Miss Trelawney must have suffered terribly from the cold, before we reached the farm."

"No, indeed, thank you," said Maude; "that was impossible; for I knew nothing and felt nothing, till the heat of the fire brought back my senses a little. I had no idea"—she stopped, for her head was weak, and she felt confused; what had she been going to say? She wanted him to understand that she had been quite unconscious of being touched or carried by any one. He knew that perfectly well; she need not have troubled herself. Mrs. Trelawney relieved her by coming to the rescue.

"Maude knew nothing of the care and kindness bestowed upon her till long afterwards," she said, "and she has been quite distressed to hear of all the trouble she gave."

"Then I wish she never had heard of it," was the prompt reply. "If nothing ever gives me more trouble than Miss Trelawney did, I shall have an easy life of it."

"I hope your dog was none the worse for his exertions; I should very much like to see him," said Maude; with a sudden, unaccountable feeling, that it would be easier to thank Rover than his master.

"Rover!—oh, he is all right, thank you; he is outside waiting for me. If you could come to the window, you would see him."

But Maude could not come to the window; and Mrs. Trelawney asked if Rover might not come in.

"He is so dirty—all over mud," Mr. Ellicombe said.

"Oh, never mind that," said Maude; "let him come in; he won't hurt any thing here."

"Very well; I am sure he is highly honoured," said Mr. Ellicombe,—and he went down to fetch Rover; causing him, however, to undergo a cleansing process, by means of a cloth borrowed from Hannah, before he brought him up-stairs. The moment he entered the room, he bounded upon Maude, with evident recognition; thereby nearly upsetting her, chair and all.

T

"Rover, you brute! lie down directly, sir," exclaimed Mr. Ellicombe. The dog hung down his ears and his tail, and obeyed; but evidently felt aggrieved at being scolded for so very innocent a manifestation of pleasure.

"Poor fellow!" said Maude, stooping down, and putting out her hand to him; whereupon, though afraid to get up after his master's reproof, he wriggled himself sufficiently near for her to pat his head. She opened a box on the work-table at her side, and, taking out a bit of red-velvet ribbon, tied it in a bow round his collar.

"There!" she said, "I have nothing else to give you." Then, turning to Mr. Ellicombe, she asked how soon he was going to Italy, and if Rover was to accompany him.

Now, Herbert had intended to avoid the subject of Italy altogether, for it was one on which he could hardly speak without showing something of the enthusiasm he felt; and Father Wilfrid's last words to him had been:

"Remember that Miss Trelawney is most likely a hot Garibaldian; and don't go off into the heroics about victories to be achieved in future by the gallant Zouaves, or the past glories of Castel Fidardo."

"I go early next week," he said. "Poor Rover!—no; I must leave him at home; he would hardly be acceptable as a camp-follower."

Hearing his name mentioned, the dog looked up and wagged his tail, and then, as if conscious that he had found a friend, curled himself round against Maude's footstool, and laid his head upon her feet.

Maude was not particularly fond of animals, and had never made a pet of one in her life; but perhaps she felt that a dog which had rescued her from great peril, if not from death, was an exceptional case, and she looked down at him, and smiled, as she said:

"I hope he will be well taken care of; you will be sorry to part from him?"

Herbert was on the point of saying that he was too eager to be gone, to care much what he left behind, but recollected himself just in time (perhaps Rover's scarlet bow reminded him of a red shirt), and, by way of an improvement on his first impulse, said:

"If you have any fancy for him, Miss Trelawney, I shall be happy to give him to you, and then I am sure he will be taken good care of; he seems inclined to put himself under your protection already. But I beg your pardon," he added, seeing that Maude made no sign of acquiescence; "of course he will only be a trouble to you,—he is not a lady's dog,—and he will be in very good quarters at Abbotsleigh."

What was the matter with Maude? She looked down at Rover, but said nothing. Mrs. Trelawney thought she saw the difficulty, and hastened to remove it by saying:

"If you would really like to leave Rover with us, Mr. Ellicombe, either Maude or I will be delighted to have the care of him during your absence. I have often wished for a dog; so if you think he will be happy here with us, it will be a great pleasure to us to have him."

Maude roused up now, and said:

"I shall consider him my special charge, M Ellicombe, and shall be ready to give him back to you whenever you return from your campaign. I don't think it will be a very long one."

"Don't you?" he said, smiling; "I think there seems every prospect that it will; there is little chance of surrender on either side."

"Surrender!" repeated Maude, firing up; "no; Garibaldi will never surrender."

"Neither shall we," said Mr. Ellicombe quietly.

"But you will be defeated—you *must* be; what can a mere handful of men, even if they were all as brave as Bayard, do against the united army of Italy?"

Well, if she *would* challenge him, it could not be helped; she must take the consequences,— which was precisely what she intended to do.

He tried hard, however, to restrain himself within moderate bounds, as he said:

"I fear, Miss Trelawney, you are much deceived in what you call the united army of Italy. I know a good soldier should never depreciate his enemies; but a set of bandits, renegades, and desperadoes of every sort can hardly be disciplined into a regular, and far less into a united, army. Garibaldi, though he may be—pardon me—a bold ruffian, is not an experienced general; and a small handful of men, with right on their side, and the blessing of God to help them, will be, I fully believe, more than a match for a whole horde of marauders, who fight on no principle but that of seizing by main force all that they can lay hands upon, and of utterly subverting all order and authority." :

To Mrs. Trelawney's astonishment, Maude betrayed no indignation at this slight to her favourite hero, but answered, with great quietness :

"Do you mean to say that you really and seriously believe that any power on earth can save the temporal authority of the Pope ?"

She had fairly thrown down the gauntlet now, and he was not going to let it lie on the ground ; but he spoke briefly,—for argument would have been out of place.

"No, Miss Trelawney," he said, "I do *not* think that any earthly power can save it—if it depends on that alone, it is doomed ; but I believe that God can save it, and that He will save it ; and whether the human instruments that He uses are weak or strong can signify very little, for they act in His strength, and not in their own."

"And you have faith enough in your cause to risk your life for it ?"

"To *risk* my life for it !" he repeated, no longer attempting to restrain himself. "I would gladly, thankfully, *give* my life, and every hope I have in life, for it."

There was a bright, unearthly gleam in his eyes, and a tremulousness in his voice, which was evidently not that of doubt or indecision, but of strong suppressed emotion. Mrs. Trelawney looked nervously at him ; she feared the effect on Maude. But Maude herself, to her mother's extreme astonishment, raised her eyes to meet his, with an expression of ardent admiration and sympathy.

Had he worked a sudden revolution of her whole being, simply by his eye and his voice? Such things have been; for only too true is it for their own peace, that

"Some fall in love with voices, some with eyes;"

but such was not the case with Maude: she was not so easily overcome; and if Herbert Ellicombe thought that her sympathy was given to the cause he had advocated, he never was more mistaken in his life. Maude was as *Italianissima* at heart as ever, but her whole soul went out to meet real, true enthusiasm wherever she found it; it was an instinct of her nature; she could not help it. In theory she was as fierce a Covenanter as Habakuk Mucklewrath himself, and yet one of her favourite heroes was "that de'il o' Dundee," as he rode out of the gates of Edinburgh to his mad self-sacrifice at Killiecrankie. In theory she was a Puritan, a Cromwellite, and hated the "malignants;" and yet she could not choose but admire that bold "Rupert of the Rhine," who, as a modern historian tersely says, "always won *his part* of the battle." Was she inconsistent? Was there a single English soldier, officer or private, in the Crimean army, who did not gaze with pride and admiration on that memorable light-cavalry charge at Balaclava? And yet did not every one of them know that it was a mad, reckless, senseless infatuation; that Canrobert characterised it truly when he said: "C'est magnifique, mais ce n'est pas la guerre"?

Enthusiasm, even in a bad cause, is apt to be infectious; but when it speaks in the highest and holiest of all causes, it has an inherent power of attraction which is irresistible to such a mind as Maude Trelawney's.

But her sympathy was with Herbert himself, not with his cause—no, not for a moment—she had not even the very smallest grain of sympathy with it; she looked upon him as the victim of a "magnificent error," an infatuated and fatal delusion; she could not despise him for it: he was too real and genuine an enthusiast for her contempt; but she did what was hardly less flattering, and much more dangerous—she pitied him.

She did not long give him the chance of misunderstanding her look; for she said, after a moment's pause:

"It seems very hard that so much zeal should be wasted on a hopeless cause."

"I see I cannot convince you," he said, rising to go; "but at all events, if we are enemies, let us sign a truce till our next meeting; by that time either the Garibaldians will have plundered and sacked Rome, or we shall have rescued her from the hands of the most unprincipled and determined robbers in the world, as they will soon prove themselves to be even to you. Meanwhile, can we agree upon the subject of Rover?"

Maude had sunk back into her chair, looking wearied: she felt too physically weak to contend with him, and, but for this direct question, would not have answered him at all. She roused herself now sufficiently to say:

"I hope so; but it rests with you: I shall be delighted to have the care of him."

"Very well," replied Mr. Ellicombe; "then I will send him and his kennel too next Tuesday, if that will suit you. I must really say good bye now: it is quite late."

And five minutes later he was trotting fast up the sunk fence, with Rover (scarlet bow and all) scampering on in front.

Maude was very silent all the rest of the evening, and obstinately refused to take her sleeping-draught at night, saying she "could rest better awake."

CHAPTER XXIII.

"Oh, let no wind wake up for other ears
   The sad confessions trusted to thy keeping;
But, by the Cross that pardons, and the tears
   That win us grace, dear mountain, leave them sleeping."
                              F. W. FABER.

ANNIE CROFTON did not forget her offer of taking Maude for a drive when she should be strong enough; but, after her unlucky speeches on that first day, she felt a little shy of calling again. She had proposed her plan about the school to Father Wilfrid, and obtained his sanction for it: so that matter was settled; and as Maude seemed rapidly recovering, though she still continued weaker than could quite satisfactorily be accounted for, the time was fast approaching for her removal to Teignmouth—that place having been finally agreed upon, as being less hilly, and consequently less fatiguing, than Torquay.

Father Wilfrid had not called again; and she had expressed no wish to see him, or, indeed, to see any one; she had become more silent and reserved than ever, and always seemed happiest alone; so that Mrs. Trelawney began to feel free to go a little oftener to the church. She strongly suspected that Maude read many things when thus left to herself that she would not have cared to acknowledge taking any interest in; but her grounds for this supposition would certainly have been rejected as evidence in any court, civil or ecclesiastical, seeing that they consisted chiefly in the fact that Maude would read *nothing* when she was at home, and always said it tired her. How this could be construed into a proof that she did read when her mother was out, Mrs. Trelawney best knew.

Except that strange, sudden inquiry about black Masses, Maude had never asked a single question, or expressed the very slightest interest or curiosity about any thing; and the only person who had reason to think she had felt any was Father Wilfrid: but whether or not she knew that he was aware of her stolen visit to the church on the morning of the Helstone-bog disaster, he had no means of ascertaining; neither could he know whether she had any desire to repeat her visit, as it was of course now impossible for her to do so. Had he been able to read her thoughts, he would, with all his experience of human nature, have been a little astonished; for it was neither interest nor curiosity that had actuated her on that day, but a very much less creditable motive—a motive, however, which in itself betokened so very morbid a state of mind, that perhaps she ought hardly to be held morally responsible for it. Hating the Catholic faith, and even, with the exception of her mother, all who professed it, with a fierce, bitter hatred, as having been the cause of her father's sufferings and death, she yet was profoundly ignorant both of its principles and practices, and consequently found herself in the illogical position of being utterly unable to give a reason even to her own mind for the hatred that was in her, except the merely personal one, which of course was worth nothing as an argument. She had found the inconvenience of this lately on more than one occasion, when hard pressed to account for the harsh bigotry which even most of her Protestant friends thought extravagant and uncharitable; and once she had even been reduced to the humiliating confession, that she did not in the least know what was either said, done, or taught in Catholic churches, as she had never been inside one in her life. As a matter of choice or taste, she would as soon have gone inside a gin-palace; but she had come latterly to the conclusion, that this particular form of indulging her disgust was a mistake, and that it would be wiser to convince herself by means of oral and ocular proof that there was sufficient cause for her hatred, and that her disgust had a *raison d'être*. It never so much as glanced across her mind for the minutest portion of a second, that there was a possibility of any other result; she *wanted* to be disgusted with whatever she might see or hear, and she felt absolutely certain that she should be ; how could it be otherwise, with a set of senseless and absurd ceremonies, performed by fantastically dressed priests, and accompanied by a jargon of monkish Latin (which, by the way, Maude had a special and separate contempt for, as being vulgar and unclassical)? These things could have but one effect, and therefore she felt no interest or curiosity about them,— only, it would be a satisfaction as well as a convenience to know by proof that she had a right to hate her mother's religion. Her mother's religion! Yes; after all, that was the head and front of its offending, that it had beguiled and cast its deceitful glamour over her mother. At the bottom of her heart, Maude had an uneasy suspicion that she had done wrong in separating from her mother; and yet the pain of living with her, under circumstances which shut out all sympathy between them, was so great, that she could not school herself to endure it. She wanted, therefore, to justify her conduct to her own restless conscience; she wanted to see with her eyes and hear with her ears that her mother was enslaved to a degrading superstition, which every enlightened Christian ought to abhor, abominate, and fly from. She came to Stonebridge with the determination to accomplish this purpose,—to see, to hear, to read all that she possibly could,—but also with the further determination to do it secretly and cautiously; not for all the world would she have let her most intimate friend suspect that she was " examining" the Catholic religion, even with such very strictly Protestant intentions : in fact, she really had the grace to be just a little ashamed of herself; and had she not been, as we have said, in a thoroughly morbid state of mind, she would have been a great deal too much ashamed of her plan to prosecute it at all. That she did begin to prosecute it, however, we have seen, and also with what immediate results; the ultimate consequences will perhaps reveal themselves later. The Helstone episode had frustrated any further direct pursuance of it for a time, and also complicated matters by putting her under personal obligation to a priest; for though it had the advantage of bringing her into closer intercourse with him than she would otherwise have endured, even to gain her own object, the commonest gratitude makes it a little difficult to feel unmitigated aversion for a man who has been instrumental in saving one's life. Let Father Wilfrid be what he might, Maude could never again with full consciousness repeat the look she had bestowed upon him in Helstone Farm. She might still think him every thing that was bad, every thing that was contemptible, but she could not altogether hate him; and, perhaps for that very reason, she shrank from seeing him again. Did she hate Herbert Ellicombe? He was not a priest, certainly, but he was something almost as bad — a papal Zouave; he had saved her life, it was true, but only as he would have saved that of any stranger whom accident had thrown across his path: whereas Father Wilfrid had recognised her, which made the obligation more personal. On her own principles, she ought to have detested Mr. Ellicombe; but — alas for the inconsistency of human nature!—she did not even dislike him. Instead of hating him for his zeal in the Pope's cause, she only pitied him for it,—and pity is said to bear a dangerous approximation to another feeling; but perhaps there are exceptions to that rule: at all events, Maude would have indignantly denied the very possibility of any warmer feeling than pity for a Zouave.

Nor did she express even that feeling; for, after his visit, Herbert Ellicombe's name never crossed her lips. On the following Tuesday, according to promise, a servant brought Rover's kennel in a dog-cart, accompanied by the animal himself, still wearing (Maude noticed that) the scarlet ribbon, though its brightness was considerably tarnished. The man said his master had left for London that morning, and proceeded to give Maude, who listened with amusing gravity, various directions with regard to the food and general treatment to which Rover had been accustomed; finally leaving the dog chained to his kennel in the yard behind Mrs. North's house, where he soon began to howl dismally, as was only natural.

"Poor fellow!" said Maude; "of course he won't be happy till he knows us a little, and feels at home. Do you mind having him in the house for a little while, mamma?"

Mrs. Trelawney did not object; and Rover was accordingly admitted as a drawing-room guest for the remainder of the day, where his behaviour was so unexceptionable, that he was subsequently allowed to spend his evenings habitually there, though the kennel was his home during the night and daytime, except when taken out for a walk.

He seemed to attach himself at once to Maude, who always took him his food herself; and amazed her mother greatly, the third day after he came, by asking if Catholics allowed their dogs to eat meat on Fridays. Though assured that not to do so would be an absurd scruple, Mrs. Trelawney noticed, with some surprise, that Rover's Friday dinner never contained the smallest portion of animal food. Whether the dog himself appreciated this delicate attention may perhaps be doubted; as, also, whether he understood Maude's explanation of it, when, on the first Friday, she patted his head, as she put down his plate, and said:

"There, doggie, you must not disgrace your master and turn Protestant. You haven't got a soul—so it can't hurt *you* to be a Catholic."

This speech was certainly only intended for Rover's private edification; and, unless he found some means of repeating it, no one else was likely to be the wiser.

Towards the end of that week, Maude being now sufficiently recovered to venture upon a drive, a note came from Annie one fine, bright morning, to say that, if the day suited them, she would send the carriage at two o'clock; and begged that Mrs. Trelawney and Maude would make what use they liked of it. She had fully intended coming herself; but her courage failed her at the last moment: "For, if I make a fool of myself in the carriage, I can't jump up and run away, as I did in the house," she thought; "and, besides, I daresay they would rather go by themselves, and do what they like:" in which supposition she was perfectly correct.

Maude, who had been particularly listless and idle all the morning, roused up and seemed pleased at the thought of a drive. So the offer of the carriage was gratefully accepted.

"Do you care where we go, mamma?" said Maude.

Mrs. Trelawney had no choice — all roads were alike to her; and Maude proposed that they should go to Helstone Farm, saying that she had not yet had an opportunity of thanking good Betty Luscombe for all her kind offices "that night."

Betty had been abundantly both thanked and rewarded; but it certainly was a natural feeling on Maude's part; and, though Mrs. Trelawney was a little afraid of any thing that recalled the scenes of that night to her mind, the only objection she could reasonably make was, that the road was a very rough one for a gentleman's carriage. Maude laughed.

"Do people keep London carriages and horses here, then?" she said; "it is very foolish of them if they do. Well, never mind; if Miss Crofton sends an elegant landau, with a pair of spanking blood-bays, we will drive in state on the Exeter turnpike-road, and hire a fly some other day to go to Helstone."

But Annie was not such a goose. When her father had first proposed to keep a carriage for her that would be fit for night- as well as day-work, she had said:

"I don't see what I want it for, papa; we sha'n't often go out to dinner; and, when we do, I would much rather put on a coachman's great-

coat and go in the phaeton, if it rains ever so hard,
than be boxed up in a nasty close carriage."

But Mr. Crofton did not approve of this plan:
perhaps he thought a coachman's great-coat would
not benefit her evening dresses; and, finding that
he really insisted upon it, Annie contented herself with stipulating that the said carriage should
be "strong enough for any thing," and drawn by
Devonshire horses, who would stick at nothing
in the shape of either steepness or roughness.

"I should like," she said, "to have horses that
will trot down Berrynarbor Hill without the drag
on;" and any one who ever saw Berrynarbor
Hill will appreciate the force of the expression.

Accordingly, at two o'clock, a strongly built
brougham, drawn by a pair of small, sturdy
brown cobs, appeared at Mrs. North's door, and
both Mrs. Trelawney and Maude were at once
aware that they might drive not only to Helstone
Farm, but to the very edge of Helstone bog, if
they pleased, without any fear of injury to Mr.
Crofton's equipage. To say the truth, Annie had
had a shrewd suspicion that they would drive on
some part of Dartmoor, and had specially charged
the coachman not to frighten the ladies with any
nonsense about rough roads, in case they should
propose it.

"You know very well, Deane," she said, "that
you delight in deluding people into the idea that
a road is dangerous, just to get more credit for
driving them safely over it. Miss Trelawney has
been very ill, and I will not have her frightened
by any such nonsense; so, if you are ordered to
drive down the quarry-road, just do it, and say

nothing about it; the horses have done it safely enough before."

"Ay, sure, ma'am," replied Deane, his pride in his horses roused by Annie's concluding words; "them 'osses would take you safe down Botallack Mine:" rather a bold assertion, which he would probably have declined to put to the proof; but, then, it must be taken into consideration, that there was not the smallest chance of his ever being called upon to do so.

On this occasion he was not even called upon to drive down the quarry-road, the direction he received in reply to his:

"Where to, if you please, ma'am?" being:

"To Helstone Farm."

"And that be a bad road, sure enough, too!" thought the man; but, after Annie's caution, he did not venture to make any remonstrance.

There was a little debate as to whether Rover was sufficiently at home with them to follow the carriage, but his own strongly expressed desire to be let loose carried the day, and the coachman promised to keep an eye upon him; but he gave no trouble, and kept always well in sight.

When they were fairly on the moor, Maude put down the window, and leaned out, taking a long breath of the pure mountain-air, and also, if the truth must be owned, trying to discover the whereabouts of the famous bog,—for she had not really the remotest idea how far she had wandered on that memorable evening.

The rough, stony road seemed to stretch farther and farther, and higher and higher, interminably; and at last, in utter consternation at the distance

U

(though it was really scarcely three miles), she asked how much farther it was to Helstone.

"Just handy by now, miss," said Deane; "down yonder's the bog;" and he pointed with his whip towards a hollow on their left hand.

"How near does the road go to it?" asked Maude.

Within about a quarter of a mile, it appeared; but the obliging Deane suggested that, the ground being now tolerably hard by reason of a frost, it would be easy to drive over the turf to within about a hundred yards, if the ladies pleased.

"No, thank you," said Mrs. Trelawney; "we can see quite enough from the road:" but, to her astonishment, Maude said very quietly:

"If you please, mamma, I lost a ring there, and I should like to look for it,—if there really would be no difficulty," she continued, addressing herself to the coachman, "in driving as near as you said."

"Never fear, ma'am," returned that worthy, rather flattered with the idea that he, too, was going to have a finger in the pie which had supplied food to the gossip of Stonebridge for the last ten days.

"You can't possibly walk into the bog to look for your ring, Maude," said Mrs. Trelawney; "and you would have little chance of finding it if you could,—it is sure to have been seen and picked up by some of the curious people who have been to look at the place you have made so notorious."

It was an unlucky speech, as she felt the moment it was too late to recall her words: all gossiping tales had been, of course, carefully kept from Maude, and she had never realised *this* consequence of her imprudence.

"That *I* have made notorious!" she repeated. "Do you mean that people talk about me, and make up stories about me? For goodness' sake, let us go to Teignmouth, or any where else, out of their way, as fast as we can; I am quite well enough to travel now."

Mrs. Trelawney had some difficulty in quieting her; and, in fact, was obliged to represent Charley's expedition as the great event of the night in the Stonebridge estimation—which was not altogether untrue.

"That boy will make an awful fool of himself some day," said Maude, by way of reply; "but it won't be my fault: I'm sure I did my best to snub him."

By this time they had reached the farthest point to which the carriage could venture; and Deane, dismounting from the box, presented himself at the window to signify the same to the ladies.

"Let me out, please," said Maude.

Mrs. Trelawney laid her hand on her arm, and looked imploringly at her; but Maude only said:

"Let me go; I shall be back in five minutes;" and jumped out on the spongy turf, which was only slightly crusted over by the frost.

Mrs. Trelawney felt instinctively that she must not follow her; but she also got out of the carriage, and watched her anxiously, ready to fly to the rescue at the first sign of danger—for not only was the ground very unsafe, but Maude was very weak. She seemed, however, wonderfully clever at picking her way; or perhaps the credit is due to Rover, who, seeming to divine her intention, or having some private speculation of his own on the subject, made his way, by the firmest path he could find, straight for the point where he had first discovered Maude, who now followed him; but, on reaching the last piece of solid footing, instead of looking for her ring, she appeared to leave that task to the dog, who groped and scratched with all his might, and stood gazing fixedly up at Hillsborough Tor, which rose up against the sky some four or five miles off. She was presently interrupted in this occupation by Rover, who had found something which he came in great delight to show her,—not her ring, but a narrow, soft, shepherd's-plaid necktie. Mr. Ellicombe must have dropped it there. Maude stooped down, and took it from the dog's mouth.

"Good Rover!" she said, patting him; and rolling up the dirty little scarf into a ball, she put it in her pocket.

She then stooped down, and let her eye run over the surface of the bog; but no ring was to be seen, and it was impossible to search more thoroughly.

She came back to the carriage, and, merely saying,

"I cannot see it," got in, and they proceeded to the farm.

On arriving there, the first thing they saw was Father Wilfrid's pony tied up at the gate;

he had come to see how old John's rheumatism was getting on.

Maude looked annoyed; what business had he *dans cette galère?* Quite as much as she had, probably; but that was not the point.

The consequence was, that she would not get out of the carriage, but spoke to Betty at the window for a few minutes, and then begged to be taken home.

CHAPTER XXIV.

> " More changes still! and are good hearts like thine
> Bound by the ebbs and flows of common life?
> Ah, yes, full many a mark and random line
> Show where the world has marred thee with its strife."
> F. W. FABER.

MAUDE and her mother were gone to Teignmouth, and Father Wilfrid had never seen Maude again. It would have been impossible for her to have gone again to the church unperceived; and when he had called, the day before their departure, to say good bye, only Mrs. Trelawney made her appearance, bringing a message from Maude that she had a very severe headache, and begged he would excuse her.

"I am very unhappy about Maude," Mrs. Trelawney said; "she starts and screams frightfully in her sleep, and complains that she never gets any rest; but she will not take opiates,—and, indeed, she was worse when she did take them, so I do not press her."

"Her nerves are unstrung," said Father Wilfrid; "it will require time to restore them to a natural state."

"Perhaps," said Mrs. Trelawney; but she was evidently not satisfied with the explanation: nor did Father Wilfrid, in his heart, think that it accounted adequately for the sort of mixed restlessness and languor of Maude's condition. She seemed to have the greatest possible dread of going to sleep, and often, when evidently quite wearied out, would try to rouse herself by talking, or working, or walking up and down the room; but when not feeling tired or sleepy, she would sit gazing dreamily into the fire for hours, saying nothing and doing nothing. She would neither read (at all events, not in her mother's presence), nor be read to; and as for writing, she left even the necessary task of asking for further leave of absence from the Vivians to her mother.

Mrs. Trelawney believed that she sat up during a great part of the night, for she often heard her poking her fire, and moving about in the room; but as Maude always locked her door, she had no direct means of ascertaining this. Neither had she the smallest idea what were the contents of a square box which stood on her table, and of which the key was never to be seen any where. It was a small fireproof box, in which her father had been accustomed to keep important papers.

To all this Father Wilfrid listened attentively; but he could only suggest that, as Dr. Wilson had recommended, change of air and scene should be tried without loss of time; perhaps an entirely new place, devoid of all associations, might give Maude the rest she evidently so much needed.

"You will bring her back here afterwards?" he said.

"If she will come, certainly," replied Mrs. Trelawney; "but I cannot answer for it: she may be anxious to get back to Miss Vivian as soon as she is well enough."

"She must come here on her way, at all events," said Father Wilfrid decisively, and so pointedly, that Mrs. Trelawney did not venture to remind him that Stonebridge was very considerably *out* of the way from Teignmouth to Carew Castle. Perhaps he had not a topographical turn of mind; it was not worth while to discuss the point just then.

So, one bright, clear, frosty morning, Mr. Crofton's carriage, which Annie had insisted on sending, took them to the Stonebridge Station, *en route* for Exeter and Teignmouth. The schoolchildren wept over the departure of their mistress, to whom they had all become devotedly attached, and Annie Crofton reigned in her stead, feeling uncomfortably conscious of her disadvantageous position; for, though the children all liked her, she was quite aware that her authority over them was very insignificant, compared with Mrs. Trelawney's.

To her great relief, Father Wilfrid came almost every day, and heard sometimes one class, and sometimes another, himself; and though Annie did tell him that she knew he only did it because he could not trust her to keep order, and that it was both an insult and a "tremendous mortification," she was glad enough of the help and support.

She had told him of her prospects for the spring, and of her disgust at the whole affair; but she had not "advised herself," as the French say, to ask him, as she had asked Mrs. Trelawney, if he thought it would be very wicked to flirt, "just a little, you know."

In the first place, she knew very well beforehand what his answer would be, and, in the next, "What could he possibly know about it? *he* had never played naughty tricks, not even *just a little*, —of course not! Were not priests always brought up in seminaries from the time they were six years old, and never allowed even to know of the existence of such a questionable amusement as flirting? They might hear plenty about it afterwards, to be sure, but that was different."

It so happened that Annie's facts as well as her arguments were at fault in this case, for Father Wilfrid had not been originally educated as a priest, but as a merchant; and it was not till after his twenty-first year, that, being seized with a disgust for the calculating, money-making spirit of mercantile life, he had, like the seraphic St. Francis, thrown all his worldly prospects and earthly ties and affections overboard (all that these latter included, only himself knew), and betaken himself to the Benedictine monastery of Subiaco, in Italy; whence, after a few years of study and discipline, he had been sent back to England as a missionary priest, with the black mantle and hood of St. Benedict, and the red scarf girding his cassock, which is the missionary's declaration of readiness for martyrdom. But he never spoke of his early life; and, for all Annie knew, he might have been brought up at Subiaco from the time he was six years old.

Perhaps, however, if she had enlightened him with regard to her intentions of "paying off" Aunt Hanmer, he might have found rather more to say than she expected on the subject.

As it was, she only said:

"The whole thing is an unmitigated nuisance; but I shall try to get a little amusement out of it if I can;" by which he innocently supposed her to mean that she would try to enjoy the balls, operas, &c., in spite of her dislike to them, and replied:

"Well, my child, enjoy yourself if you can,— I am not afraid of your getting too fond of dissipation; but the opera, did you say?—shall you go there?"

"I suppose so," said Annie; "why? do you object to it?"

"Very much," he said, "as a matter of private opinion; but I have no right to forbid you to go: it is not a sin, unless special circumstances make it so. I don't think it is likely to do you any harm; but I am sorry you should go to it; even at the best, I think it must blunt the delicacy of a sensitive conscience."

Annie looked at him with wide-open eyes.

"I have not the very remotest idea what you mean," she said, "and I'm sure I have not a sensitive conscience, as *you* ought to know well enough; however, if you don't like me to go to the opera, I won't; I don't care much about it: so don't imagine I am making a martyr of myself."

It had been Mrs. Hanmer's wish to have Annie

with her in London, where she inhabited a large and splendidly furnished house in Grosvenor Square; but Annie had absolutely refused to give in her adhesion to the London plan at all, unless her father would go with her; and, for various reasons, the Hanmers did not choose to include him in their invitation. Consequently, as Annie stoutly objected to lodgings, Mr. Crofton engaged rooms for her and himself at the Great Western Hotel; and thither they betook themselves about the middle of April: "a month too late," Mrs. Hanmer said; but she could by no means persuade them to come before Easter.

Arthur Hatton was half wild at the idea of Annie being "let loose upon London," as he called it; but she only laughed, and told him it was not very flattering to be spoken of as if she were a wild beast, and that if he provoked her too much, he might find she could scratch. He would have gone, too, to mount guard upon her; but he was too good a son to leave his mother in solitude at Stinchcombe, and a London season would have been a very purgatory to Mrs. Hatton.

Before Annie had been two days in London, she found herself drawn into a perfect whirlpool of gaieties of all kinds; and it was greatly to her credit that, in spite of late hours and weary limbs, she always contrived to get to the eight-o'clock Mass at the Rosary Chapel, which was only five minutes' walk from the hotel.

One Friday evening, having, for a marvel, no engagement, she persuaded her father to take her to the sermon and Benediction at Bayswater; the discourse happened to be an energetic exposition and denunciation of worldliness in all its forms, flirting included, though not, of course, exactly under that name.

Annie went to bed early that night, saying that the church was insufferably hot, and had made her feel faint; and the next morning, for the first (and, we are bound to add, also the last) time, she missed going to Mass.

She had denied the possession of a sensitive conscience, so how could the sermon have affected her? Not according to its intention, certainly, for it did her harm instead of good; but, to explain this, we must go back for a few days. She had been now for nearly a fortnight launched on the full tide of London society; and though she had been half disgusted and half amused at its unreality and conventionalism, the constant whirl was beginning to tell upon her in the shape of a feverish excitement which supplied the place of pleasure, and made her eager in plunging into every gaiety that offered itself: she did, in fact, really and genuinely enjoy many things to which she had looked forward as simple nuisances; and notably she enjoyed dancing, at Mrs. Hanmer's very select evening parties, with a certain Colonel Blount, who kept time and step to perfection, and always knew exactly how to find his partner the very seat she wished to occupy, and when to offer her an ice; and riding in Rotten Row between her father and the same gallant colonel, who rode a fiery chestnut charger, which Annie was never tired of admiring, till one day he offered to have it trained to carry a lady, if she would accept it; and Mr. Crofton, leaning across Annie, said, rather coldly, that he was much obliged, but he could not think of allowing such a thing; and that evening Annie received a mild curtain-lecture (Mr. Crofton could never be really angry with her), to the effect that she must be more prudent in her manners and conversation with gentlemen; whereat she only pouted her lip, and said she could take very good care of herself. She had the bit fairly between her teeth now, and was determined to have her own way.

God only knew from how much of evil she was preserved by her regular frequentation of the Sacraments, and daily attendance at Mass; for, after all, she was only thoughtless and childish—she meant no harm, she did no actual harm; she only exposed herself to danger and to misconstruction, partly from ignorance, partly from that utter disregard of consequences which was a part of her character.

Robert Hatton—who, of course, saw a good deal of her in London—was pained and troubled by what seemed to him an unbecoming levity of conduct in an already affianced wife; and though, for many reasons, he shrank from the least appearance of interfering, he did venture once to suggest to Annie, that Arthur might be vexed if any rumours reached him of Colonel Blount's constant attendance upon her; but she had replied, very sharply, that if Arthur could not trust her, he had better come and take care of her himself, and that she had a right to amuse herself as she pleased. Robert said no more, but he did his best negatively, by occupying Annie's attention himself as much as he could, by providing her with other partners at the balls (he never danced himself), and by contriving to be almost always one of the riding-party. The amount of suffering he thus entailed upon himself would have scared Annie, had she known it; but she was in blissful ignorance on that, as well as on some other points. Robert's letters to his brother occasionally contained such words as, "I wish you could run up to town for a few days;" or, "Annie is very much admired; I hope she is proof against flattery;" which—taken together with Annie's own hurried scrawls, always written just when she "must run and put her habit on, as the horses were waiting;" or, they were "just starting with a delightful party for one of those charming Saturday concerts at the Crystal Palace"—made Arthur echo his brother's wish that he could run up for a few days to town, and judge with his own eyes of what was going on; and, in fact, he had very nearly made up his mind to do so.

Things were in this state, when Annie—who was now accustomed, night after night, to the stifling atmosphere of a crowded London drawing-room—found the church at Bayswater so "insufferably hot," that, instead of the hour's comfortable chat with her father which he had looked forward to on their return to the hotel, she pleaded the conventional headache—which does duty for so many other aches, bodily and mental—and, after pouring out his tea, retired to her own room.

A riding-party had been arranged for the following day; and, as Annie had expressed a desire for "a breath of country air, to take out the taste of London smoke," it had been agreed to go to Harrow, and get a good blow on the top of the hill. The party was to consist of Mr. Crofton and Annie, Robert and Colonel Blount.

What connection there was between this arrangement and certain words that she had heard that evening at St. Mary of the Angels', we will not pretend to explain; but certain it was, that Annie's last thought that night was:

"Well, perhaps it will be a wet day, and then we can't go; and that will settle every thing comfortably."

But, instead of being a wet day, it was brilliantly fine; and, soon after three o'clock, Annie, resting her little foot for a moment on her father's hand, sprang lightly into her saddle. Colonel Blount's chestnut pirouetted on the pavement, exciting the terror of a little girl and the wrath of a policeman; Mr. Crofton and Robert mounted their respective steeds, and the whole party rode off at a brisk trot up Eastbourne Terrace, over the Bishop's-Road bridge, and turned down the Harrow Road. Through Kensal Green, past the Cemetery, and on to Harlesdon Green, they trotted and cantered; and then Annie declared that it was much too hot to ride so fast, and slackened her pace to a walk; Colonel Blount did the same, and for a moment they were alone, as the other two riders were a few yards ahead.

"I want to show you the cricket-ground," he said; "and there's sure to be a match going on to-day—it's a half-holiday; it will not be much out of our way going home, only it is a steepish hill down to it. Shall you mind that?"

Annie laughed, as she said:

"I don't believe in steep hills out of Devonshire; I should like to see what you mean by a steepish hill. Let us go, by all means."

By this time the others had joined them, and no more was said.

As they drew rein by the white railings at the foot of Harrow Hill, Annie turned to Colonel Blount and said:

"Do you call *this* a hill? It would be good trotting-ground at Stonebridge."

"Wait till you see Hog Lane," he replied.

"Hog Lane!" exclaimed Mr. Crofton; "it does not sound a tempting locality."

"Oh, but that is only its name in the vulgar tongue," said Colonel Blount; "it was originally Hogarth Street, and I believe it is now called, in polite language, Crown Street, or some such name; but it was Hog Lane when I was a boy, and I never call it any thing else."

"Is *every thing* the same to you now that it was when you were a boy?" asked Annie, with a bewitching little smile.

He returned it by a look which brought the colour into her cheeks, though she hardly knew why, as he said:

"No, Miss Crofton; when I was a boy, I had no higher aspirations than cricket and football; *now* I have a higher ambition than to be head of the school eleven."

Her good angel surely befriended Annie at that moment, or, for very mischief, she would have led him on. Or perhaps a recollection of something she had heard (and resented the evening before, swept over her mind; at all events, she struck her horse lightly with the whip, and cantered on without making any reply, till they came to the "King's Head," where she looked up at the signboard, shook her whip at it, and said :

"O you horrid old monster! shouldn't I like to tear you down, and trample you in the dust! Is Henry VIII. the patron saint of Harrow, Colonel Blount?"

"Not exactly, I think," he said, laughing; "we have Cardinal Wolsey's farm two miles farther on; perhaps that would suit you better for a halting-place?"

But the two miles farther on were a serious objection, even had there been no other; so they left their horses to bait, and walked on to the school and churchyard, school-chapel, library, and new racket-courts.

"What a glorious Catholic college it would make!" exclaimed Robert; "there is every thing here except the *life;* it is a body without a soul!"

"Ah!" said Colonel Blount, rather contemptuously,—he was a Broad-Church Protestant,— "don't you wish you may get it! Not much chance for you, I fancy; and as for *life*, there's plenty of it here, as you shall see directly in the cricket-ground."

Robert did not care to begin a useless discussion; and as the horses, which had been ordered to meet them at the library, were now waiting, they mounted, and turned homewards;

but on arriving at the top of "Hog Lane," Colonel Blount said, pointing to it:

"Is *that* a hill, Miss Crofton? Will you trust your horse down it?"

There seemed no question on that point, for the whole party turned down the steep, stony hill; so Annie only said:

"If you ever come to Stonebridge, Colonel Blount, we will show you the quarry-road; I don't think you will care to trust your beautiful chestnut down that."

"I will trust myself any where, if you lead the way," was the reply, spoken so low that only Annie distinctly heard it; and a little flash of triumph lighted up her eyes. But there was no fear, no misgiving; she thought herself quite secure, and at liberty to amuse herself to any extent within the limits of her chain. She supposed, too, that Colonel Blount knew of her engagement, and would respect it—poor little, innocent Annie! —but in this she was mistaken, for Mrs. Hanmer had taken very good care that he should know nothing of the kind; he was heir to a baronetcy and a large fortune.

They stood for some time at the bottom of the cricket-ground, watching the game, till Robert's horse began to grow restive, and he said he would ride on: "Up the National-School hill, I suppose?" he said; he had often been at Harrow before, and knew his way.

"I only want to wait till we see how many more runs that boy gets," said Annie; "we will follow you as soon as his wicket is down."

But the runs seemed interminable, and the

wicket stood as firm as a rock; and presently Mr. Crofton moved off, saying he was tired of waiting, and would catch up Robert; they would wait at the top of the hill for Annie and Colonel Blount, who could ride on faster after them.

What was he thinking of? He seemed for the moment to have forgotten who was Annie's companion, or perhaps he thought that five minutes were of no great consequence; any how, he rode on.

For a few moments Colonel Blount was thoughtful and silent; he was going to make a desperate plunge, without feeling quite sure of his ground; just as he was about to speak, down went the wicket.

"Seventy-four runs!" exclaimed Annie; "did you ever see any thing like it! But now *we* must run;" and she shook her rein.

"One moment, Miss Crofton," he said; and she subsided to a walking-pace, rather wondering what was to come next. What did come next was a hurried, eager, impassioned offer of his "hand and heart," which fairly took her breath away with astonishment and indignation. Flashing upon him eyes scorching with anger, she exclaimed:

"How dare you insult me so!" and, without adding a word of explanation, she struck her horse sharply on the shoulder, and tore up the hill at a mad pace, dashing past her father and Robert, who were waiting quietly at the top; but as soon as she could check her horse, she wheeled round and joined them.

"Why, Annie!" said Mr. Crofton, "has that brute run away with you?"

"Very nearly, I think," said Annie, speaking now quite coolly; "something started him off."

"And where is the gallant Colonel?"

"I don't know; behind me, I suppose."

But he did not appear, having in fact fought shy of rejoining the party, and gone round by Northolt, Greenford, Perivale, and Acton.

"Never mind him," said Annie; "he told me there was another road; I suppose he has taken it."

"H'm! very odd of him," said Mr. Crofton. Robert made no remark, and they rode quietly home.

CHAPTER XXV.

"Cependant, on ne voit pas, sans en être piqué,
Possédé par un autre, un cœur qu'on a manqué."
MOLIÈRE.

BUT Robert had only delayed his remark; he staid to dine with the Croftons, after their return to the hotel; and later in the evening, when Mr. Crofton was indulging in an after-dinner nap, he came and sat by Annie; who instinctively felt what was coming, and armed herself accordingly.

"What had that fellow been saying to you, Annie?" he began. "You are too good a rider to be run away with by any horse short of a determined bolter; so don't try to impose upon me by that story; besides, in that case, he would have followed you."

"Upon my word," she replied, drawing herself up to her full height,—which was not very much, after all,—"I don't see what business it is of yours, Robert; have you been appointed Grand Inquisitor lately?"

He gave her a reproachful look, which went to her heart, as he said:

"You are right, Annie; it is no business of mine; but I cannot forget that I am Arthur's brother,—and whatever would pain him, must pain me."

"What have I done to pain him?" said Annie. "Is he so unreasonable, that he would grudge me a little amusement? I do think you men are the most inconsistent creatures; you take any amount of liberty yourselves, but if *we* step a hair's breadth out of the beaten track, we are forthwith branded with all manner of hard names. I declare you are enough to make one go in for the rights of women, out and out!"

"Good heavens, Annie!" exclaimed Robert, amazed and horrified. He knew too little of women, to understand the pleasure they often take in *trying effects*, by saying things they don't the least mean; neither did he make allowance for Annie's innate love of teasing.

She burst out laughing.

"Why, I have actually performed a miracle!" she exclaimed; "I have made you swear. Did you ever do such a wicked thing in your life before?"

"Very often," he answered; so quietly and gravely, that his very calmness startled her.

"Well, you don't seem much ashamed of it," she said; "and I am sure, if London has taught you to swear, you needn't be shocked if it has taught me to amuse myself a little. I don't care for Mrs. Grundy; and no one else has a right to object, that I know of. Miss Marsden says"— but here Robert broke in impatiently:

"For goodness' sake, Annie, never speak to that woman; you don't know what she is; she would corrupt an angel, if she could."

"You are charitable!" said Annie. "I only heard Miss Marsden say, that the time would soon come for women to claim their rights, and use their powers and energies."

"Yes," said Robert, "she took care you should hear no more then; she is a cautious trainer. If I were to tell you what rights and powers and energies she means, you would — well, thank God! you would not understand me."

"You are wonderfully mysterious," said Annie. "However, if it is any comfort to you to know it, I have not the smallest desire to have a vote, or to be a doctor, or to go into Parliament— what funny speeches I should make!—or even to matriculate in a ladies' college, or—or any thing at all of that sort; so now don't be cross with me any longer. Do you know you are making yourself outrageously disagreeable this evening?" and Annie softened down into her old Stonebridge tone and manner; for, after all, the other was too unnatural to be kept up for long.

Robert was silent, and looked so disturbed, that Annie took compassion on him, and said:

"Come, now, I will be good, and tell you what

you asked me just now: Colonel Blount made a fool of himself, and of me too, this afternoon; and I ran away from him. I suppose Arthur really would be vexed if he knew, so you need not tell him; and I don't think Colonel Blount will care to repeat the story; so we can keep it to ourselves. But, Robert, I never thought any one calling himself a gentleman would dare to ask a lady to break her engagement. I will never speak to him again."

"I don't suppose he knew you were engaged," said Robert, "unless you told him so."

"I told him so!" exclaimed Annie. "Are you out of your senses, Robert? Of course, I took it for granted that he knew it; he must have seen that I always treated you like a brother. Why, Robert," she continued, a sudden light breaking upon her, "if he didn't know it, he must have thought I flirted desperately with you!"

Poor Robert! his self-elected guardianship of Annie certainly brought no particular consolation to himself. Seeing her, however, in a more manageable mood than she had been lately, he took advantage of it to say:

"You flirted with *him*, Annie; was that right or honourable?"

Her fit of pride was over for the time, and she hung down her head as she replied:

"No, Robert, it was naughty of me, I know; but it was such fun! And you know I could never *really* care for any one but Arthur, so it is very ridiculous of him to be jealous. By the way, he is coming up to London with our mother; I heard from him this morning;—I wonder what for? I know she hates London. Have you been telling tales of me, and urging him to come and act sheep-dog? It strikes me you have taken that office on yourself lately, and you certainly deserve credit for discharging it faithfully."

Robert smiled. Though Annie's words had given him a sharp pang, the pain was only for himself, not for her, and he did not mind it; he felt happier about her than he had done for a long time.

"No," he said, "I have told no tales; but I am very glad they are coming; I suppose I shall hear to-morrow all about it; they will want rooms or lodgings looked out for them. But I must go now; it is Saturday night."

"'Saturday night, *and all*,' as our old nurse used to say," answered Annie, laughing. "Well, you had better make haste, or you will find all the churches shut up."

She felt very much inclined to go with him; but, in spite of her contempt for Mrs. Grundy, she did not propose doing so; perhaps knowing it would be quite useless, as he would certainly have refused to take her. She contented herself, therefore, with getting up at six the next morning, and marching off to Bayswater; returning in time to accompany her father to the Homer-Row Chapel at eight o'clock.

The next morning brought a letter from Mrs. Vivian to Annie, saying that they were coming that week to London, for the benefit of a first-rate physician's advice for poor Maggie, whose malady seemed to increase, and that Miss Trelawney would accompany them. It was a long time since

Annie had heard any thing of Maude. She had come back to Stonebridge with her mother, after a three weeks' sojourn at Teignmouth, but only for two nights, after which she had gone back to the Vivians. That one day Annie had seen her, for she had rushed up to Mrs. Trelawney's the moment school was over; but it had not been a very satisfactory visit. Mrs. Trelawney was out of spirits at the prospect of parting with Maude the next day, and Maude herself was more cold and reserved than ever, though there was genuine gratitude in her tone of thanking Annie for all her past kindness, and for supplying her mother's place in the school. To inquiries about her health, she replied that she was quite well, only not very strong, because she slept so little that she felt always tired; nor did Annie obtain much more information afterwards from Mrs. Trelawney, who only said that Maude had got well wonderfully quickly at Teignmouth, and been able to go out almost every day; as to the sleeping, she said she believed it was partly her own fault, for always drinking very strong coffee, or green tea, at night,—but that she could not induce her to give it up.

Father Wilfrid had also called that day, and had seen Maude. Rather to his surprise, and very greatly to her mother's, she gave him a small packet, saying that it contained a rosary made of Devonshire marbles, which she hoped he would accept in remembrance of Helstone bog, "and our first meeting," she added, fixing her eyes upon him; but he did not return her look, or give any sign that he understood it.

"Good," thought Maude; "if he did see me, he is to be trusted." Presently after, she said:

"Mamma, where is that photograph of the new convent at Teignmouth?—perhaps Father Wilfrid would like to see it."

It was at the bottom of her mother's box, as she knew full well, and Mrs. Trelawney immediately went in search of it.

Maude seized the opportunity. "Tell me," she said quickly, "how did you recognise me that night? Had you ever seen me before?"

He raised his eyes, and looked kindly at her, as he replied: "I had seen you twice before, once walking with your mother, and once in the church."

"Does any one know that you saw me there?"

"No one," he replied emphatically.

"Thank you," she said; "I am more grateful to you for that than for saving my life"—as if he did not know it! "Can you interpret dreams?"

Before he had time to answer this very unexpected and rather startling question, Mrs. Trelawney came back with the photograph, and he turned his whole attention to it. Maude walked off to the window, and resolutely stood there during the remainder of his visit, which, however, was only a few minutes.

"I hope we shall hear of your getting stronger before long, Miss Trelawney," he said, as he rose to go. "Are you a good correspondent?"

"No, indeed," said Mrs. Trelawney, answering for her. "Maude is very naughty about writing; she dislikes it so much."

"I only write when I have something to say,"

replied Maude, " or something to ask. What is the use of a hundredth part of the letters most people write and keep ?"

"Ah, well! I never *keep* letters," said Father Wilfrid; "I follow the Duke of Wellington's good example: answer them all by return of post, and then burn them."

"If there is a railway-accident to-morrow," said Maude, "you will hear of it by telegraph ; if not, I will write the next day and announce my safe arrival." She spoke to her mother, but came forward at the same time to say good bye to Father Wilfrid.

She did write to announce her safe arrival to her mother, and the same post brought a letter to Father Wilfrid, with the Stretton post-mark, which he answered by return of post and burnt ; but he never heard any thing again of Maude, except through her mother, who always spoke very despondingly about her.

Annie had, of course, only the same means of information, and, though she saw a great deal of Mrs. Trelawney, very little was ever said between them about Maude ; it was a painful subject, and they both avoided it.

But now Maude was coming to London, and Annie would be able to judge for herself how far she was still suffering from the effects of "the shock to her nervous system."

Mrs. Hatton and Arthur came first, and established themselves in very comfortable lodgings in Gloucester Terrace. Annie had written to propose rooms in the hotel, but "the mother" preferred the quiet of a private house, and they were so close by that it made very little difference.

Arthur showed such unmistakable intentions of "acting sheep-dog," as Annie called it, that all her spirit of mischief and antagonism was roused; and, though Colonel Blount had put himself *hors de combat*, and kept at a respectful distance, others were not wanting to take his place,—for Mrs. Hanmer took care to surround Annie with a constant succession of young men of birth and fortune, in hopes that she might take a fancy to some one who would "put that stupid Arthur Hatton out of her head." She utterly and persistently ignored the engagement; and when poor Colonel Blount asked her for an explanation of Annie's conduct, saying,

"I quite understand that I have been unfortunate enough to offend Miss Crofton, but I am at a loss to conceive in what sense I have insulted her," she laughed, and said:

"Oh, that's all nonsense; Annie is a country-girl. I daresay she has old-fashioned notions about its being proper for you to speak to her father first; that will rub off before the end of the season: wait a little, and then try again."

"No," he replied; "pardon me, but I know how to accept a refusal."

"Oh, very well; you men are always so proud and hasty," she said; but she could not persuade him to change his mind.

Arthur's arrival in London disconcerted Mrs. Hanmer greatly, for it was not likely *he* would make a secret of his engagement to Annie; but she succeeded in persuading the latter that it would be extremely bad taste, and, in fact, "quite improper," to "parade it in public,"—that it might be all very well to walk or ride alone with Arthur at Stonebridge, but that in London it would be quite out of the question, nor must they on any account engage too much of each other's attention in society.

Arthur protested vigorously at first; but Mrs. Hanmer was a clever woman: a hint, mysteriously dropped, that he might compromise Annie's character for modesty, effectually served her purpose. He would have submitted (and she knew it) to any restraint rather than risk that.

With Annie herself, the task was easy enough; she fell into the snare at once. It gave her all the better opportunity of amusing herself by making Arthur "just a little bit jealous, to see what he would do."

"Do, my dear?" said Mrs. Hanmer; "why, return the compliment by amusing himself with somebody else, to be sure, if he has any sense."

But this suggestion did not seem quite to suit Annie. She answered sharply:

"No, he won't."

Mrs. Hanmer only laughed, and said no more to Annie; but to *herself* she said:

"Won't he? We shall see."

She did see, rather sooner than she expected; but not, perhaps, exactly what she was prepared for.

It was unfortunate for Annie that Mrs. Hatton's extreme aversion to gaiety of all kinds prevented her from going at all into society: not that she was in the very least of a morose or melancholy, and still less of a puritanical, disposition ; but she preferred a quiet life, and the society of real friends, to the mere show and glare of fashionable life, nor did she think it becoming in a widow to take part in it,—a " crotchet" which some of her friends had tried in vain to laugh her out of, and for which, in their hearts, they respected her. Consequently there was no watchful motherly eye to protect Annie. Mrs. Hanmer was her *chaperone;* and, though quite a trustworthy one for all ordinary purposes, she saw no harm in many things that Mrs. Hatton would have used her utmost influence to guard or warn against.

Robert, as we have seen, was not given to telling tales ; but knowing his mother's great love for Annie, and influence over her, he did tell her that he feared Annie's high spirits and innocent gaiety of heart were leading her further than she herself was aware of ;—and Arthur, after the first few days they spent in London, complained bitterly to her that " the Hanmers and all that set were spoiling Annie, and turning her into a fashionable monstrosity ;" but neither did he specify any thing in particular,—so that Mrs. Hatton, not seeing any alteration in Annie, who was as simple and loving and affectionate to her as ever, and whose manner, among the few friends who occasionally assembled at her own lodgings or in Mr. Crofton's rooms, was every thing that could be desired, was under the impression that her sons were a little over-exacting, and told them that as, according to the old saying, " boys will be boys," so, likewise, girls will be

girls, and will, if they have good health and
spirits, and no cares or anxieties, enjoy themselves
in society, and take pleasure in all such amuse-
ments as fall in their way. Neither Arthur nor
Robert cared to enlighten her further; and, indeed,
Arthur could not have given expression to a
horrible suspicion that had lately come into his
mind, and which he knew very well he ought to
have put away instantly as a suggestion of the
devil, but which, having once allowed it to fasten
upon him, he could not shake off.

He had noticed Robert's watchful care of
Annie, his readiness to interpose between her and
any one whose attentions became troublesome to
her; and he had also noticed, as he imagined, that
Annie accepted this care with more eagerness,
more gratification, than she exhibited to himself
under similar circumstances : and, having naturally quick feelings and a hasty temper, he misinterpreted both her and Robert.

As to Robert, of course he admitted that he
had a right to act a brother's part towards her ;
but why on earth could not Charley act for
himself? Confound the boy ! he was gone abroad
with a tutor. How stupid to take himself off just
when he might have been of some use! What
could have possessed Arthur ? He knew that his
brother was the most single-minded and pure-
hearted of men, scrupulously straightforward,
chivalrously honourable ; but "jealousy is cruel
as the grave ;" and the dark thought that had
flashed into his mind, only to be immediately cast
out, on Christmas-day, at Stinchcombe, came back
now with a rebound, and, alas ! was not imme-

diately cast out, but suffered to rankle and fester.

But Annie?—did he not trust her? Could e love her, and doubt her? He hardly knew himself; he did trust implicitly to her truth, to her honour: he could never have thought her capable of deceiving him; but he was not so absolutely certain that she had ever really loved him as a woman loves but once in her life. She was so young, so childish; had she really known what she was about, when she engaged herself to him? And, if not, was it not possible that she might be learning it now, and learning it in a way fatal to his happiness? Such thoughts tormented him night and day. He did not take into consideration the fact that every woman resents the imputation of having been easily won, and will often, if the imputation be a true one, *work off* her resentment in the form of a vigorous sham-fight; neither did he make allowance for, probably he was quite ignorant of, the sort of *shyness* which every pure-minded woman feels of a strong affection, and which often leads her not only to disguise, but apparently to ignore it.

And on one point he was inexorable: he looked upon the very faintest shadow of coquetry as a sin,—in which he would hardly have been borne out by any theologian; for though, doubtless, it can very seldom be indulged in without leading to sin, yet much that goes by that name is merely a natural and harmless desire to please others, quite apart from vanity or any other wrong feeling; and where there is no malice, there is no sin.

In Annie it was simply exuberance of animal spirits, and that inveterate love of teasing, which might be mischievous or imprudent, but could hardly be called sinful.

But Arthur took a very different view of the matter, and one day found a "convenient season" for manifesting the same to Annie, who happened to be in a particularly mischievous mood just then. The result was, that she told him, if he did not like her to enjoy herself, he had better put her under lock and key; for that, as she had been dragged into a London season against her will, she would at least make the most of it.

CHAPTER XXVI.

" Full many a shaft at random sent,
Finds mark the archer little meant;
And many a word at random spoken,
May hurt or heal a heart half broken."

ANON.

ON the morning following the little *breeze* mentioned in the last chapter, Mr. Crofton sat at the breakfast-table waiting for Annie, who had not yet come in from Mass; he generally went with her, but some accident had hindered him that morning. The post was just in, and he was in the act of reading a letter from Charley, dated simply "Boulogne," when Annie came in, looking something like a brown squirrel, with her sable-trimmed cloak and muff.

"Charley will be here to-day," said Mr. Crofton; "he seems to have missed my Cologne letter, advising him to stay another week in Germany, and join us at home instead of coming here. However, here he will be now by the tidal train from Folkestone; so you had better see about engaging a room for him. I suppose there are some to be had in this huge hotel?"

"What fun!" exclaimed Annie. "I told him in my last letter that the Vivians were coming to town; and here he comes, like a loadstone to the magnet, to bask in the sunshine of Maude Trelawney's great, glorious eyes, as he calls them! They were to come yesterday; I shall go and call to-day, and prepare Maude to receive her *preux chevalier*."

"You mischievous sprite!" said her father, not over-pleased, though he treated it as a joke. "And, pray, does Miss Trelawney encourage this pretty tomfoolery?"

"Maude, papa! Maude encourage any thing foolish, or romantic, or funny, or amusing! Why, she would as soon swing in a merry-go-round at a fair. Oh, dear, no; Maude is a highly sensible, well-conducted young woman, quite superior to all the weaknesses of ordinary mortals."

"Then I think you might do well to profit by her example," said Mr. Crofton. "I don't want to vex you, child, and I have seen nothing really to blame; but as long as you are engaged to Arthur Hatton, I think you should be a little more reserved in your manner to others."

Annie sprang to her feet as if her chair had suddenly become red-hot.

Y

"*As long as* I am engaged to Arthur! What do you mean?" she said, quite fiercely.

"Gently!" said Mr. Crofton; "don't excite yourself"—as if she could help it! "Engagements, especially long ones, are broken off sometimes without any fault on either side."

"Papa!" said Annie, coming close to him, and looking straight into his face, "what have I done, that *you* should say this to me? Others may think, Arthur may think, what they please; but *you* ought to know me better. Listen! sooner than break off my engagement, sooner than give up Arthur,"—and the deep colour mounted to her forehead as she said this even to her own father,— "I would give up my eyes and ears and tongue, and be blind and deaf and dumb for the rest of my life."

"There! come, don't distress yourself, birdie; I didn't think you would take it so seriously. Keep Arthur, and keep your eyes and ears too; he might object to a blind and deaf bride."

"Not if he cared for her," said Annie; and then ran away rather hastily, to take off her things and read a letter of her own, which she had picked up from the table and put into her pocket unopened. It was from Arthur, and her brow contracted as she read it. Her father, too, kind and indulgent as he was, even he had reproved her for her freedom of manner. Had she really been so very wrong?

"But I cannot stay to think about it now," she thought to herself, and went back to take her place at the breakfast-table.

After breakfast, she had to arrange about Charley's room, to look over and select some music which Robert had ordered for her, and to write some letters for her father; her own, she thought, would do just as well in the afternoon, even if there were any necessity to answer Arthur's absurd nonsense at all. Robert, too!—it really was too ridiculous.

At the unfashionable hour of twelve, she set out to see if her friends, the Vivians, had arrived, and found them in all the confusion of unpacking. They had taken rooms in Dover Street, for the convenience of being near Maggie's doctor. Annie was on the point of congratulating them on its nearness to Farm Street, but recollected herself just in time.

She asked to see Maude, who was accordingly sent for, and who appeared, looking so pale and thin, that Annie asked if she were still suffering from the effects of her illness at Stonebridge.

"Indeed, yes," said Mrs. Vivian; "I don't know what you all did to Maude at Stonebridge; she has never been the same since she went there."

"The same as what?" asked Maude, with a little, low laugh, which struck Annie as something quite different from her old manner.

Mrs. Vivian felt pulled up in her grammar, and was rather embarrassed thereby.

"The same as you were before, I mean," she said.

"I don't sleep so well—that is the only difference; I suppose it is the reaction after all those strong opiates they made me take," said Maude.

Was it the only difference? Annie looked at Maude, and doubted it; the sharpness seemed gone out of her manner, the sting was extracted; but, like the poor bee, she seemed to have parted with it at the cost of all vital power; her head drooped as though she had no strength to raise it, and there was a dreamy, far-away look in her "great, glorious eyes," as if she saw, or tried to see, something invisible to others.

"What can have happened to her?" thought Annie. "I wonder if Mrs. Trelawney knows, and if I may ask when I go home?" Yes, she might ask; but Mrs. Trelawney could not tell her, for she did not know.

Anxious to speak of something that would embarrass nobody, Annie inquired for Rover, who had been allowed to accompany Maude to Carew Castle, where, no doubt, he was much happier, with a Newfoundland and a Scotch terrier as companions, than cooped up all alone in Mrs. North's back yard.

"Rover is quite well," said Maude; "I think his master will be satisfied with him whenever he reclaims him."

"Reclaims him!" exclaimed Annie; "I don't suppose he will ever do that."

"Very little chance of it, I should think," said Mrs. Vivian. "I don't believe a single Zouave will come home alive; they are committing suicide as deliberately as if they threw themselves off the top of the Monument."

Maude did not speak, but Annie saw her lip tremble, and the faint colour that had been in her cheeks die out of them. But what could it matter to her if every Zouave were killed? Were not all her sympathies with "the united army of

Italy"? Had she not taken Garibaldi's part against a Zouave to his very face, and tied a scarlet bow on his dog under his very eyes?

Annie remembered, and looked, and wondered; but her month "in the world" had given her a little experience of life, and she did not draw any hasty conclusions. Maude might very naturally feel an interest in the man who had saved her life, without including any other feeling, or any sympathy with his cause.

"I didn't mean that," she said, addressing Mrs. Vivian; "I thought Rover was a present, not a loan. As for the Zouaves, if they are all to be killed, I envy them; they will die martyrs, and go straight to heaven without any purgatory."

Mrs. Vivian laughed. "I didn't know," she said, "that the Pope had enlisted the noble army of martyrs in his service: is that your last new doctrine?"

"Bother!" thought Annie; "how stupid Protestants are!"

But she was saved the trouble of answering by a most unexpected interruption: Maude looked up, and asked, in the quietest possible tone:

"Why should martyrs have no purgatory, Miss Crofton?"

"Because they don't," said Annie bluntly. She hated being brought to book about any thing.

"Why don't they?" persisted Maude, evidently not inclined to accept assertion for proof.

"Why? oh, let me see—I always forget the reason of things; I know now: it is because martyrdom is like baptism,—washes out all the stains, and leaves nothing for the fire to purify. Is that what you mean?"

Perhaps these few words conveyed as much meaning to Maude's mind as St. Catharine of Genoa's treatise would have done; at all events, she seemed satisfied, and rather more than satisfied; for, answering briefly,

"Thank you; yes, I think so," she excused herself on the plea that Maggie would be wanting her, and left the room.

"Miss Trelawney looks ill," said Annie.

"Yes, she is nervous and excitable. If I believed in such things, I should think she had seen a ghost in that strange adventure of hers on Dartmoor; perhaps she fancies she saw one, which is all the same, you know. But now tell me about yourself, and what you have been doing."

And forthwith there ensued a long conversation on the doings of the last month, which it would be only wearisome to record; and the consequence of which was, that, finding it already nearly two o'clock, Annie agreed to stay to luncheon, when of course she again saw Maude,—but the conversation was only of the most ordinary kind; and immediately afterwards, Annie said she must make haste home, as her father would be expecting her, and Charley very possibly might be arrived.

In Oxford Street, she caught sight of Robert Hatton, and, stopping her cab, beckoned him to the window: it was only to tell him what music she had chosen, and to ask for another song that she wanted.

"I am afraid that is out of print," he said;

"but a friend of mine has it in one of his books: I will copy it for you."

"Oh, thanks," she answered; and surely the spirit of mischief was upon her, for she added, "Come and try it over with me to-morrow morning; I shall be quite alone."

"I can't promise," he said; "I will come if I can; good bye."

"Why, I do believe Arthur has been plaguing him too; it is too bad! I meant to have written him a penitent letter, to the tune of 'I will be good;' but now I sha'n't: he doesn't deserve it."

Just as she drove up to the door of the hotel, another cab, containing Charley and his luggage, drove up also; and for the moment her letter was driven out of Annie's "scatter-brained" head.

"Very glad to see you, my boy," said Mr. Crofton; "but why didn't you answer my letter from Cologne?"

"Because I didn't get it; I haven't been to Cologne. I came straight from Strasburg to Paris."

"You changed your route, then, at the last moment?"

"Yes," said Charley, looking rather confused; "I was getting tired of it all out there, and wanted to get back to old England again."

Later in the afternoon, the brother and sister were talking together in Annie's room, and he asked if the Vivians were in town.

"Oh, yes," said Annie; "and Maude too, which is what you really mean; but she is quite changed, and looks dreadfully ill. You won't admire her magnificent eyes any more; so you had better turn your attentions elsewhere."

"Don't be a fool, Annie!" was the very unceremonious reply. "How are the Hattons? I think I'll run over and see them presently; it's close by, isn't it?"

"Yes, only just in Gloucester Terrace. Oh, by the by, if you are going there, you can take a note for me to Arthur; just be quiet for five minutes, while I write it."

"All right," said Charley; "fire away; I won't speak a word."

Annie took her morning's letter from her pocket, and read it over again, and mentally added to it Robert's last words; then, after a few moments' consideration, she took a sheet of the smallest note-paper, and wrote as follows:

"DEAR ARTHUR,
"I really have never taken the trouble to measure by the foot or yard the exact extent of my affection for Robert, or to examine very closely into its quality; but you seem to be suffering from a severe attack of jealousy; and as I am rather nervous about infection, and don't wish to catch the complaint, I must beg you to keep at a distance till the dangerous stage is over. Meanwhile, with every hope for your speedy recovery, I am yours compassionately,
"ANNIE."

"Here, Charley," she said, twisting it up, and quite forgetting to direct it, "don't forget to give it to him. You're not given to keeping notes in your waistcoat-pocket, are you?"

"Not if I know it," he said, laughing. "Never fear; your *billet-doux* is all right with me: perhaps, though, it's a *billet-dur;* you looked rather savage while you were writing it. Talking of waistcoats, though, I must go and change mine; I can't go out like this in London," indicating with one finger a fur waistcoat which he had worn for travelling. "Here, give us the note. Why, you haven't directed it! I think I'll give it to some one else by mistake, eh? Wouldn't it be a nice kettle of fish if I did?"

"I'll put *you* into a nice kettle of fish if you do," said Annie; "give it me back directly!"

"No, no, nonsense; all right," he said, stuffing it into his pocket, and taking himself off.

Presently he looked in again, to ask what time dinner would be; and saying he would be back for it, went out.

Annie never troubled herself any more about her note; her affection for Arthur Hatton was too real and too deeply rooted for any other to come near it, though she did not choose to make any display of it even to himself: she *felt* that she could quite safely afford any amount of friendship to others; and as for Robert, to her simple and childlike mind, *his* brother was the same to her as her own. What could he possibly mean by such ridiculous nonsense? She had not even the remotest conception of the meaning of the jealousy she laughed at, and imagined that Arthur's letter must have been written in joke. Moreover, never having suffered herself, it was

difficult to her to realise that others could suffer;
and she could not understand that what to her
was an innocent diversion, or the mere amusement of an idle hour, should be magnified by any
one into a deliberate unkindness, or a serious
fault. She had perfect confidence in Arthur, and
could not believe it possible that he did not in
his heart trust her equally; she thought he was
only teasing her a little; and as she was perfectly
conscious of teasing him a good deal, she took it
as *quid pro quo*, and only thought that he might
have hit upon a less disagreeable method of inflicting the punishment.

"Well, Charley," she said, when he came in,
"did you give my note?"

"Of course I did; what fidgets you girls always are! I very nearly did forget it, though—
in fact quite, to say the truth; so I dropped it
into the letter-box outside afterwards."

"Without any address on it! O Charley,
how could you! why, the servants will all read
it."

"No, they won't," said Charley; "I scratched
'A. Hatton, Esq.,' on it, and rang the bell, and
told the servant to take it up to Mr. Hatton immediately."

"Then why did you put it into the box at
all?" asked Annie, rather puzzled at such a
roundabout proceeding.

"Well, because I forgot there was no seal; so
then I rang, and sent it up-stairs, and watched
the servant all the way to the drawing-room door.
Are you satisfied now?"

"I suppose so," she said. "Then he has read

it by this time. I am so glad! thank you so much, Charley."

"What a baby you are! You really must try to grow into a woman before you are married. By the by, when is that happy consummation to take place?"

"I don't know," replied Annie demurely, and with a little blush, which perhaps proved her to be less of a baby than her brother imagined.

They spent a quiet evening, talking over Charley's travels, looking at the photographs he had brought home, and arranging a plan for the next day, which was to include a visit to the Crystal Palace. The Hattons were expecting some friends, so they would not be able to join the party; and as they were people Annie particularly disliked, she intended to keep aloof from them for a day or two. That Arthur would take her at her word, and "keep at a distance," she never for a moment imagined; but even if he did, she could "get on very well without him," she thought.

As she said her Rosary that night, there suddenly flashed into her mind the remembrance of a certain intention she had once asked Father Wilfrid to say Mass for, and had refused to explain to him; what did it mean by coming and looking her in the face now?

CHAPTER XXVII.

"As if a morning in June, with all its music and sunshine,
Suddenly paused in the sky, and, fading, slowly descended
Into the east again, from whence it late had arisen."
                                    LONGFELLOW's *Evangeline.*

THREE days passed, and nothing was seen or heard of Arthur. Annie had not been to Gloucester Terrace, but had sent a little note to Mrs. Hatton, saying she would come and see her as soon as the Maxwells were gone. She was rather surprised that neither Arthur nor Robert came to her; but with regard to the latter, she supposed that " he had been badgered, and didn't like it;" while as to Arthur, she said to herself:

"Well, he has a real good fit of it this time; never mind: he'll be all the better afterwards."

On the fourth morning, however, she began to feel a little dull, and was half inclined to cry *peccavi,* and send Charley with a note or message of reconciliation.

"No, I won't, though," she concluded; "it is too humiliating: he shall not think I care so much about it."

That afternoon she was surprised by a visit from Maude, who came alone. Mr. Crofton and Charley were out; but as it was pouring with rain, and Annie felt altogether rather "whisht," as her Stonebridge friends would have said, she had staid at home, and was found by Maude lying on the sofa, reading a novel.

"Miss Trelawney," she exclaimed, as Maude

entered, "what a day for you to come out! is any thing the matter?" she added, suddenly struck by a strange expression in Maude's face.

"No," said Maude, "nothing is the matter —nothing wrong, at least; I came to tell you something that will give you pleasure: I am a Catholic."

She spoke in a measured tone, as if she were repeating a lesson; but Annie instantly sprang up, threw her arms round her neck, kissed her on both cheeks, and exclaimed fervently:

"Thank God! but—perhaps, though, I ought not to ask any questions."

"There is not much to tell," said Maude; "it was not my own doing."

"Not your own doing!" repeated Annie, amazed; "I don't understand you. Have you been received in your sleep, or under chloroform, or something? What do you mean?"

"I don't mean that," said Maude, still in the same constrained tone. "I mean that I have not convinced myself; my father has converted me: no one else could."

Annie looked at her speechless with astonishment; was she crazy?

"Take off your wet cloak," she said presently, "and let me give you some tea,—you look quite cold, though it is such a hot day,—and then tell me quietly about it."

Maude smiled; for she saw the impression she had given, and obeyed orders by divesting herself of her cloak.

"Yes," she said, "I am rather cold; I have never quite shaken off the chill I brought from

Helstone. I *will* tell you, Miss Crofton, for you were kind to me when I behaved very ill to you, and you have been so good to my poor mother."

"How happy you will make her now!" said Annie.

"I hope so; I must try, if only as an act of restitution," was the reply.

Annie rang for tea; and when it had come, and there had been silence for a few minutes, Maude, without waiting to be asked again, began:

"That night I was brought home from Helstone—you know when I mean—I had a horrible sort of nightmare,—I thought it was the effect of the opiate—I suppose it was, partly. I saw flames all round my bed, and voices came out of them, crying, and calling out strange, uncouth words, that sounded like muttered Latin prayers. I know now what they were, but I did not know then—I knew them again, when I saw them in a prayer-book of my mother's: *Miseremini mei, miseremini mei, saltem vos amici mei!* The next night, and the next, and the next, and, oh, so many nights, I saw my father kneeling at the foot of the bed, and heard him say, "Pray for me," quite distinctly; but I thought it was all that horrid chlorodyne that they made me take, and I used to throw it out of the window whenever I could, —but then the dreams, or whatever they were, were worse. Things grinned at me, and made horrid faces, and laughed hateful, mocking laughs at me, till I thought I should have gone mad, and then I tried to keep awake and not sleep at all; and then at Teignmouth sometimes I looked into the Catholic church, just for something to do,"—

Maude never told *any one* of her visit to Stonebridge Church: it was no doing of hers that Father Wilfrid knew of it,—"and one day there was a grand funeral, and they sang the Office of the Dead, and I heard those strange-sounding Latin words again, and they went round the bier and sprinkled it with holy water, and made it fragrant with incense, and a Bishop came and pronounced absolution over it, and then they chanted the Mass,—such a long, low, earnest wail of entreaty, it sounded; and the notes of the *Dies Iræ* seemed as if they must needs soothe the most troubled spirit to rest. I knew that, because I have heard it sung at a concert; but it seemed, oh, so different there! I could not understand anything else except the perpetually recurring *Requiem æternam,* but I thought it was very beautiful to treat the dead with such loving care and reverence; I thought"—for a moment Maude turned so faint, that she could hardly speak; then she went on, bracing herself up as if for a task: "I thought I should like to see *him*—my father, I mean—so tended and cared for. That night I was not so afraid to go to sleep; and when I saw him there before me, and heard him ask so pleadingly, with such an agonised look, "Pray for me"—I said, *Requiem æternam,*—I did not know any more, nor any other prayer,—and there came a sweet smile on his face, as he passed away from my sight. Then I was very much frightened for a long time, nothing else but frightened—I thought it was all the devil; and then—I don't know what made me—I asked Father Wilfrid if he could explain dreams, and told him that one, and he wrote a very kind letter, and sent me some prayers to use,—and then, you see," Maude continued rapidly, as if unable to explain or dwell longer on the subject, "I found it was all no good, without being a Catholic; so I couldn't help it, couldn't help seeing the rest of it, I mean," she explained rather incoherently, and then came to a sudden stop.

Her tale was almost wholly incomprehensible to Annie, who had neither experience nor imagination enough to follow the workings of a mind so entirely different from her own; but she understood, and was intensely thankful for, the definite fact that Maude was now a Catholic.

"Does Mrs. Vivian know?" she asked, feeling vexed with herself for so unsympathising a reply to Maude's confidence, but longing to say *something*, and not knowing what to say.

Maude felt chilled; and Annie, seeing this at once, drew her towards her, and said:

"Oh, I am so glad for you! you will be so happy now! and you must be my sister—you know I never had one. It was only that I really didn't know what to say," she added frankly, blundering out an awkward truth with her usual thoughtlessness; "it all seems so strange; and it took me by surprise."

Maude smiled; she quite *understood* that Annie didn't know what to say, and was not in the least offended by it.

"Yes," she said, "Mrs. Vivian knows now; I told her this morning. Of course she does not wish me to stay with her: but that is of no consequence; if she had wished it ever so much, I should have gone to my mother."

"What a comfort for you!" said Annie. "So many converts have to give up home and parents; it is just the contrary with you."

"Yes," said Maude, slowly and thoughtfully; "I suppose I am not worthy to suffer any thing for His Name."

"Oh, no, no," exclaimed Annie; "you must not think that, and make yourself unhappy; you suffered so much before; and, besides, you don't know,—we cannot tell what may be in the future for any of us."

Did she speak prophetically? Even at that moment the shadow of what was to come was falling across her path; the door opened, and Mr. Crofton came in.

Annie looked at Maude, uncertain whether she might venture to proclaim the good news; there was no reason, certainly, for keeping it secret: but Maude had gone through enough that day; and rising hastily, she looked at her watch, expressed surprise at the lateness of the hour, and asked for her cloak, which had been sent away to dry by a fire.

"Where is Charley, papa?" asked Annie, by way of covering Maude's retreat.

"Gone to the Hattons; he'll be back in time for dinner; I sent him to see what has become of Master Arthur: I think he has played truant long enough."

By this time Maude's cloak was brought and put on, and she bid good bye; taking the opportunity of saying to Annie, "You may tell them, if you like."

As soon as she was gone, Annie burst out:

"You sent him! O papa, why did you do that? Arthur will think—"

"Never mind what Arthur will think," replied Mr. Crofton; "I thought you despised Mrs. Grundy."

"But Arthur is not Mrs. Grundy," was the undeniable response.

"No, not exactly; but you have no need to care what he thinks."

"Haven't I? Well, people really are very hard to please: I have been scolded within an inch of my—temper, for not caring enough about what he thinks."

"Ah! that's looking at it from a different point of view," said her father.

"H'm! one is looking straight, and the other squinting, perhaps. Suppose you look at something else for a minute, papa,—look here!"

"Well," he said, "I am looking with both eyes as straight as you could desire, but I see nothing."

"Maude Trelawney is a Catholic," said Annie; "does not your hair stand on end with astonishment?"

"Nonsense!" he exclaimed; "don't humbug me with such a hoax as that."

"But it isn't a hoax, and it isn't nonsense, and it isn't humbug," retorted Annie; "it's just the truth; she has told me so herself."

"Has she been converted by a miracle, like Père Ratisbon?" asked Mr. Crofton, thinking that nothing short of that could have accomplished such a result.

But Annie did not feel at liberty to enter into particulars, and merely said:

"Not that I know of, papa. She did not say so."

"Well, that is one point in Charley's favour," said Mr. Crofton; "but the difference of age is on the wrong side—altogether very objectionable."

"Why, papa!" exclaimed Annie; "you don't, surely, take Charley's nonsense *au grand sérieux?* Why, he is only just seventeen; and besides, even if he meant any thing, I am very sure Maude does not."

"You seem very ready to answer for other people; pray, how much more than seventeen were you, when you took Arthur Hatton *au grand sérieux*, you little puss?"

"Oh, but that is not at all the same thing; I am not a boy," said Annie.

Mr. Crofton laughed, but looked a little grave too, as he said:

"True; but a boy of seventeen is not a baby. However, perhaps Miss Trelawney will take to a convent now that she is a Catholic; converts generally do, as naturally as ducks take to water."

"O papa! what a comparison! I don't think Maude is one of that sort, but of course I don't know; how should I?"

How should she, indeed? Nevertheless, she had a little idea in her own head, which she kept to herself.

But it was time now to dress for dinner, which meal they took at a private table in the large coffee-room, as Annie had vigorously protested against having their only sitting-room "turned upside down" for that purpose.

Dinner was announced, but no Charley appeared; they waited a quarter of an hour, and then decided to begin without him: very likely he was staying to dine with the Hattons. Hardly, however, had they sat down, when in he came, hung his hat on a peg, and took his place without saying a word.

"*Sans cérémonie !*" said Annie, looking at his dirty boots; but there were other tables occupied in the room, so she refrained from further banter.

"I beg pardon," said Charley; "but as you had begun, I thought it was not worth while to wait for ceremony;" and pouring out a glass of sherry, he drank it straight off—which was so unlike his usual habit, that Annie looked wonderingly at him, and saw that he was deadly pale.

"What's the matter, Charley?" she said; "are you ill, or cold, or what? have you seen a ghost?—what did it look like?"

Instead of making any answer, he poured out and drank another glass of wine.

"Charley, what are you about?" said his father, rather sternly.

"I am very cold, that's all," said Charley, "and very tired; give me some chicken, Annie—that's right; quite well, I assure you, father, only rather wet,—it rains cats and dogs."

"Are you very hungry too?" said Annie, noticing that he literally bolted his chicken; "have you eaten nothing all day? you devour your food like a starved dog."

He frowned at her, and made a sign indicative that there were other people in the room; and scarcely spoke another word while dinner lasted. Instead of remaining with his father to read the evening paper, as usual, when it was over, he followed Annie up-stairs; he looked flushed and excited.

"What is it, Charley? what *is* the matter?" she asked, feeling, in spite of herself, rather frightened.

"Don't frighten yourself, dear, but just listen to me quietly," he said,—forgetting, as every body does, that, if you want thoroughly to upset any one, the surest way to do it is to begin by telling them not to be frightened.

She trembled all over; the clouds were casting their shadows before. She thought of her intention, of the Mass that had been said for it, of her refusal to tell Father Wilfrid what it was, and so, as it were, stealing it from him; was it coming now? and in what form? In a suppressed tone, she repeated:

"What is it, Charley?"

"Ay," he said, "what is it, indeed? that's just the question; I'm sure I don't know, except that it's an awful mess of some sort; perhaps you can explain it. What was that note you sent by me to Arthur Hatton the other day?"

"What was it? nothing, a little bit of nonsense. Why? what of it? what do you mean?"

"I mean—come, Annie, you had better tell me the truth—have you and Arthur been having what is vulgarly called a lover's quarrel?"

"I should hope not," returned Annie, drawing

herself up proudly, and curling her lip with an expression of intense disgust; "we have only been teasing each other a little. But, Charley, is he really so very angry with me? Is that what you mean by all this mystery?"

"I don't know whether he is angry or not," replied Charley; "I only know that he went out of town yesterday morning, and has not been heard of since."

He was rather frightened as he made this announcement; he had been exciting his imagination by all sorts of wild conjectures, and he expected Annie to faint, or scream, or *make a scene* of some sort—a performance he held in devout horror. To his utter amazement, she only laughed, and exclaimed:

"Oh, that is famous! he is taking my advice literally. I told him to keep away till he was cured of his fit of jealousy."

"Jealousy!" repeated Charley. "So, then, that is at the bottom of it! You had better mind what you are about, Annie: jealousy is a spiteful cat to play with; it has claws, and can scratch."

"Why, what on earth do *you* know about it?" she asked.

"Never mind; nothing, perhaps. But all the same, if it is not an impertinent question, of whom is Arthur Hatton jealous? I don't envy the individual, whoever he may be."

"Of Robert! Did you ever know any thing so absurd? Just because Robert amuses me with his quaint notions, and I like to draw him out and make him talk, and because we sing duets together, Arthur takes it into his head to be jealous. Why, Charley, he might as well be jealous of you! I'm sure I like you better than Robert. I daresay he is gone to see that crazy old aunt at Brighton, and amuse himself with meditations on 'What are the wild waves saying?' till he ventures to appear in my presence again. How foolish of you to look grave, and try to frighten me about such nonsense!"

"You certainly have an inveterate propensity for looking on the bright side of every thing; but just listen, Annie—he is not at Brighton."

"Well, then, he's somewhere else, I suppose; he really is old enough to take care of himself. I daresay he'll come all right on Monday, if not before."

"I tell you," said Charley, getting out of patience at her coolness, "he is not in England at all; and before he left home, he said something to Robert that neither of us could make head or tail of, but that I begin to understand a little now."

The clouds were gathering in the horizon; Annie felt the sunlight growing dim around her; but still she was not going to give in yet: and there was more of curiosity than of anxiety in her tone, as she asked:

"What did he say to Robert?"

"He said, 'You may direct your wedding-cards to me at Constantinople, if you like.' Robert was so scared, he could not ask him what he meant, and he has not the very smallest conception. He says Arthur has been very strange for the last two days, and has several times asked Mrs. Hatton if she had seen you, or had any message; and yesterday morning, when he came home from Mass, he found a cab at the door packed with heavy luggage, and Arthur just getting into it; he looked up at Robert, said what I have told you, and drove off; Robert noticed that the luggage was directed to Dover and Paris, and heard him tell cabby to go to the London-Bridge Station."

Annie was thoroughly subdued now; she asked in a low voice:

"Was that *all* he said?"

"Yes, every word of it. Poor Mrs. Hatton is in a dreadful way; she was at Blackheath for a couple of days, and only heard of it on her return this afternoon. Can you explain it, Annie?"

"I!—no. Are you sure, *quite* sure, you gave my note that evening?"

"Quite positive; I saw the servant take it upstairs with my own eyes; indeed, Robert says he saw him receive it."

"Did he see him *read* it?" said Annie; "did he notice any thing then?"

"No; he says Arthur went out of the room with it in his hand unopened; he did not come down again till after the dinner-bell had rung, hardly eat any thing, and went to bed early with a bad headache. Can you throw *no* light upon it, Annie? it is too serious for trifling, and Mrs. Hatton is looking anxiously for your explanation. If you wrote any thing in a passion, you had better say so honestly."

"In a passion!" she repeated. "You were in the room when I wrote the note; did I look in a passion? I only wrote, that I had never troubled myself to analyse my feelings for Robert; and that if he was so jealous, he had better keep away from me till the fit was over. What in the world can he mean about Constantinople and wedding-cards?"

"You must have given him some ground for his jealousy; *he* is in earnest, Annie, whatever you may be—that I am very sure of."

"You had better go and tell papa," she said; "I will come down and make his tea presently;" and she glided swiftly and noiselessly out of the room.

CHAPTER XXVIII.

"The smoothest seas will sometimes prove
To the confiding bark untrue;
And if she trust the stars above,
They can prove treacherous too."
WORDSWORTH.

A FEW days after his sudden and unaccountable departure had caused such grave uneasiness to all his friends, and the deepest anxiety to his poor mother and Robert, Arthur Hatton was pacing up and down the deck of a French steamer, bound from Marseilles to Civita Vecchia. He intended to spend a short time in Rome, from which place he meant to write to his mother, and give such explanation of his conduct as he thought needful to offer; for even in his unreasoning passion he was a dutiful son, and already felt pain for the suffering he knew he was inflicting upon her. His subsequent intentions were to visit Constantinople and the Holy Land, remaining abroad till after he supposed the union between Annie and Robert, which was now an *idée fixe* in his mind, would have taken place.

"We shall have fine weather to-morrow, if that sky may be trusted," remarked a fellow-passenger.

"Never trust any thing; you will only be deceived," replied Arthur, in a bitter tone.

"Is that your experience of life, sir?" asked some one who passed them at the moment—an English priest, also bound for the Eternal City.

"It is most people's experience, sooner or later, I suppose," replied Arthur; and he crossed over to the other side of the vessel, feeling no inclination for conversation, especially if it was to become of a personal nature.

The priest had asked a very unnecessary question, as far as he was himself concerned; but he had hoped for an opportunity of offering a few kind words of sympathy or help, where he saw plainly that one or the other was much needed. Finding his good intention frustrated by Arthur's manner, he made no further attempt in that direction, but proceeded quietly to pace the same side of the deck as before, and occupied himself with his Office.

Arthur seated himself on a heap of luggage, a little apart from the rest of the passengers, and took out of his pocket a small piece of paper, neatly folded up in the shape of a three-cornered note, but bearing no address whatever. It contained only two lines of manuscript, and they were the following half-stanza from Longfellow's "Psalm of Life :"

> "Trust no future, howe'er pleasant;
> Let the dead past bury its dead."

They were unmistakably in Annie Crofton's handwriting.

There was no signature, no date, nothing but the bare handwriting itself to identify it; but it was the very identical missive which the servant had brought into Mrs. Hatton's drawing-room a few evenings before, with a blundering explanation that "Master Crofton had left it without an address, but it was from Miss Crofton, and to be delivered immediately." At first it had simply puzzled him, and he thought it was some mistake, that there must have been some other note with it which had been forgotten to be delivered; but the next morning he had spoken to Charley coming out from church, and had ascertained, beyond possibility of further doubt, that Annie only gave him one note, a three-cornered one. The subject of the absence of address did not happen to be mentioned between them.

There could then be no mistake; the more he thought over the circumstances which had caused his suspicions about his brother, the more he felt convinced that he had sufficient grounds for them, and Annie's light-heartedness had blinded him to the real depth of her character. Men, unless they are priests, and so have it supernaturally, are not generally gifted with much penetration, especially of women's characters.

It was a cruel, heartless way of jilting him,

certainly—at least, it would be so in any one else; but Arthur Hatton had (or thought he had) a keen sense of justice, and he partly excused Annie on the ground that she did not know what a strong affection really was, or understand the nature of the pain she was inflicting. And yet— and yet, she was so truthful, his confidence in her had been so unbounded, so *restful*, it was hard to give up his faith in her. He clung all that day to the hope that there might yet have been some mistake, that he should hear something more from her. But no; there was no word, no sign; and, as if in confirmation of his worst fears, Robert said, at luncheon-time, that he was going to ride with Charles Crofton, and should take the opportunity of giving him a piece of music he had been copying for his sister.

Circumstantial evidence was certainly strong against poor Annie, as it is against many who are unjustly condemned. Arthur did not even give her the benefit of a "not-proven" verdict, but, without giving himself any time for thought, condemned her absolutely, and rushed away from her.

The fine evening sky was false to its promise; a stiff gale came on in the night, with a heavy swell, which made the vessel roll frightfully; and the sights and sounds in the cabin were not of a nature to make it a pleasant resting-place for one who, like Arthur Hatton, was neither frightened nor sea-sick. Sleep, of course, was out of the question, and the hours of darkness were passed in the company of thoughts hardly less dark than themselves. His fellow-passengers were mostly either ill, or given up to mortal terror; and from time to time, impelled by common charity, he tried to reassure them; but his mental comments on them were somewhat in the following form :

"What fools Frenchmen are! they are as sick as dogs the moment they feel the sea under them, and as frightened at a breath of wind as a pack of women!" With the first gleam of daylight, he turned out of his berth, and with some difficulty gained the deck. Only one other person was there, —the English priest, who had spoken to him the day before; he was sitting under the lee of a high pile of luggage, wrapped in a sailor's great-coat, and quietly saying his Office, apparently to the great astonishment of the crew, who were not accustomed to see a passenger as indifferent to wind and weather as one of themselves.

Arthur tried to walk up and down the deck, but it was no use; he had not his sea-legs on, and only made himself an object of ridicule by reeling about like a drunken man; so, after two or three fruitless attempts, he looked for a seat; but the priest seemed to have monopolised the only part of the deck where there was any thing like shelter, and Arthur did not "desiderate" companionship.

"At all events, however," he thought, "he can't talk while he is saying his Office."

Fortifying himself, therefore, as well as he could against the cold, by the help of great-coats and railway-wrappers, he sat down as far as circumstances would permit from his companion.

"How soon shall we get into port?" he asked

presently of a sailor, who was dragging a heavy rope along the deck.

"*Peste! je ne sais pas,*" replied the man, with a genuine French shrug of his shoulders.

"*Mais comment? vous ne savez pas!*" said Arthur, in a tone of annoyance.

The man looked round, and, probably having some private reason of his own for thinking his questioner worth speaking civilly to, replied respectfully, and of course in French:

"Well, you see, sir, we ought to be alongside the quay at Civita Vecchia by noon; but it's dirty weather, and the boat—plague her!—sprang a leak last night."

"Do you mean to say the water is coming in?" exclaimed Arthur, rather alarmed.

"Ay, sure! she lets in water: how can she help it, with a hole in her bottom?" said the man, looking at Arthur with a slightly contemptuous laugh at the ignorance of his question.

He, on his part, could hardly refrain from laughing at the very undeniable *argumentum ad hominem;* but he proceeded to ask if they were in any danger.

"Danger! bless you, no, sir," replied the man; "it is but a small hole, and we can pump the water out faster than it comes in; only, it keeps two men constantly at work, and we want all hands on deck."

The priest, who by this time had finished his Office, here looked up, and said:

"I will take a turn at the pumps, my friend, for an hour or so, if you will show me the way down below; that will give you one more hand on deck, at all events."

It was evidently no surprise to the sailor that a priest should make such an offer; he came from Marseilles, and had known more than one good father there who had spent his early boyhood "before the mast;" but Arthur's astonishment was extreme at hearing such a proposal from one who bore the unmistakable marks of an English gentleman, as well as those of a Catholic priest; and we fear we must add, that his sense of propriety was somewhat scandalised: though practically he would have done the same himself under the circumstances, yet theoretically and naturally he had rather strong feelings about *caste* and distinction of rank. Perhaps Father Price saw something of this in his face; for he turned to him, and said, with a pleasant smile:

"I suppose I must not ask you to accompany me? I am accustomed to rough work, and do not mind it; but you would find it very fatiguing."

"Well, it can't be very rough work to pump water; I suppose I can do that, any how," replied Arthur, ashamed to refuse, though by no means pleased with the employment which seemed thus in a manner forced upon him.

"*Allons, donc!*" said the priest, rising as he spoke.

The sailor looked somewhat dubiously at Arthur, as he prepared to follow, and, with a muttered exclamation of, "*Bah! ces Anglais!*" led the way down to the hold, and pointed out the pumps, at which two men were working lustily. A few words sufficed to explain to them that they were to resign their places to the new-comers, and a few moments effected the exchange.

"Do you know how to set about it?" asked Arthur, who found the pumps more unmanageable than he had expected; "I have not the remotest idea."

"I think so," was the reply; "at least, I have had a little experience. I have been three times nearly lost at sea, and I worked a whole day at the pumps each time;" and Father Price soon contrived to set Arthur going in his work.

Arthur himself began now to feel a little more sociable; his interest was excited, and he soon found himself listening with pleasure to Father Price's recital of various strange adventures. He had been a missionary for some years in Africa, and seemed to have been as familiar with perils of all kinds as was St. Paul.

"You see," he remarked at last, "I had, perhaps, as much reason as you to distrust a fair sky; and yet, I confess, I did not expect this change of weather after last night's sunset."

"It is like being deceived by God Himself!" exclaimed Arthur bitterly.

"Nay, my good friend," replied the priest gently. "When and where did God ever promise a fine day after a red sunset? Certainly not in Holy Scripture; nor, that I am aware of, through any private revelation."

"He never promised that it should be cold in winter and hot in summer, I suppose, did He?" replied Arthur, in the same bitter tone; "and yet one has a right to trust that water will not freeze in July."

"He did promise something very like it; for He solemnly declared that summer and winter, seed-time and harvest, should never cease," said Father Price; "and, moreover, He has established certain natural laws, which He will not break, because He is unchanging and unchangeable; but who shall dare to say that He has not the right, on any occasion that He pleases, to set them aside if He chooses? Does He not, as a matter of fact, sometimes do so, as if for the very purpose of showing His power? I have myself known a severe thunder-storm on one of the coldest days of March. If such a thing were to happen as a sudden hard frost in July, should you therefore lose your confidence in God?"

"I don't know," replied Arthur; "but I do know that if one person deceives me, I can never trust any one else."

"It must surely depend a little on who it is that deceives you; it would be hard to condemn the whole world for the fault of one person."

"But," said Arthur, "if that one person is perfectly truthful, perfectly guileless, innocent, simple-hearted as a child—"

"Stop, stop!" interrupted the priest; "you are supposing an impossibility: such a person could not deceive. You might mistake or misunderstand something in his conduct; in that case, there would be no fault on his part."

"I am not supposing at all; it is a fact," said Arthur. "But it is no use talking; you don't know her, you never saw her, you cannot understand it."

No, certainly, Father Price did not know, and had never seen, Annie Crofton; but he did know a few other things that might have helped him to an understanding of the difficulty—the mere fact of the feminine pronoun told him a good deal; but he felt unwilling to intrude and take by storm a confidence that was not freely given, glad as he would have been to offer any help or consolation in his power. But Arthur relapsed into silence, and the pumping went on uninterruptedly for some time.

At length Father Price remarked:

"We shall find Rome very full."

"Shall we?" replied Arthur. "I should have thought the winter visitors would have nearly all left by this time; it must be getting very hot there now."

"The English and Americans, you mean?—oh, yes, no doubt they are nearly all gone, except the few who are Catholics like ourselves, and who, of course, will stay."

"Stay for what?" asked Arthur.

Father Price looked up in unfeigned astonishment that such a question should be asked at such a time, for it was the end of May 1862: but being too polite to express surprise, he only said quietly:

"For the canonisation of the Japanese martyrs."

Arthur coloured deeply. He was ashamed of having betrayed to what an extent his own private troubles had put out of his mind a subject which was just then of such special interest to the whole Catholic world.

"I had forgotten," he said. "I suppose it will be a grand ceremony; it is to take place on the Feast of Pentecost, is it not?"

Good Father Price—who had hitherto been under the full impression that Arthur was, like himself, going to Rome for the express purpose of assisting at the ceremony—was rather taken aback, but answered at once :

"Yes ; I believe that is quite settled now. *A grand ceremony !*" he continued, his countenance lighting up with enthusiasm ; " it will be very much more than that. I should not have left my work, and spent more time and money than a year's hard labour will repay me for, only to see *a grand ceremony.*"

" I beg your pardon," said Arthur apologetically, fearing he had given offence. " May I ask why you attach so much importance to these particular twenty-six martyrs ? I am ashamed to say I am not very well up in the lives of the Saints, and I know very little about them."

" It is not so much to the Saints themselves —though I happen to have a great devotion to the twenty-three Franciscan martyrs—that I attach importance," replied Father Price, " as to the fact of their canonisation just at this time. God be praised," he exclaimed fervently, " for this signal triumph over the enemies of the Holy See !"

Arthur looked up in astonishment at this sudden burst of emotion. A month ago he would have heartily sympathised with it ; but of late the evil spirit of jealousy had tainted his mind, and blunted the fine edge of that " sensitiveness to the interests of Jesus" which is one of the most distinguishing marks of a heart in perfect union with God. Father Price did not seem to remark his surprise, but, after a few moments' pause, went on more calmly :

"Who but the Vicar of Christ could presume to call upon the Church to declare solemnly, as the living, speaking voice of the Holy Ghost, that twenty-six martyrs are added to her catalogue of Saints? Protestants may ridicule it; but Catholics can hardly dare, after this, to think lightly of the power and authority of the Holy See."

"There seems to be a very general opinion," said Arthur, "that the Pope is taking advantage of this occasion to draw his friends together for political purposes; that, in short,—begging your pardon if I speak irreverently,—the canonisation is to be made a sort of cat's-paw, a dodge for strengthening the temporal power."

"If I thought you were expressing your own opinion, my dear sir, I should say you do speak irreverently," said the priest, rather gravely.

"Nay, I know nothing about it; I do not meddle with politics," returned Arthur.

"Neither does the Pope," said Father Price; "though the world, which understands only its own maxims and principles, will never believe this."

"Do you think, after all, that the temporal power will be lost or saved?" asked Arthur.

"It *cannot* be lost, unless perhaps for a time," replied Father Price emphatically. "What God has once given, neither the world nor the devil can take away."

"I never thought of it exactly in that light," replied Arthur, who, to say the truth, was getting rather tired of thinking of it in any light. "But is your back made of iron? Mine is not; and it aches frightfully."

Father Price looked round, and perceived that his companion was thoroughly exhausted. In fact, they had been working hard for nearly two hours, without any breakfast; and though Arthur was pretty well inured to all athletic exercises, and by no means of a delicate constitution, it is no joke for one who is unaccustomed to it to stand for two hours fasting, with his feet wet and cold, and the rest of his body bathed in perspiration, from hard exercise.

"They are stupid fellows not to have a carpenter on board, who could mend that hole," said Father Price; "but the water comes in much less now that the sea is going down; and they cannot want so many hands on deck, either; they should have come to relieve us by this time. Why didn't you tell me sooner that you were tired? Do go now, and see if any breakfast is to be had; and send some one else down here. I will join you in the cabin as soon as I can resign my post."

Both these objects were easily accomplished; but Arthur scarcely touched any breakfast, and, in reply to Father Price's inquiries, said that he felt ill, and thought he must have given himself some internal strain, he had such a terrible pain in his side.

Father Price felt uneasy about him, and, as they landed at Civita Vecchia too late to go on to Rome that evening, he took a room for himself in the same hotel. Arthur threw himself on his bed without undressing, and, overcome by physical and mental exhaustion, burst into a paroxysm of tears, very much to his own astonishment and mortification.

CHAPTER XXIX.

" The more that yesterday hath loved,
The more to-day can sacrifice."
F. W. FABER.

"CHARLEY, have you an old waistcoat that you could let me have for a poor man? I am perpetually asked for coats and trousers, as if they were the most natural articles in the world for me to possess."

The speaker was Annie Crofton, and the time a fortnight from that of Arthur's mysterious disappearance; the place was still London, for there seemed more hope of hearing something of him there than by returning to Stonebridge, which had been their first impulse; but nothing had as yet been heard. They had tried every means of inquiry they could think of, including, of course, advertisements, and Robert had even employed a private detective, though he dared not tell his mother so; but the utmost they could discover was that Arthur had gone to Paris, and had left it again in a few hours, but in what direction it was impossible to ascertain. There was no trace of him at any railway-station or *diligence*-office;

he had left the hotel at which he dined, late in the evening, in a *fiacre*, but no one knew either the carriage or the driver.

The anxiety, the uncertainty, the suspense, the many harrowing doubts which would not bear putting into words, had told fearfully upon Annie in those few days; and yet outwardly she was, in some respects, less changed than might have been expected. She had a brave heart, and a woman's strong power of endurance, and, better still, she knew how to cast her care where the burden would be more than half borne for her. She was not thinner, and only very little paler, and her eyes still, at times, flashed brilliantly; but the elasticity of her step, and the ringing joyousness of her voice and laugh, were gone; she glided about like a quiet shadow, and spoke in low, silvery tones, always cheerfully, but never merrily,—the spring was gone out of her life. She never alluded to the past, never asked any questions, never made any separate attempts on her own part (at least, so far as any one knew) to obtain information about Arthur; but she listened with strained eyes and sustained breath to all information (such as it was) brought by others; and the sight of Robert was so distressing to her, that Mr. Crofton had been obliged to forbid his coming to the house,—nor would she go to see Mrs. Hatton, saying always that she could be no comfort to her, and could not bear to see the misery of which she felt herself to be the cause. But this was a feeling which the loving and generous-hearted Mrs. Hatton herself did all in her power to overcome; *she* came to see Annie, and would take no refusal, but she found it quite impossible to silence the poor child's self-reproaches.

With her father, Annie made an effort to be as little changed as possible; she knew that *his* chief distress would be to see *her* suffer, and she always took the brightest possible side of things in talking to him, saying that perhaps Arthur only wished to retaliate a little by making her anxious, and that he would be sure to turn up again before long, and laugh at them all for their trouble. Mr. Crofton tried to believe her, but he could not altogether blind himself to her anxiety; in short, every one was keeping up a painful outward cheerfulness for the sake of every one else. Strangers, who saw Annie, remarked that a peculiar gentleness had taken the place of her former careless gaiety of manner, that an almost morbid sensitiveness about the feelings of others had wholly quenched the brilliant satire and witty repartee which had hitherto been the great charm of her conversation; and that a natural tendency to self-defence on all occasions had given way to an exactly opposite spirit. But none knew that the source of this change was the consciousness of an accepted sacrifice,—for Annie knew now that her prayer had been heard, and her intention granted, and that from henceforth a life of suffering was her appointed lot on earth. From the first moment that she had realised Arthur Hatton's desertion of her (for so she regarded it), she had recognised this; and, controlling by a strong effort all natural emotions, she had knelt down before her crucifix, and said calmly and simply:

"Lord Jesus, Thou hast taken me at my word; give me grace to be thankful."

From that day she looked upon her past happiness as something which it would be a sacrilege to wish restored, and made an act of perfect renunciation.

It never for a moment occurred to her to doubt that the note she had sent by her brother was the cause of Arthur's conduct; and though she blamed herself for having written thoughtlessly and unfeelingly, she could not help thinking that he had judged her hastily and unkindly.

"But I must conquer this feeling," she had said in her letter to Father Wilfrid; "for since it is clearly the will of God that I should lose him, I have no right to let my mind dwell upon what has been a mere instrument in bringing it about."

(Father Wilfrid knew by this time for what intention he had said the Mass which Annie had once so mysteriously asked of him.)

But we have kept poor Annie waiting a long time for an answer to her question about the old waistcoat. Charley thought he had one to spare, and went up-stairs to look for it. After tumbling over about a dozen, for he was somewhat addicted to extravagance in the matter of waistcoats, he fixed upon a thick, warm one, which he thought looked too shabby to wear again.

"Holloa! here's something in the pocket!" he exclaimed; "I must turn that out first."

It was a crumpled-up note, and Charley gazed with an expression of blank horror as he looked at it. Yes, it was impossible to doubt or deny it; it was the very note Annie had given him on that memorable evening, a fortnight ago, for Arthur Hatton.

"What on earth can I have sent him instead?" he cried out in a perfect agony of grief.

"Charley, dear, do make haste; I cannot wait any longer," Annie called up the stairs.

A bedroom-door was flung open, and a waistcoat was thrown over the banisters, and fell at Annie's feet. She ran off with it, and hardly noticed that Charley rushed past her on the staircase and out into the street; it was fortunate she did not see his face, or she certainly would have followed him, regardless of appearances, for it was as white as a sheet, and his eyes seemed starting out of their sockets.

The servant at Mrs. Hatton's lodgings stared in stupid amazement at the scared youth, who breathlessly demanded to see Mr. Robert immediately, instead of giving him any answer; and Charley, without giving her time to recover herself, sprang up the stairs, burst open the drawing-room door, and exclaimed:

"Robert! where is Robert?" Happily, Mrs. Hatton was a person of strong self-control, and also, from a long habit of perfect abandonment of herself to the will of God, she was not easily startled or agitated; for nothing so insures calmness and evenness of mind, as this kind of self-annihilation. Yet she turned pale, and trembled from head to foot, as she said:

"For God's sake, tell me what it is! My son? Arthur?—have you heard any thing?"

"No, no, there is nothing. Forgive me for

frightening you. I have heard nothing,—indeed, I have not,—no one has; I would not deceive you. But can I see Robert? I have some urgent business with him."

He tried his very best to speak calmly, but he had never in all his life "practised to deceive," and he was a bad hand at concealing his feelings. Mrs. Hatton, who lived now in hourly dread of some sudden shock, saw plainly that *something* was the matter.

"Robert will not be at home till late this evening," she said; "but if it is any thing of importance, can you trust me with it? You are in some trouble, I am sure," she added kindly; "will you not let me try to help you? You have part of my burden to bear, let me have part of yours."

Charley hesitated a few moments; but the tender, loving tone, so like his own dear mother's, was irresistible to him.

"Can you bear to talk to me about Arthur?" he said gently; "if so, perhaps you can help me."

A slight inclination of her head was the only reply; but Charley noticed, with keen self-reproach, that the tears started involuntarily to her eyes.

"Do you know," he said, "have you any idea, what were the contents of the note I brought him from Annie, on the Thursday evening before he went away?"

"I only know what Annie has told me," she said,—"that she wrote thoughtlessly, in a moment of pique, something that she did not mean him to understand seriously. Stay," she added, "I remember seeing a slip of paper in Arthur's hand the next day, with two lines of poetry, that looked something like Annie's handwriting; but that could not have been the note she sent by you."

"Two lines of poetry!" repeated Charley, confused and puzzled; then, with a sudden exclamation of anguish, that pierced the poor suffering mother's heart, he flung himself on his knees at her feet, and, bursting into tears, tried in vain for some moments to speak.

"My poor boy!" she said, stooping down and gently stroking back the hair from his forehead, as if he had been her own child, while she tried to put aside her own intense anxiety; but Charley only sobbed the more bitterly, and shrank away from her.

"Do not be afraid to tell me," she said, knowing well that it was the only thing which it was of the smallest use to say.

At last he found voice enough to say, in broken accents:

"It is all my doing, my fault; I left that paper, those two lines of poetry, by mistake; I found Annie's note in my pocket to-day; see, here it is,—the other was a memorandum of my own, in her handwriting. Oh, what shall I do? what will become of me?"

Bewildered, agitated, frightened almost beyond power of endurance, Mrs. Hatton yet endeavoured to speak quietly, as she said:

"But what was it? what were the words? what can Arthur have understood from them?"

"They were two lines from Longfellow; I wish

he had been dead before he wrote them !" replied Charley, with somewhat Hibernian inconsistency; "you must know them:

> 'Trust no future, howe'er pleasant;
> Let the dead past bury its dead.'

Arthur must have understood from them that she meant to give him up. Oh, it is too hard, too cruel! Here, take the note; it must be sent to him at once—it *must;* we *must* find him," cried Charley, forgetting that perhaps, all things considered, the note itself would hardly mend matters, unless accompanied by some explanation.

Mrs. Hatton took the note mechanically, and crumpled it in her hand.

"Robert must go to Dover," she said,—"to Paris, I mean,—and try himself to find some further trace. Perhaps he can hear something through the police; perhaps"—she shuddered, as a horrible vision of the Morgue rose before her eyes. "At all events, it must be tried; we must leave nothing undone, *nothing.*"

"Robert!" exclaimed Charley; "no, no; *I* must go. Do you think I could bear to stay here, and wait, wait, wait, and hear nothing? Do you think I can bear to see Annie again? Do you think I could tell her? Do you think I can ever go back to them?"

. "She ought to be told," said Mrs. Hatton gently, but firmly; "and it would be a relief to her; it would be less pain than she is suffering now, less self-reproach."

Ah, yes; the self-reproach would all weigh upon poor Charley now.

"I cannot tell her," he cried; "I cannot do it; don't ask me; don't make her hate me."

"Hate you, my poor child! Is not yours the heaviest burden of all now? Does not that make us love you more than ever? No, no, Annie will bless you for it; she will begin to forgive herself—"

"Herself! yes, but not me," said poor Charley, almost choked by his tears.

"Yes; you first, and herself after: indeed, indeed, it will be best and happiest for you both. Poor boy!" she said, "yours is the hardest part now; and yet it was no fault, it was a mere accident; you must try to take that comfort—you must not blame yourself."

Charley was hardly in a state fully to appreciate the unselfishness of these words; to realise that the heaviest burden was, in truth, and must always be, hers—the mother's; and that only the perfection of Christian charity could have enabled her so to speak to one who, though by no greater fault than a slight act of carelessness, had brought this great sorrow upon her.

He only repeated, as if he could not leave off saying it:

"I cannot, I cannot, I cannot see her; I cannot tell her; I cannot go back to the hotel. I must go at once to Paris."

Mrs. Hatton was silent for a few minutes; then she looked up at him, smiling through her tears,—for she was anxious by any means to rouse him from this terrible agony,—and said:

"Then you must let me tell her for you. May I come and spend the evening with Annie?"

"May you!" he repeated; "how can you ask? Do anything—anything you think best and right."

"Then listen to me," she said, in that tone of quiet authority which scarcely ever fails to insure submission. "Go back yourself now; speak to your father—you need not see Annie; prepare what you require for your journey, and then return here. Robert must go with you; you may want his help: two can always do more than one. You can go by the night-mail to Dover, and reach Paris to-morrow. God grant you may find him, and bring him home! Write to me every day; tell me *every thing*, keep *nothing* back from me; you understand?—*nothing*." He understood only too well, and shuddered. "As soon as you return, I will go to Annie; her father will tell her, of course; but it may be a comfort to her to see me."

"Oh, yes; it will, it will," said Charley. "Oh, how good you are to us all, instead of hating us as you ought."

Mrs. Hatton smiled sadly.

"That is a new-fashioned act of charity," she said; "I have not learnt it yet; so I must be content to keep to the old one. But now, my dear boy, go; it is getting late, and you have a good deal to do. Remember, you must be here again soon after seven, or you will lose your train."

She rose to leave the room, and Charley, hardly knowing what he was about, went slowly out, and walked, not towards Praed Street, but in an exactly opposite direction. He was seized with an unconquerable fit of moral cowardice; he could not bear to meet his father, and tell him the truth; besides, how could he get rid of Annie, without exciting suspicion? They had but one sitting-room in the hotel; there was no convenient study or library where he could see his father alone. He thought he would wait till Annie should be gone to dress for dinner; but his carpet-bag—it would never be ready in time; well, what matter? he could go without it. However, a few grains of common sense at last came to the rescue; he went to the hotel, packed his bag, and watched to hear Annie go to her room to dress. The moment her door was shut, he ran down, and stopped Mr. Crofton from following her example, by exclaiming:

"O papa, we know it all now; it was all my fault—I did it. I must go directly and find Arthur—now, to-night, by the night-mail. I left a wrong note by mistake; I only found the right one to-day. Mrs. Hatton knows; she is coming this evening to tell Annie: she will tell you all about it. Don't ask me any more now. I will write to-morrow from Paris. Good bye;" and he was rushing off; but Mr. Crofton, who had scarcely understood a word of his incoherent outburst, seized his arm, and asked eagerly:

"Is Arthur found? Is that it?"

"No, no, not found; I am going to look for him," said Charley. "Please let me go; I shall lose the train. Mrs. Hatton will tell you every thing: she will be here almost directly;" and he tore himself away, and ran, carpet-bag in hand, to Gloucester Terrace, where he found a cab at the door, and Robert ready to start. Mrs. Hatton was also at the door, with her bonnet on.

"We can drop you, mother; it won't be out of our way," said Robert; and they all got into the cab. But not a word more was spoken; their hearts were all too full for words. Mrs. Hatton got out at the hotel, and the two young men went on to London Bridge, and thence, as fast as steam could convey them, to Folkestone, Boulogne, and Paris, that being a shorter route than by Dover.

Mrs. Hatton found Annie in the act of listening to Mr. Crofton's still more confused repetition of Charley's confused explanation, and soon put them both in full possession of the real facts of the case.

Annie drank in every word eagerly, and sat with hands tightly clasped, and compressed lips; then, without speaking one word, she quietly rose and went up to her own room, where Mrs. Hatton thought it wisest to leave her undisturbed for a little while. She forced herself to share Mr. Crofton's dinner with him, for *his* sake; and some was sent up to Annie, which came down again untouched. Later in the evening, Mrs. Hatton ventured up to her, and was admitted without any hesitation.

"My darling," she said, "you see you *must* forgive yourself now; it was no doing, no fault, of yours."

Annie clasped her lovingly in her arms, and said very calmly:

"No, not my doing, but God's doing; He has taken away what I loved too much, and I will never ask for it back again."

Mrs. Hatton looked at her, expecting some further explanation of what seemed to her a misconception; but Annie gave none,—nor would she listen to another word on the subject.

"Let us go down to papa," she said.

CHAPTER XXX.

> "Oh, that they would not comfort me!
> Deep grief cannot be reached.
> Wisdom, to cure a broken heart,
> Must not be wisdom preached."
>
> F. W. FABER.

A WEEK or ten days passed, and still the daily letters received from the travellers reported only the disheartening intelligence:

"We cannot find any trace beyond Paris."

Several false traces they had found and followed, but only to meet fresh disappointments; still, as yet, this only served to increase their energy and activity: and doubtless it was less hard to bear for them, than for the watchers and waiters at home, who could only pray in silent anguish.

One morning, two foreign letters were put into Mrs. Hatton's hands; one was from Lyons, and the handwriting was Robert's. With that terrible heart-sickness of hope deferred, she opened it, and read:

"Another disappointment! Dearest mother, my heart aches for your daily renewed sorrow. We had every reason to believe that we were on the right track this time, for an Englishman whose description exactly corresponded with Arthur had arrived here two days ago from the neighbourhood of Paris; but, alas! though we found him at the hotel, he was a perfect stranger to us; and now we hardly know which way to turn. Poor Charley seems utterly disheartened, and I find it hard work to make efforts to cheer him. He was much comforted by your account of Annie: I think that has done more for him than any thing else. He even smiled for the first time since we left England, and said, 'Annie has the spirit of a Red Indian in her: she would come down with the shaft of a poisoned arrow in her arm, and sit down to dinner as if nothing had happened, rather than distress other people by telling of it.' *I* say it is the spirit of a Christian martyr. But, mother, this was some days ago, before our last disappointment; the journey to Lyons seemed to give him energy and hope,—now nothing rouses him; and if this is to go on much longer, I fear we shall have another serious anxiety: if he breaks down, I will bring him home at once, and then do the best I can by myself."

Mrs. Hatton put down the letter with a sigh and an act of resignation to the will of God, which was becoming daily more difficult and more meritorious.

Charley wrote but little himself, and then only to his father. He could not bear to write to Annie, though *she* wrote most lovingly and tenderly to him; nor did he write to Mrs. Hatton: he knew that she heard every particular daily from Robert; and what more was there to say? He had no heart to write to any one.

The other foreign letter was directed in an unknown hand; but she had so many correspondents abroad, that it had somehow not occurred to her to connect it in any way with her son; besides, she did not expect news of him from a stranger. He was not likely to commission others to write for him, unless—ah! a sudden undefined fear came over her as she took up the letter again. The post-mark was Rome; she had several friends there, amongst others Herbert Ellicombe, who occasionally sent her intelligence of a more trustworthy nature than that wherewith "our own correspondents" sometimes favour the journals; but this was not his handwriting, nor that of any one she knew. She opened it with trembling hands. Two enclosures dropped out of the cover, both in the same handwriting; but one was signed, in an almost illegible scrawl, *Arthur Hatton*. The letter fell from her hands, as she sank upon her knees, and exclaimed:

"Thank God! thank God!"

It was some time before she was able to do more than this; for she felt instinctively that the shadow of some great trial was upon her, and she prayed for strength before going forward to meet it.

With that sort of nervous dread which is so unreasonable, and yet which at times we are all subject to, she could not begin to read what she most longed to know.

At length she took courage, and braced herself to the task; of course, Arthur's letter was her first thought. It was very short—only a few lines, written evidently from dictation, in the same handwriting as the other enclosure:

"My own dearest mother, can you forgive me? can Annie? can any one? Father Price's letter will tell you all. I am disobeying the doctor even in dictating these few words, and perhaps losing my only hope of seeing you. For the love of God, come to me as soon as you can, and, if possible, bring Annie and Robert. I should like to see them together. Do not blame Annie, mother; there was no formal engagement between us; she was free: and he is more worthy of her than I ever should have been.

"Your affectionate and penitent son,
"ARTHUR HATTON."

No formal engagement! Not, perhaps, in the strict sense of the words, if a formal engagement implies a ceremony of betrothal; but a solemn promise had been given and taken on both sides; and if Annie had acted as he believed, she would unquestionably have broken her word and her troth. Had Arthur forgotten this? No, surely not; but he had forgiven her too fully, too generously, not to shield her from every shadow of blame.

Mrs. Hatton turned in anxious haste to the other letter; it was a long one, though Father Price had written as briefly as circumstances permitted, for he knew well that every unnecessary word would be worse than useless. He explained, with the greatest possible sympathy and consideration, that, on the morning after his arrival at Civita Vecchia, Arthur had been seized with an attack of pleurisy, brought on by over-exertion and exposure to wet during the voyage; that the attack, though rather severe, had not been pronounced dangerous, and that, as soon as the worst symptoms had subsided, he had, with the consent (though certainly not by the advice) of his physician, continued his journey to Rome; but that, on his arrival there, a very serious relapse had taken place, rendered still more alarming by the rupture of a blood-vessel in the left lung; and that, though the physician gave every hope of his ultimate recovery, it was impossible to deny that the case was a very serious one, requiring the utmost care, as the slightest imprudence might cause a return of hemorrhage, and be fatal at any moment. Father Price did not attempt to disguise this: he knew it would only be a false kindness.

"I shall never forgive myself," he went on to say, "for having been, though involuntarily, the cause of your son's sad illness. But for my persuasion, he would never have undertaken the laborious work for which I ought to have seen at once that he was quite unfit. God only knows how deeply I reproach myself for this, or how gladly I would repair my carelessness at the cost of my own life, if that were possible. But these will be as idle words to you. I have engaged the best nurse I could procure from the doctor's recommendation, who of course never leaves your son night or day; my own room opens out of his, and I never leave the house, except to say Mass, and for necessary business. I need hardly add, that I offer the Holy Sacrifice daily for him, and for you, that our dear Lord may grant you strength and grace for all your needs under this terrible affliction. It is indeed a heavy cross. Rest assured, my dear madam, that nothing which is in my power shall be left undone for your son's comfort; but I earnestly hope you will lose no time in coming to him. He reproaches himself bitterly for the grief and anxiety he must already have caused you; and, during the delirium on the first night of his illness, his entreaties for your forgiveness were most heartrending. He is quite calm now—thank God!—and fully understands that the slightest exertion or mental agitation would entail the most serious consequences. For *your* sake, he is perfectly submissive to every order of his physician, and has only twice disobeyed the injunction not to speak—once to make his confession, and once to dictate the few lines which I enclose at his request. Believe me, madam, with the truest sympathy,

"Yours very sincerely,
"James Augustine Price.
" Hôtel Minerva, Rome, June 5th, 1862."

Mrs. Hatton did not know till long after that Father Price was himself suffering severely from Roman fever when he wrote that letter; she did not know that, ill as he was, he watched by Arthur's bedside for several hours, night after night, sending the nurse away to sleep, and never allowing himself more than two hours' rest. She did not know that he prepared with his own hands the blisters and other remedies necessary for the invalid, fearing lest a foreigner (he had not been able to procure an English nurse) might not be so scrupulously nice in her habits as the fastidiousness of our insular taste demands. All these things, however, she learnt afterwards from the nurse; but there were many other things that she never knew, and never will know. She never knew the earnestness, the agonised intensity, of the intercession that rose unceasingly from the priest's heart to the Throne of Grace; she never knew how, daily, in the Holy Sacrifice of the Mass, he offered himself, his own life, if it might be accepted, in exchange for Arthur's, in reparation for the thoughtlessness which he never ceased to reproach himself with, as the cause of all this misery. She never knew, she would never have guessed, the severe self-discipline and rigorous penances he imposed upon himself to punish himself for having been, as he called it, "unsparing to another." In this respect he certainly took to himself far more than his just share of blame, for he did not in the very least attempt to *persuade* Arthur to work with him at the pumps; but his humility led him to accuse himself of having suggested it to him in such a manner as almost to compel his consent by wounding his pride on the subject, and he further blamed himself for not having sooner noticed Arthur's fatigue. But the truth was, Arthur had not felt fatigued till just at the last, when he spoke of it himself. He was neither physically weak, nor unaccustomed to hard exercise; and probably, had there been no mental agitation to disturb him, no injury would have ensued; but those strange possessions of ours, nerves, which seem to be half mind and half body, will often, if they are unhinged, throw the whole machinery out of order.

There was another thing, too, which Mrs. Hatton never knew: Father Price never told her that he had given up the one object that had brought him to Rome, to watch by Arthur's dying bed. Yes; on that memorable 8th day of June, the Feast of Pentecost, 1862, at the very moment when the inspired notes of the *Veni Creator* rose from the hearts and lips of such an assembly of prelates as, perhaps, even Rome had not till then witnessed —at the very moment when the voice of the Sovereign Pontiff pronounced the solemn canonisation of twenty-three Franciscan and three Jesuit martyrs—a poor English priest, who had with great difficulty undertaken a long journey, for the sole purpose of being present at the ceremony, out of obedience to the understood (though unexpressed) wish of the Holy Father, was listening anxiously to the almost inaudible accents of the last words Arthur Hatton ever spoke on earth. All the whole sorrowful tale was told, and he seemed to derive comfort from the thought that now there would be no obstacle in the way of Robert and Annie, nothing to give them any feeling of hesitation or scruple. Father Price did not contradict him in this, though his own impression on the subject was a very different one. From what Arthur had told him of his brother and Annie, he greatly doubted if the idea of an attachment between them was not altogether a mistake; but Arthur was so firmly convinced, that it was useless to discuss the subject, and the good priest could only earnestly hope and pray that Annie herself might come in time to remove the misunderstanding.

But it was not to be. The sun that set over

Rome on the evening of that glorious Feast of Pentecost, lighted up a dying chamber, and cast a red glow on the page from which Father Price read, in low, quiet tones, the commendation of a departing soul.

In reply to the question whether he had any messages to leave, any special requests to make, Arthur had only said:

"I did wish *very, very* much to see them; but I offer that to God, with all the rest. Tell them I die at peace with God, a faithful Catholic; tell them I know they have forgiven me; tell Annie I forgave her with all my heart,—it is all for the best; tell Robert he must never leave our mother, he and Annie must live with her at Stinchcombe always—it will be a happy home at the dear old place;" and one involuntary sigh bore testimony to the dreams of future happiness in which he had so often himself indulged,—sharing them, too, as he had fondly thought, with Annie. "Tell our mother I am happy; she must not grieve; tell her to love Annie very much, to be a mother to her, as she has always been, and"—but here the dreaded effect of any exertion took place: a stream of blood burst forth, and his utterance was choked. A few minutes later, and all was over, without pain, without a struggle. If there were any conflict, it was silent and unseen.

It was only two days later when the four anxious travellers arrived in Rome—Mrs. Hatton, Annie, Robert, and Charles; Mr. Crofton had gone back to Stonebridge, to do or to prepare whatever might be required before their return. Only two days; but according to Roman custom, and the necessity of the climate, even the lifeless form of their loved one was already taken away out of their sight.

No second letter, of course, had reached them, for Mrs. Hatton and Annie had started a few hours after receiving the first one, and Robert and Charley had been summoned by telegraph, and had joined them at Marseilles; but though they had heard nothing, they were fully prepared. Annie had said at once:

"We shall not find him alive;" and, though Mrs. Hatton had, for the sake of others, seemed to hope, her heart had always belied her words.

Father Price met them at the door of the hotel, but he saw at once that the worst was already known; that he had only to satisfy that saddest of all anxieties, the longing to hear every word, every detail, every the very minutest circumstance, of those last days and hours.

When he gave Annie that fatal paper, containing the two lines which had worked all this sorrow, and underneath which Arthur had written, with his own hand, "God bless you, dear Annie; pray for me always," a low cry broke from her:

"Oh, it is too hard to bear! If he had only known the truth before he died!"

"He knows it now, my poor child," said Father Price, divining at once what "the truth" was; "be sure he knows it all now."

"Oh, do you think so? do you really think so? Are you sure of it?" exclaimed poor Charley, who had hitherto sat as if stupefied, and never spoken a word.

"I do, indeed," replied the priest; "I cannot doubt it; I cannot believe it possible for any misunderstanding or doubt or distrust to pass into the calm land beyond the sea. If one could not believe this, life would be almost too heavy a cross to bear."

But Charley could not as yet be persuaded to take the comfort offered him; anxiety and over-fatigue, and, above all, remorse, had told fearfully upon a constitution which inherited much of his mother's delicacy; and for the next month they were detained in Rome, watching and nursing him through an attack of fever, which at one time threatened to prove fatal. Mr. Crofton, of course, joined them; and perhaps, though they would hardly have acknowledged it, the present interest and anxiety was the best relief they could all have had from the pressure of the past sorrow. They saw no one but Father Price and Herbert Ellicombe, who had been often with Arthur during his illness, and whose heartfelt sympathy and ready kindness were invaluable to them. He was to return to England for three or four months, as there seemed no immediate prospect of war; but would resume his volunteer soldier-life in November.

Careful nursing gradually restored Charley's bodily health, but it soon became painfully evident that his mind was unhinged and shattered in no ordinary degree. They returned home in July; but for more than a year it was Annie's chief care to watch over and minister to his comfort, making him understand clearly, not by words, but by acts, that he was dearer to her than ever.

CHAPTER XXXI.

"Sorrow and silence are strong, and patient endurance is godlike."
LONGFELLOW's Evangeline.

THE month of August, with its bright, hot days, its valleys standing thick with corn, and its joyous harvest-homes, had passed away, and the September evenings were drawing in, with their own peculiar soft twilight and golden haze of sunset. The shortening days were a great relief to Annie; she could creep down to the church now late in the evening without being noticed or recognised, and as yet she had been nowhere else, except to Stinchcombe: she knew that would be Arthur's wish, and, painful as it was, she would fulfil it. He had said that she and Robert must live with his mother always, but that could never be, in the sense that he had meant it; others might perhaps think such a result possible in the dim future, but to themselves the bare suggestion was as a sacrilege.

And yet it was impossible but that some thought of Arthur's dying words should be in their minds the first time they met at Stinchcombe, and Robert understood only too well the meaning of Annie's sudden paleness and nervous trembling when he came into the room, and found her sitting with his mother.

"Dear child, you will be none the less a daughter to me," Mrs Hatton was saying; and Annie's only reply was a pressure of the hand, and a loving kiss, more eloquent than words.

Robert came forward, and, taking the hand she held out to him, said, in his own simple, manly, straightforward manner:

"Do you remember the day he first gave you to me for a sister, Annie? We have been brother and sister ever since; we shall be the same still, shall we not? and always? There will be no change? You will be as a child to our mother always?"

Annie looked straight up into his eyes, though her own were brimming over with tears, and in that one look they understood and trusted each other perfectly.

"Yes, yes," she said; "the same, always the same;" but she could bear no more, and rose to go. Mrs. Hatton saw how it was, and did not try to detain her; she only said:

"Remember, darling, Stinchcombe is always *home* for you, whenever you come to it."

"Home!" thought Annie, as she walked slowly and sadly down the shrubbery,—that very shrubbery, or rather wood, in which Robert had cut the evergreens for Christmas, and she had so thoughtlessly told him that she would like to vex Arthur a little, "just to see what it would be like." And she had done it, and had seen what it would be like.

This was her misery, her anguish; not that she had lost him,—that was the least part of the trial (least where *every* part was so intense),—but that her own reckless folly had brought misery and death to him, and—keenest pang of all!—that he had died misjudging and misunderstanding her. Oh, if she could have been allowed but one moment to tell him that it was all false; that she loved him, and him only on earth, with all her heart! Father Price had said he knew it now; Father Wilfrid had said that the souls of the faithful departed were at rest, perfect rest, from all earthly cares and anxieties,—that whatever their pain might be, they could no longer suffer doubt or distrust; but Annie longed, with a yearning she would not have dared to express, for some means, *any* means, of communication, were it but for one moment, with that disembodied spirit; she would have done any thing, *dared* any thing, for it, except mortal sin. But what *could* she do? There are *no lawful* means of *seeking* intercourse with the souls of the departed, though it has sometimes been permitted by a special miracle. St. Teresa did not *ask* to see St. Peter of Alcantara after his death, though it pleased God to console her with that marvellous testimony to the blessedness of a life of penance from his mouth.

Home, in one sense, Annie knew that Stinchcombe would always be to her—as far, that is, as the most loving affection could make it so; but home in the sense she had felt it to be, when she pointed it out to Mrs. Trelawney from Hillsborough Tor, and said, "You have no idea how lovely those woods are—*and then it is home*," neither Stinchcombe nor any other place on earth could ever be to her again as long as she lived. It was well, and she knew it was well, to be homeless on earth, but, oh, it was very dreary, and she could not quite be *thankful* for this beginning of conformity with the life of Jesus on

YET.

that he u

rd ; " wha
ever fellow
rkable abou
ing able t
 with you
l ever do
the man's
t !"
hat was n
the other

earth—*not yet;* but it would soon come, for she knew that she had received a great grace, hidden in the outward form of a great sorrow ; and she knew that the first step in correspondence with any grace is to give thanks for it. Already she had begun to pray for the spirit of thankfulness, and to meet depressing thoughts with the words of the *Magnificat,* though they would die away on her lips.

Robert, of course, was now settled down for life at Stinchcombe; he had given up his profession immediately on his change of position, and was only too glad to be able to do so, for it had become most uncongenial to him, and for some months he had entertained serious thoughts of exchanging it for some other mode of life. A friend had one day found him at his chambers, venting his disgust in such very strong language, that he had asked what special circumstance had occurred to ruffle his ordinarily even temper to such an extent.

"Read that," said Robert, pointing to a thick, dingy, small-print, and altogether most uninviting-looking book, which lay open on his desk. It contained full-length reports of various trials for murder; the one to which Robert specially directed Mr. Ford's attention, set forth how a certain eminent counsel had succeeded in obtaining a verdict of acquittal for his client, who was accused of having wilfully murdered his wife's brother: "the learned counsel being, however, fully aware that his client was really guilty of the crime imputed to him, inasmuch as the man had confidentially acknowledged this fact to him from the first day that he undertook the cause."

"Well?" said Mr. Ford; "what of it? The learned counsel was a clever fellow; that's all I can see in any way remarkable about the matter. Do you despair of ever being able to do the like? is that what's the matter with you?"

"God forbid I should ever do the like!" exclaimed Robert. "Why, the man's whole defence was a lie, and he knew it!"

"Of course it was; that was no affair of his: his business was to get the other fellow off, and he did it."

"By deliberately putting a lie into other men's mouths, after repeating it about a hundred times himself first. A nice sort of conscience he must have had!"

"My dear Hatton," said his friend, "you are—begging your pardon—altogether under a mistake. A counsel's business is not to decide whether or not his client is really guilty, but whether the evidence brought forward is sufficiently conclusive to prove him so."

"I know that," replied Robert; "but if he knows for certain, to begin with, that his client *is* guilty, how can he possibly in conscience try to prove him innocent?"

"What else would you have him do?" asked Mr. Ford; "he is paid for making the best case he can for the man, and he is bound to do it. Would you have him betray his client's confidence, and lose his reputation as well as his cause?"

"No," said Robert; "he has no right to do that."

"Then what, in Heaven's name, *is* he to do?" asked Mr. Ford, beginning to be rather provoked at what he considered his friend's "queer crotchets."

"Throw up his brief," answered Robert very quietly.

"Throw up his brief! Good gracious, Hatton! do you happen to be a lineal descendant of Don Quixote?"

"Not that I know of," replied Robert, laughing.

"Well, I hope you have no ambition to be Lord Chancellor, or Chief Baron, or Judge," said Mr. Ford, "for you certainly don't stand much chance of either, at that rate. Throw up your brief because your client pleads guilty! O ye gods! to think that the walls of Lincoln's Inn should be compelled to echo such words! I can tell you one thing,—if you let the world at large know that "them's your sentiments," you won't get any briefs at all; so you will be spared the trouble of giving them up. I advise you to keep your own counsel, if you can't keep your client's, and say nothing about such very unorthodox doctrine."

Robert did keep his own counsel for the future about it; but it was with a feeling of intense relief that he finally "threw up," not a brief, but his law-books and chambers altogether, exchanging them for a life so much more congenial to his taste at Stinchcombe.

At first he thought it would be a trial to him to be so near Annie; but he had subdued himself even more thoroughly than he was fully aware of. It was emphatically "not a victory, but a conquest," that he had won; and he had so long looked upon Annie as Arthur's wife, that now it had become simply impossible to him to regard her in any other light; she was his sister—would be always his sister—and nothing more. He had told his mother this plainly, lest she should ever entertain any other hopes and desires, and so suffer a second disappointment; and Mrs. Hatton felt and understood it, and had only said:

"But you will let Annie feel at home here, till Stinchcombe has another mistress?"

"Mother!" exclaimed Robert, "what are you saying? Annie must *always* be at home here; Stinchcombe shall never have a mistress who would exclude her."

For the present, however, Annie was too much tied at home to be able to spend much time at Stinchcombe. Charley's state was a painful and anxious one, and required the most tender care; he was not ill, but so fearfully depressed, so morbidly sensitive, that Annie had hard work to comfort him out of her own sore heart; but she did make a vigorous and generous effort, and her natural elasticity of character came to her help. She tried her best to be cheerful, to let Charley see bright smiles, and hear happy tones,—to be once more, as she had always been, the sunshine of the house. And, as far as it could ever be possible for her, she succeeded; for she had a brave heart, and something else better still—something that Robert had characterised as "the martyr spirit."

One day, about a month after their return

home, she came down to luncheon in her riding-habit; it was the first time she had worn it since all that terrible time in London; the first time she had shown the slightest inclination to go out any where, except to the church or to Stinchcombe; she had not even seen Mrs. Trelawney or Maude yet, except in church, though kind notes had been written and answered on both sides.

Mr. Crofton was delighted to see his child look once more "a little bit like her old self;" and his happy smile, as he kissed her, amply rewarded Annie for any pain the effort had cost her.

"That's right, my child," he said; "a good blow on Hillsborough will do you all the good in the world. Why didn't you tell me in the morning you would like to ride? I will have Selim saddled, and go with you."

"I didn't think of it this morning," said Annie; "but it has come out such a lovely day; and I thought, if I could persuade Charley to go, it might do him good; he is not so well to-day—not inclined to come down to luncheon, and you know how important it is to rouse him. Jessie and Nabob are eating their heads off in the stable, and getting as fat as pigs; they want exercise terribly. You know Charley can't bear to see them looking like farmers' nags, as he calls it; so I thought of proposing to him to take compassion on them."

"I wish you may succeed," said Mr. Crofton, "but I fear it is too soon yet; besides, are you sure it would be safe? Charley is very weak, and Nabob pulls nineteen to the dozen."

"He is too fat to run away now," replied Annie, " and I have had him well exercised this morning too, to take the spirit out of him ; he is as quiet as a mouse now—a baby could ride him ; and besides, papa, though Charley seems so weak, I believe he would find plenty of strength if he only had something to call it out, some little exertion that he *must* make. I quite expect, when he finds himself on Nabob's back, he will be able to hold him as well as ever; the only thing is to get him there."

"Well, perhaps you are right; but I think I shall go with you," said Mr. Crofton.

To this, of course, Annie had no objection ; and as soon as luncheon was over, she departed on her errand to Charley.

He started when he saw her in her habit, and passed his hand across his eyes, as if to shut out some painful vision.

" Going out, Annie?" he said, in a dreary tone.

"Yes," said Annie; "I am going to exercise Jessie a little ; she will be too fat to stand soon, and Nabob is nearly as bad ; they both look like dwarf dray-horses. I am going to take Jessie just one canter across the heath-field, to see if she has forgotten the use of her legs."

" Nabob getting fat ! how disgusting !" and Charley half roused himself out of his easy-chair, but only half.

"Yes," said Annie, " very disgusting. I must take him out to-morrow, unless you will save me the trouble by coming with me to-day; why shouldn't you ? if we go by the back lane, we shall meet no one."

"Why should I?" replied Charley listlessly; "why should either of us go? What are grooms for, but to exercise one's horses?"

"And spoil their paces. I never allow any groom to ride Jessie. But I really feel inclined for a ride to-day; won't *you* come with me?"

Charley began to raise all sorts of objections: he must change his boots, he had not on the right sort of trousers for riding, he didn't know where to find his whip, his riding-gloves wanted mending; but by the time the gloves were mended, and the whip was found, and the boots were brought, he had gone to attire himself suitably; he was, however, very near giving it all up when he saw Selim brought round with the two ponies.

"Can't we go alone, Annie?" he said.

"Yes, dear, if you wish it; but poor, dear papa would be so hurt; he has set his heart on coming with us."

Charley submitted instantly, without a word: he would do *any thing* now that was pleaded for out of consideration for another person's feelings.

Annie came down with a thick crape veil tied over her hat, and covering her face; she never went out now without it. In the first paroxysm of her grief, she had declared that she would wear widows' mourning for Arthur; and on being told that she had no right to indulge her feelings in that manner, had replied:

"Right! don't talk to me of right! If I had my rights, I should be hanged for a murderess!"

Gradually, however, she had been prevailed upon to content herself with the deepest black she could procure, of an ordinary kind, and with the solemn declaration that she would never wear any thing else as long as she lived—a resolution which no one but herself believed that she would persevere in.

Father Wilfrid, who knew her recklessness, had warned her against making any rash vows, or promises, or determinations ; and, out of obedience to him, she had refrained, except on this one point, which he did not attempt to contest with her—probably thinking it of no great importance whether she chose to wear a black gown or a brown one.

"Shall we have a little blow on Hillsborough?" said Mr. Crofton, as they rode slowly up the back lane.

"Annie said only a canter across the heathfield," answered Charley, to whom the prospect of a little additional exertion was more wearying than the exertion itself would be.

"Suppose we do that first, and then see how we feel about going farther," she said.

Her expectations with regard to Charley's riding powers were fully realised. "Spotted Bob," as soon as he felt the turf under his feet, felt also a renewal of the spirit which had been "taken out of him" in the morning, and began to play various tricks that would have been rather trying to a nervous rider, and for the first moment even Annie shared a little of her father's anxiety ; but Charley soon put an end both to their fears and to Nabob's restiveness, by himself proposing a gallop across the centre of the heath, and suiting the action to the word. To say the truth, he felt no great inclination for it; but he saw Mr. Crofton's anxiety expressed in his face, and his pride was roused, if nothing else was.

"Papa shall never say I funked my own horse," he thought; nor, indeed, would it have been in the least true. Charley had Nabob perfectly under command, but he was a little afraid of turning giddy during the gallop.

Annie, however,—who had learnt watchfulness by this time,—kept close at his side, and subsided into a walk long before the heath was crossed. On arriving at the other end, she said:

"Shall we leave Hillsborough for another time? I think we have had enough for to-day."

And this being unanimously agreed to, they rode quietly home.

CHAPTER XXXII.

"When the shore is won at last,
Who will count the billows past?"
Christian Year.

MRS. TRELAWNEY and Maude now inhabited a small house in Stonebridge; for Maude's health required constant care, and it was quite necessary for them to have a servant of their own. It was not exactly that she was *ill*, but she never seemed to have recovered the deadly chill of Helstone bog, and even in August would sit crouched over a blazing fire in the evenings, though in the day-time she was tolerably active, and helped her mother in the school,—but it was evidently not the kind of work that suited her; and Mrs. Trelawney sometimes had serious thoughts of giving it up for Maude's sake, and engaging a regular schoolmistress at her own expense, which she could very well afford to do: she and Maude would then be free to devote themselves to other work in the mission—of which there was plenty of all kinds to be done.

But nothing was yet absolutely decided. Mrs. Trelawney thoroughly *liked* her school-work; her heart was in it, and she was in no hurry to give it up. Maude sometimes laughed at her, and said:

"Mamma, I am sure you have an inordinate attachment to that school, and all those horrid, dirty little brats!" but, at the same time, she never made the slightest attempt to urge its being handed over to some one else. Father Wilfrid, from motives of delicacy, said nothing; he could not advise a step which would entail expense on Mrs. Trelawney; and he had no wish for any change in itself—it was not likely to be for the better: therefore, though he would have been glad, for her own sake, to see Mrs. Trelawney set herself free, he left the matter entirely in her own hands.

Matters, however, threatened to arrive at a crisis before long; for Dr. Wilson—whose interest in Maude continued, though he now visited her only as a friend — said that her spending the winter in England was quite out of the question; she must go to a warmer climate.

Mrs. Trelawney took fright at once. A warmer climate than Devonshire, which was always so much recommended for consumptive people! Was Maude in so very critical a state?

"Not at all, my dear madam," said the worthy doctor; "not a bit of it. Miss Trelawney is no more consumptive than I am; she has no organic disease whatever of any kind,—her heart and lungs are all right enough; you have not the smallest cause for anxiety: but she is like a room with damp walls, that wants a fire day and night to dry and warm it. The bog is sticking to her still, and we must get rid of it. I hope one winter in a warm climate will thoroughly warm her through, and then she will be all right for Siberia, if you like, next winter."

Maude herself heard this sentence with a sort of quiet indifference, which rather puzzled her mother; she said:

"I daresay I can find some one to go abroad with me for the winter, if it is necessary; there is no need for you to uproot yourself."

But Mrs. Trelawney had no idea of parting with her child, now that she had at last got her, now that she seemed given back to her. Surely now she might keep her; surely that one earthly consolation was to be allowed her?

"No, indeed, dear, if you go, we will go together; what should hinder us? I can easily get a mistress for the school, and there is nothing else to tie me here. I cannot part from you again, my child; do you wish it? Would you rather go with strangers?"

"With strangers! Oh, no, I didn't mean that," said Maude (then what did she mean?); "I only don't want to be a trouble to you. But never mind," she added, rather incoherently; "we needn't think about it just yet; it is only the first week in September: there are two months, at least, yet; and one never knows what may happen."

Father Wilfrid could not quite make out Maude to his satisfaction; there was a mixture of frankness and reserve in her manner to him which occasionally suggested the idea that she had something either in or on her mind that she would like to tell him, but could not. She did not, as Mr. Crofton had expected, "take to a convent," or show any disposition to do so; and yet there was an intensity of self-devotion and self-sacrifice about her which seemed as if it could only find its full scope in the religious life; her one great aim, since becoming a Catholic, seemed to be to annihilate self in every possible way. The more troublesome or irksome any duty was to her, the more joyfully she performed it; and every natural impulse and inclination was mortified with almost scrupulous severity.

"I was so obstinate and self-willed before," she used to say; "I must make reparation for it."

But when Father Wilfrid had once asked her if she ever felt any attraction to the religious life, she said, in rather a hesitating manner:

"I think not; I don't think I should ever be fit for it."

She had not lost her old wandering propensity, though she seldom indulged it; but now and then she would stroll up the sunk fence, and out upon Hillsborough, with only Rover for a companion—Rover, whom Herbert Ellicombe had *not* claimed, though he had been now nearly two months at Abbotsleigh. It was not because he had forgotten him: he had called on Mrs. Trelawney a few days after his return, on which occasion his faithful animal's expressions of affection had been so inconveniently demonstrative, that Maude had been obliged to lead him away by main force, and chain him up in the yard; but he would not hear of taking his old friend back,—he must return to Rome in November or December, he said, and therefore it would be useless; besides, he was evidently in such good hands, that if Miss Trelawney really liked to have him, he was only too glad to leave him with her. Maude very decidedly did "really like," and that settled the question.

He had heard from Mrs. Hatton in Rome that Maude was a Catholic, but was hardly prepared for the evident enthusiasm with which she listened to all he had to tell about Rome, and the prospects of the Holy Father's cause.

"And you really have no little sneaking bit of admiration left for Garibaldi?" he asked.

Maude coloured furiously, for which there did not seem to be any particular reason, as she replied, with a little of the old bitterness of tone:

"It is ungenerous to remind people of their mistakes and follies, Mr. Ellicombe. If I had the chance now, I would shoot Garibaldi with my own hand."

He laughed.

"I see," he said, "you go on the principle of a firm friend and a bitter enemy. But you may perhaps have the chance, if you come to Rome this winter; we don't know yet, but things look rather warlike. I shouldn't wonder if we have a scrimmage or two before we can get rid of the red-shirts. Will you come for the chance? I assure you a few English Catholic ladies would be invaluable there in case of a battle, as useful as ever they were at Scutari a few years ago."

"Would they?" she said; "would there really be any thing for them to do?"

"Plenty, I fancy," he replied, "in any case, if they would only take the trouble to do it; but in the event of war breaking out, a few brave-hearted women, who wouldn't faint at the sight of blood, and could dress a gun-shot wound,—no easy accomplishment, I assure you,—would be the greatest possible blessing."

Maude's eyes kindled, and her heart beat fast, but she made no answer; she thought she could answer for not fainting, but as for the gun-shot wounds—well, she knew nothing about them, it is true, but surely she could go to a hospital and learn. However, this was before there had been any talk of a milder climate for the winter; so Maude kept her thoughts, whatever they were, to herself.

Herbert Ellicombe's visit was repeated several times; and before the conversation we have recorded between her and her mother took place regarding their winter plans, she *knew*, though nothing definite had been said,—" for quickly comes such knowledge,"—that it would soon rest with herself to decide whether she would go with Herbert Ellicombe to Rome in November as his wife, there to devote herself to corporal works of mercy, and especially to the care of sick or wounded soldiers of the Papal army. Most assuredly no other manner of wife would the ardent young Zouave have taken out with him,—no one who would be less devoted than himself to the one object he had at heart,—nay, no one who would be less ready than himself to labour and suffer for it, if need were. But he had satisfied himself that Maude would be such a wife, and he was only waiting for an opportunity of telling her so, and she knew it.

The opportunity soon came: in one of Maude's solitary rambles on Hillsborough, he met her, and, without further circumlocution,—for, as we have seen, he was not of a romantic turn of mind,—asked for a few minutes' conversation. She knew at once what was coming, but she did not refuse his request, and, by granting it, decided her future destiny.

The "few minutes" lengthened out into two hours; but the "conversation" would probably not greatly interest any one but themselves.

At last Maude, looking at her watch, exclaimed:

"Six o'clock! Indeed, I must run home. Mamma will be frightened to death, and think I have got into Helstone bog again;" and she darted off, followed by Rover, who quite understood to whom he belonged.

"Then I may come to-morrow morning, and see Mrs. Trelawney?" Herbert called after her. Maude was too far off for her answer, if she made any, to be heard; but it didn't much signify.

Herbert did call the next morning, and found Maude had already told her own tale; in fact, she had been compelled to account in some way for her long absence, and had found it both easiest and pleasantest to tell the truth about it.

Mrs. Trelawney could not help being glad and thankful and happy, for Maude's sake; but it did seem a little hard to lose her so soon.

"I don't want to take her from you," Herbert had said; "come with us to Rome." But Mrs. Trelawney was too wise to put herself in such a position; and besides—yes, but she could not express the *besides;* so she only said that she thought they would be better without her,—that she would work on at Stonebridge for the present. Next summer, if they came to England, they would all know better how to decide for the future; perhaps she might join them at some future time, but not yet.

To Father Wilfrid, she said:

"I know now that our Lord has taken all I love into His own hands, and set me free to serve Him alone; but I do not know yet what service He may require of me: I can make no plans for the future."

He understood fully all that she meant and implied, and willingly consented to let her continue her present mode of life as long as it should seem to be the will of God for her.

Just about this time, Annie had written, asking Maude to go and see her. *She*, of course, knew nothing of the change in prospect, and poor Maude felt sadly troubled. How could she, the very first time of seeing Annie, intrude upon her sorrow with a tale of happy love? and yet it would be almost more unkind to say nothing about it.

In her perplexity, she appealed to Father Wilfrid, and asked him to break the news for her, which he willingly consented to do. Annie heard it with unfeigned pleasure; she was far too large-hearted and unselfish to grudge happiness to another because she had lost it herself; and indeed, after all, it was only one—and that not the highest—kind of happiness, as she was already beginning to find out.

When Maude went to pay the visit she so much dreaded, she found all difficulty and embarrassment vanish at once; for Annie, whose naturally ready tact had not deserted her, at once took the initiative, and in a few simple words, very quietly spoken,—for they did cost her something,—congratulated her friend on the happy life that seemed opening out before her.

"You will be almost as good as a Zouave yourself," she said; "I call it a great privilege. And then you will be almost always in Rome; I feel half inclined to envy you that."

For a moment Maude forgot the sad attraction which Rome must always henceforth have for Annie, and said:

"Do you? I thought you were rooted to Devonshire, heart and soul."

Annie tried to smile, but rather failed in the attempt.

"Heart, perhaps, I was," she said; "but never soul. Are *you* not Roman enough yet to echo that old song of triumph: *O Roma! tu sei prima, e non avrai secunda*"?

"I never heard it," said Maude; "but I think I do feel what you mean. But why should you not spend this winter at Rome, if you wish it?"

"For many reasons," replied Annie. "I cannot leave papa, and *he* cannot leave Stonebridge; and then, you know, it would be so bad for Charley, reminding him so of every thing; and he is my chief care now."

Maude could have bitten her tongue out with vexation at her thoughtless speech. She had been so long in the habit of trampling upon other people's feelings, from sheer bitterness of heart, that it became almost a second nature to her; and she did it, not only without intending, but actually without knowing it at the moment.

"I forgot," she said. "Forgive me; I did not mean to pain you."

"It is nothing; no pain, I mean," said Annie bravely, with the arrow quivering in her heart all the time. "Would you like to see Charley? I think it might do him good, if you don't mind. He knows all about you, and is tolerably reconciled to his fate; so you need not be afraid. By the by, did you ever hear of his famous ride to Helstone in search of you? I assure you, he wished Mr. Ellicombe at Jericho with hearty good will that night. You know, he was desperately in love with you then."

"No," said Maude; "not with me, only with

a fancy of his own, which happened to take my form, because it came readiest to hand."

A perfectly true explanation of the matter; but Annie wondered how Maude should have hit upon it.

"*I* should never have found that out. I wonder if it is true," she thought.

They did go to see Charley, who seemed so pleased and cheered by Maude's visit, that she often afterwards repeated it; and before November she had the happiness of seeing him so much better, that, of his own accord, he proposed being present at her wedding—though, of course, only *incog.*; and, in fact, he really did go, concealing himself in the organ-gallery, but having an excellent view of the whole ceremony.

As her anxiety about him lessened, and she was consequently more thrown back upon herself, Annie found it harder to maintain her cheerfulness constantly,—or, rather, it required a more supernatural effort; for she did maintain it so successfully, that at last Mr. Crofton began to hope that a time might come when he might once more look forward to leaving her in a home of her own.

One day he had ventured gently to hint this, but was rather startled by the vehemence with which the reply came:

"No, papa; once for all, no. Don't deceive yourself; that is impossible."

"Then you mean to establish yourself in Stonebridge as a respectable old maid, I suppose?" he said, on another occasion.

"Well, I will try to be as respectable as I

can," she replied, laughing, and dexterously evading the question; for the prospect of old-maidism in Stonebridge was not a particularly attractive one to her, and yet she could not suggest any other.

Father Wilfrid had given no encouragement to her proposal of entering a convent,—in fact, she privately accused him of having "snubbed her cruelly" about it; which was not quite a fair way of putting it. He had only said that, if she really had a vocation, it would show itself in time, but that he saw no sign of it at present; that perhaps, a few years hence, he might be able to give a more definite opinion, but not yet; and that, meanwhile, her duty was clearly to remain with her father and Charley, both of whom in different ways required her care. The truth was, he knew that her impetuosity of disposition would require a vocation to be tested with double severity in her case.

"Not yet, not yet!" repeated Annie; "it is always not yet: and to-morrow never comes."

"But to-day will have an end, and the rest will come," he replied. "You know,

> 'Be the day's toil never so long,
> At length it ringeth to evensong.'"

THE END.

Levey and Co., Printers, Great New Street, E.C.

BOOKS

PUBLISHED BY

BURNS, OATES, AND CO.,

17 PORTMAN STREET, AND 63 PATERNOSTER ROW.

NEW LIBRARY OF FICTION,

In Vols. at 3s. 6d.

Suited for Libraries, Presents, &c.

1. **Tales from the Diary of a Sister of Mercy.** By C. M. BRAME. 3s. 6d.
2. **In the Snow; or, Tales of Mount St. Bernard.** By Rev. W. H. ANDERDON. 3s. 6d.
3. **Nellie Netterville:** a Tale of Ireland in the Time of Cromwell. By CECILIA CADDELL, Author of "Wild Times." 3s. 6d.; cloth elegant, 5s.
4. **Edith Sydney:** a Tale of the Catholic Movement. By Miss OXENHAM. 3s. 6d.; cloth elegant, 5s.
5. **Angels' Visits:** a Series of Tales. By C. M. BRAME, Author of "Diary of a Sister of Mercy." 3s. 6d.

Eudoxia: a Tale of the Fifth Century. Cloth elegant, 4s.

Grantley Manor:

The well-known and favourite Novel

By LADY GEORGIANA FULLERTON.

Boards, 2s. 6d.; cloth, 3s.

"The skill with which the plot of 'Grantley Manor' is constructed, the exquisite truth of delineation which the characters exhibit, and the intensity of passion which warms and dignifies the subject, are alike admirable. . . . The depth of passion which surrounds the story of Genevra is the result of unquestionable genius. No heroine that we can remember excels this lovely creation in purity, deep affection, a solemn sense of the sanctity of duty, and a profound feeling of the beauty and holiness of religion."—*Times.*

Sea Stories:

Tales of Discovery, Adventure, and Escape. A new and choice Collection, containing several striking Narratives, mostly unknown to English readers. Cloth, 3s.

"The best volume of the kind we have ever met with."—*Churchman's Companion.*

Romantic Tales of Great Men:

ARTISTS, POETS, SCHOLARS, STATESMEN, &c.

Cloth, 3s.

₊ This volume will be found to convey information as well as amusement, all the tales being founded on historical facts.

The Betrothed: a Romance of the Seventeenth Century.

By MANZONI. Boards, 2s. 6d.; cloth, 3s.

This unrivalled romance, which stands quite alone in the literature of fiction, is now brought within the reach of every reader in this very neat and portable edition.

"*I am not sure*," says Rogers, "*that I would not rather have written the 'Betrothed' than all Scott's novels.*"

"It has every quality that a work of fiction ought to have."—*Heir of Redclyffe.*

Hendrik Conscience's Tales.

Complete in Six Volumes. Fcap. 8vo, cloth, 3s. each.

- The Lion of Flanders.
- The Curse of the Village, &c.
- Veva; or, the War of the Peasants.
- The Miser; Ricketicketack.
- Tales of Flanders.
- The Demon of Flanders.

"Had our writers of fiction preserved the healthful tone which characterises these volumes, they would not have been a proscribed class. Each of the tales may be read by the most modest without a blush, and by the most fastidious without scruple."—*Eclectic Review.*

"There is a truthfulness in his pictures which is perfectly delightful; while the whole moral of his works is such as to make them a valuable addition to the light-reading division of a library."—*Notes and Queries.*

Tales of the French Revolution:

A Series of Historical Tales and Episodes of this eventful period, combining the interest of History with the charm of Romance.

New Edition, 3s.

The Adventures of Jules Gerard, the "Lion-killer,"

Of Northern Africa, during his Ten Years' Campaigns among the Lions of Algeria; including the details of more than Forty Encounters, Adventures, and Episodes, and a variety of interesting Sketches of Arab Life. Twelfth Thousand. Cloth, 2s. 6d.

"We hope this charming little volume will meet with the popularity it deserves. We have seldom seen a *manlier*, a *more simple-hearted*, or a more *amusing book.*"—*Saturday Review.*

The Vessels of the Sanctuary, and the Manor of Mount Cruel:

Tales of French Life. By ELIE BERTHET. Cloth, 2s. 6d.

Two of the best Tales of this fertile and popular Author.

The History of Jean Paul Choppart;

Or, the Surprising Adventures of a Runaway. Illustrated with twenty-two Engravings. Fcap. 8vo, cloth, 2s. 6d.

"'Jean Paul Choppart' is a translation of a work which has become very popular on the Continent; and is destined to receive a large share of favour in this country, should parents and instructors of children become aware of the excellent moral which its pages convey through the medium of a story which is most piquant and catching for the youthful mind."—*Court Journal.*

The Thousand and One Days;

Or, Arabian Tales. A select and thoroughly unexceptionable collection of highly entertaining Tales, illustrative of Oriental Manners and Customs, carefully revised and adapted for the Young. With a Preface by Miss PARDOE. Fcap. 8vo, with numerous Engravings, cloth, 3s. 6d.

N.B. This is an indispensable companion to the "Arabian Nights."

Father Connell.

By BANIM. A New Edition. Cloth, 2s. 6d.

"'Father Connell,' the Irish 'Vicar of Wakefield.'"—*Literary Gazette.*

Cheap Popular Books for Lending-Libraries.

	s.	d.		s.	d.
The Isle of the Dead. By SOUVESTRE	1	0	Pictures, Tales, and Parables	3	0
The Book of 300 Anecdotes	1	0	Tales of the Crusades	2	6
			Breton Legends	2	6
Columbus and La Pérouse	1	4	Tales of Wonder. By HAUFF	2	6
Schoolmaster's Adventures, and other Tales	1	0	Andersen's Select Tales	2	0
Preciosa. By CERVANTES	1	0	Robinson Crusoe. Pocket Edition	2	0
Tales of Kings and Queens	1	0			
Tales of Joy and Sorrow	1	0	Arctic Voyages	2	0
Tales of France	1	0	Du Guesclin; or, the Hero of Chivalry	2	0
Adventures in the Forest	1	0			
Book of Poetry for the Young	1	0	Tales of Celebrated Women	2	0
Book of Ballads for the Young	1	0	Tales of Celebrated Men	3	0
The Two last in One Volume	2	0	Tales of Enterprise, Peril, and Escape	3	0
			The War in La Vendée	4	6
Popular Poetry	2	0	The Patriot War in the Tyrol	4	0
Selections from the Poets. By DE VERE	3	6			

Marie;
Or, the Workwoman of Liège. By Miss CADDELL, Author of "Nellie Netterville," &c. &c. 3s. 6d. [*Just ready.*

Verses on various Occasions,
Now collected for the first time. By JOHN H. NEWMAN.
Fcap. 8vo. Second Edition. 5s.

*** The Poems added to this edition may be had by purchasers of the first for a penny stamp.

The Dream of Gerontius,
Separately, 6d.; cloth, 1s.

By the same Author.

The Church of the Fathers. New Edition. 5s.

Callista. Fcap. 8vo, cloth, 3s. 6d.

Loss and Gain. Fcap. 8vo, cloth, 4s.

Lectures on the Turks. 4s.

Occasional Sermons. Fcap. 8vo, cloth, 5s.

Parochial and Plain Sermons. From the Text of the last Editions. Crown 8vo, in eight vols., 5s. each.

Now ready, neat cloth, 3s.
The Seven Ages of Clarewell:
A History of a Spot of Ground. By the Rev. W. H. ANDERDON, M.A. Age I. The Monastery foretold; II. Built; III. Occupied; IV. Dissolved; V. Secularised; VI. Desecrated; VII. Restored.

A Manual for Serving-Boys at Low Mass.
From the Italian of CARPI. Edited by the Rev. R. W. BRUNDRIT, M.A. Neat cloth, 6d.; wrapper, 4d.

The Witch of Rosenberg:
A Drama. With Illustrations and Music. By His Eminence Cardinal WISEMAN. Cloth, gilt edges, 3s. 6d.

Popular Devotions for the Ecclesiastical Seasons:
Being short Evening Services of Psalms, Prayers, and Hymns, suited for Singing. In numbers, at 2d.; or complete in a volume.

Contains: 1. Devotions for Advent and Christmas. 2. Devotions from Septuagesima to Easter. 3. Devotions for Paschal Time. 4. Devotions for Whitsuntide. 5. Devotions for the Sundays after Pentecost. 6. Devotions for Saints' Days. 7. Devotions for the Feasts of the Blessed Virgin.

⁎ Music for these Devotions, complete, 1s. 6d.

Family Devotions for every Day in the Week, with occasional Prayers.
Selected from Catholic Manuals, ancient and modern.

Fcap., limp cloth, red edges, very neat, 2s.

The Psalter;
Or, Psalms of David in English.
[*New Edition in the Press.*

Just out, neat cloth, red edges, 1s.; calf, 4s.
Mary in Sorrow and Desolation, Help of the Catholic Church.
With the Ritual of the Confraternity of Our Lady of Dolours.

The Apostle of Abyssinia.

Containing an interesting account of Bishop de Jacobis and Catholic Missions in Abyssinia. By Lady HERBERT of Lea. Post 8vo, cloth, 6s.; cheap edition, 3s. 6d.

By the same.

St. Francis of Sales' Mission in the Chablais. 6s.

Julia's Death:

A simple and true Account of a Catholic Child, eight years of age. 4d.

Now ready, New Edition.

Fabiola;

Or, the Church of the Catacombs. By the late Cardinal WISEMAN. Fcap. 8vo, cloth, 3s. 6d.; cloth gilt, elegant, 4s.

"Our Lady's Books."

Edited by LADY GEORGIANA FULLERTON. New Series. Uniformly printed in fcap. 8vo, limp cloth.

Vol. I. Memoir of the Hon. Henry E. Dormer. Fcp., cloth, 2s.; cheap edition, 1s.

Vol. II. A Child of the Sacred Heart; or, the Life of M. Fitzgerald. Cloth, 2s.; cheap edition, 1s.

The Doctrine of Holy Indulgences explained to the Faithful.

By the Abate DOMINICO SARRA. Translated by the Rev. A. ST. JOHN. Cloth, 1s.

Also, by the same Translator,

The Raccolta.

New Edition, with Supplement, 3s.—The Supplement alone, 6d.

Fourth Edition, in post 8vo, 2s.

Forewarnings:

Being Prophecies on the Church and Revolution, Antichrist and the Last Times. Edited by HENRY LANGDON.

Now ready, Cheap Edition.

Long Resistance and Ultimate Conversion.

By Sir CHARLES DOUGLAS, K.C.M.G. Cloth, 2s. 6d.

New Mass Music for Catholic Choirs.

It is proposed to publish a Collection of Masses of the modern school of music, fitted in all respects for the use of Catholic Choirs. In order to suit the circumstances of different Churches, the Series will be divided into two Classes, viz.:

1. UNISON MASSES, intended to meet the wants of Missions with small Choirs, Convent Chapels, &c. An Organ Accompaniment of a full and artistic character will be added; by which means an effect will be produced hardly less varied and interesting than that of vocal part-singing.
2. MASSES, of various degrees of difficulty, arranged for vocal part-singing, with Organ Accompaniment. None of these Masses will be of inconvenient length, and the several parts will be in due proportion to each other. They will also be conformed in other respects to the Instructions for Composers issued by the Holy See.

The work has the approval of His Grace the Archbishop of Westminster.

Liturgical Directions for Organists, Singers, and Composers.

Contains the Instructions of the Holy See on the proper kind of Music for the Church, from the Council of Trent to the present time; and thus furnishes Choirs with a guide for selection. Fcap. 8vo, 6d.

Aids to Choirmasters

In the Performance of Solemn Mass, Vespers, Compline, and the various Popular Services in general use. 2d.

Hymns for the Year (293).
3d.; cloth, 5d.

Melodies for the Hymns for the Year.
1s.; cloth, 1s. 6d. Together, cloth, 2s.

The Popular Hymn and Tune Book:

Containing the Vocal Scores and Accompaniments for the Melodies (250 pieces). 1 vol. cloth, 10s. 6d.; or in three parts, at 3s. each.

The Music in this work (the cheapest ever printed) comprises Tunes for the Hymns in the "Path to Heiven," the "Oratory," "Holy Family," "St. Patrick's," and all other Hymn-books.

Library of Religious Biography.
Edited by EDWARD HEALY THOMPSON.

Vol. I. The Life of St. Aloysius Gonzaga, S.J. 5s.
Vol. II. The Life of Marie Eustelle Harpain (called the Angel of the Eucharist). 5s. [*Just out.*

The Banks of the Boro:

A Story of Irish Life. By PATRICK KENNEDY. 2s.

[*Just published.*

The Path to Heaven.

(TWENTY - FIFTH THOUSAND.)

This Volume consists of upwards of 1000 *pages, and comprises:*

1. All the usual Devotions for Morning and Evening, Prayers before and after Mass, for Confession, Communion, the Sacraments, the Sick, &c. &c., with many new additions.

2. Litanies, Novenas, Devotions, and Hymns, in regular order, *for every month in the year* (including Indulgenced Prayers), intended for use in Evening Services in Churches, as well as in private. This is an *entirely novel feature*, and will, it is presumed, make the Volume a *sine qua non* in every Mission.

3. Offices: besides Vespers, Compline, Office of Immaculate Conception, &c., it comprises the "Bona Mors," Novena of St. Francis Xavier, and Sacred-Heart Devotions, used by the Jesuit Fathers; the Holy-Family Devotions used by the Redemptorist Fathers; the Devotions for the Precious Blood; also Meditations, and the **Epistles and Gospels for the Year**.

4. The most copious and varied collection of *Hymns and Sacred Songs* hitherto published (in number 293). This part of the work has been revised with great care, so as to secure its freedom from the inferior matter too often found in such collections, and thus fit it for a book of reading and meditation as well as for singing. (*Music for the Hymns*, One Shilling.)

Price, cloth lettered, Two Shillings; neatly bound, red edges, 2s. 6d.; roan, lettered, 3s.; French morocco, gilt edges, 4s.; calf, red edges, 5s.; and a variety of extra bindings.

POPULAR WORK ON IRELAND.

Now ready.

Irish Homes and Irish Hearts.

By FANNY TAYLOR, Author of "Eastern Hospitals," "Tyborne," &c. Second Edition. Handsome cloth, 6s.

Select Offices from the Ritual, Pontifical, and Breviary.

Uniformly printed, English and Latin.

The Office of Baptism. 2d.
The Office of Burial. 3d.
The Order of Laying the Foundation-stone of a Church. 2d.
The Rite of Blessing a Bell. 2d.
The Offices of Prime and Compline.
The Offices of Tierce, Sext, and None.

LONDON: BURNS, OATES, AND CO,
17, 18 PORTMAN STREET, & 63 PATERNOSTER ROW.

www.ingramcontent.com/pod-product-compliance
Lightning Source LLC
Chambersburg PA
CBHW032011300426
44117CB00008B/987